WELL SPOKEN
Oral Communication Skills for Business

Kenneth R. Mayer

WELL SPOKEN
Oral Communication Skills for Business

Kenneth R. Mayer
Cleveland State University

Harcourt Brace Jovanovich, Publishers
San Diego   New York   Chicago   Austin   Washington, D.C.
London   Sydney   Tokyo   Toronto

Cover Credit: **top left:** Pete Saloutos/After Image, 1988; **top right:** Alvis Upitis/The Image Bank West, 1988; **bottom left:** Charles Feil/The Image Bank West, 1988; **bottom right:** Alvis Upitis/The Image Bank West, 1988.

Copyright © 1989 by Harcourt Brace Jovanovich, Inc.

All rights reserved. No part of this publication may be reproduced or transmitted in any form or by any means, electronic or mechanical, including photocopy, recording, or any information storage and retrieval system, without permission in writing from the publisher.

Requests for permission to make copies of any part of the work should be mailed to: Permissions, Harcourt Brace Jovanovich, Publishers, Orlando, Florida 32887.

ISBN: 0-15-595154-8
Library of Congress Catalog Card Number: 88-82157

Printed in the United States of America

Copyrights and Acknowledgments:
Pages 4–5: Reprinted from *Management World,* January 1978, with permission from AMS. Copyright © 1978 AMS; **35–36:** Reprinted with permission of McGraw Hill. Copyright © 1957; **63:** Reprinted with permission of McGraw Hill. Copyright © 1988; **66:** Adapted from Jean H. Michulka, *Let's Talk Business* 2nd ed., with permission of South-Western Publishing Co. Copyright © 1983. All rights reserved; **105–107:** Reprinted by Permission of Kenneth R. Mayer; **118–120:** Reprinted by permission of Larry R. Smeltzer; **130–131:** Reprinted courtesy of 3M Audio Visual Division; **146, 163:** Reprinted by permission of Wm. C. Brown Publishers; **183:** Reprinted courtesy of 3M Audio Visual Division; **185:** Reprinted from *Management World,* May 1981, with permission from AMS. Copyright © 1981; **198:** Reprinted by permission of Dr. R. Alec MacKenzie, Alec MacKenzie and Associates.

PREFACE

No matter what a student's short- or long-term occupational objectives, oral communication competency will be a major component of a successful career. *Well Spoken* is a concise, comprehensive text designed to enable students to meet their goals by developing the critical communications skills they will need to be presenters, interview participants, meeting leaders, and meeting members.

Well Spoken can be used as the only text in a general or specialized speech course or as a supplement to other texts. Organized in eight chapters, it covers the full range of speaking situations in which students will be engaged in their professional, business, and personal lives. Chapter 1 reinforces the career value of public speaking and other oral communication skills and immediately relieves fears and insecurities about speaking in public. Chapter 2 provides an understanding of communication theory applied to on-the-job speaking, audience analysis, and listening skills, which lays the foundation required for strong oral communication.

The next two chapters prepare students for the challenge of extemporaneous and impromptu speaking. Chapter 3 focuses on the preparatory aspects of public speaking—planning and organizing easy-to-follow presentations, developing outlines, and practicing. Chapter 4 examines how voice, eye contact, and body language are used in a relaxed, conversational delivery style. How to use humor and how to handle question-and-answer sessions are also covered.

A thorough and up-to-date discussion of presentation aid media and how they are used effectively is presented in Chapter 5. Students are prepared to deal capably with the many interview opportunities that arise in most management- and professional-level jobs in Chapter 6.

The last two chapters focus on small group communication, rounding out each student's repertoire of oral communication abilities. Chapter 7 establishes the framework for approaching small group communication productively and for developing good meeting planning techniques. Chapter 8 presents group process techniques, followed by successful methods for accomplishing group objectives and fostering a work team rapport. An Appendix offers a speaker evaluation form and an assessment scale that professors and students may use for providing feedback and for grading oral presentations.

Special Features

Communication theory is important, but in *Well Spoken* the *application* of theory is stressed and theory itself serves to reinforce the *how* and *why* of speech. This book has a conversational style intended to interest and motivate students. Easy-to-relate-to examples dramatize concepts and help students apply them in a broad range of realistic occupational settings. Content is as up to date as possible. For example, the coverage of computer-generated presentation graphics and teleconferencing discusses today's cutting-edge technology, as well as innovations we can expect in the future.

Finally, dozens of application exercises are included. Students are challenged to put chapter concepts to work right away in interesting, career-oriented learning activities. Instructors have a variety of options for evaluating student understanding and performance and for providing constructive and concrete feedback.

Acknowledgments

This book is the product of the insights, contributions, and evaluations of many people. I want to thank members of the business communication faculty at Cleveland State University, especially John Binnion, former chair of the department and "founder" of oral business communication at Cleveland State; Margaret Bahniuk; Bella G. Parker; and Edward G. Thomas. Thanks are also extended to my business communication students. Through their experiences and reactions, I have gradually evolved this book's approach to business and professional speaking.

Reviewers shared their professional expertise with me and provided very perceptive and constructive comments for this book in its developing stages. I extend grateful appreciation to: Carol Barnum, Southern College of Technology; Sam C. Geonetta, University of Missouri, Rolla; Linda McMeniman, Glassboro State College; Jeff Schiff, Columbia College; Eunice T. Smith, Jackson State University; Ray Spitzenberger, Wharton County Junior College; and Peter Topping, University of North Carolina.

I am also thankful to the staff at Harcourt Brace Jovanovich: Susan Mease, acquisitions editor; Debbie Hardin, manuscript editor; Robert Shelburne, production editor; Ann Smith, designer; Cindy Robinson, art editor; and Diane Southworth, production manager.

Lastly, I acknowledge the continuing support and sense of perspective that my wife Mary and my baby sons Aaron and Peter provide.

KENNETH R. MAYER

CONTENTS

Preface   v

Chapter 1
INTRODUCTION TO ORAL BUSINESS COMMUNICATIONS   1
The Career Value of Oral Communication Skills   3
Speaking Opportunities   6
Presentation Modes   8
Speaking Anxiety   13
Summing Up   17

Chapter 2
ORAL COMMUNICATION BASICS   19
The Communication Process   20
Audience Analysis   25
Listening   33
Summing Up   37

Chapter 3
BEFORE YOU SPEAK: PLANNING, PRESENTATION DESIGN, AND PREPARATION   41
ESCAP-E Planning Formula   43
Organizational Patterns   48
Talk Structure   52
Persuasive Presentations   60
Note Development   64
Practicing   67
Planning and Presentation Example   70
Summing Up   76

Chapter 4
AS YOU SPEAK: DELIVERY TECHNIQUES   79
Voice   81
Eye Contact   86
Body Language   88
Using Humor   93
Handling Question-and-Answer Sessions   95
Putting It All Together   100
Summing Up   102

Chapter 5

PRESENTATION AIDS — 109
Benefits of Presentation Aids   111
Criteria for Development and Design   115
Presentation Aid Media   124
Presentation Graphics   132
Using Presentation Aids in Delivery   136
Summing Up   141

Chapter 6

INTERVIEWING — 145
What is Interviewing?   146
What are the Purposes of Interviewing?   147
What are Common Kinds of Interviews?   148
Are There Different Interview Styles?   151
How Do You Prepare for an Interview?   153
What Questioning and Responding Skills are Needed in an Interview   156
How Can You Be More Perceptive in Interviews?   162
What Other Interviewing Skills Are Important?   165
How is a Good Interview Structured?   167
Summing Up   170

*Chapter 7

PLANNING SMALL GROUP COMMUNICATION — 177
Small Group Communication Defined   179
Reasons for Working in Small Groups   180
The Other Side of Small Group Communication   182
Types of Small Group Interaction   186
Teleconferencing   188
Planning a Meeting   191
More on Agenda Planning   197
Summing Up   199

Chapter 8

USING SMALL GROUP COMMUNICATION — 201
Group Process Techniques   202
Problem-Solving Process   209
Leader's Role in Meetings   214
Member's Role in Meetings   222
Summing Up   225

Appendix   235
Index   243

---

*Application exercises for Chapter 7 are combined with Chapter 8 exercises.

Chapter 1

INTRODUCTION TO ORAL BUSINESS COMMUNICATIONS

While speaking to an audience of financial analysts from a prepared text, the president of a major steel corporation didn't realize that he had mistakenly duplicated page seven. He proceeded to read two page sevens in his most confident business voice, without noticing the repetition. Amazingly, his bored audience didn't notice either. Days later when organizing his speech folder before filing it away, he discovered his error. Thinking back, the embarrassed speaker understood why his listeners seemed uninterested and why they were polite rather than involved. He also realized that he had been plowing through his text, so disconnected with his audience and his content that he didn't realize he had repeated two pages.

This shows how many people learn the hard way that good speaking skills are essential job skills, whether you are a first-line supervisor aiming for the fast career track or a middle- or top-level executive trying to go as far in your career as possible. Skill in oral communication is one vital building block of occupational success for people in business, industry, and the professions. Speaking is the major means of working with and through people in organizations, whether the organizations be large or small, formal or informal.

Fortunately, speaking is one career skill you *needn't* learn the hard way. Business people and professionals who are considered well spoken know the principles of good speaking can be learned gradually—day by day. All of us know and probably envy people who speak logically and confidently in front of 10 or 100 people, who carry on interviews without signs of stress, and who skillfully run meetings or contribute as meeting members. They make speaking look easy. But have courage. These experts may not be much different from you, except for having had years of experience to strengthen their oral communication abilities.

This book will help you—whether you are planning a business or professional career, or even if you are already established—to build the foundation of speaking skills you need. Chapter 2 presents the basics of oral communication; you will learn to put the communication process to work on the job, especially analyzing the audience and developing your listening skills. Chapters 3 and 4 prepare you for public speaking; you will learn to prepare, organize, and deliver presentations. Chapter 5 helps you use visual aids and other types of presentation aids correctly. Chapter 6 builds your one-on-one interviewing skills. Finally, Chapters 7 and 8 handle small group communications; you will learn to plan, lead, and participate in meetings and conferences.

In the meantime, Chapter 1 encourages you to accept the exciting challenge of improving your ability to communicate orally by exploring the how and the why of speaking on the job. You will learn:

- to recognize the unmistakable contribution of oral communication skills to business and professional success,
- to capitalize on situations on and off the job that use your speaking abilities,
- to distinguish the best delivery styles for speakers,
- to overcome the anxiety of communicating in public.

THE CAREER VALUE OF ORAL COMMUNICATION SKILLS

Successful business and professional people are promoted to positions in which they are expected to communicate clearly, concisely, and persuasively, not only on paper but also in person. In many cases, however, these up-and-coming, otherwise talented employees are not prepared for their communication responsibilities—especially public speaking.

With increasing frequency today, business and professional people are called on to defend positions and policies that affect the community in which their organizations play a significant role. For example, Sally Mason, chief financial officer, is interviewed on the 11 o'clock news about her firm's announcement to divest South African investments. Or, Andrew McNally, plant manager, speaks before the Kiwanis Club on his company's progress in reducing smokestack emissions. Each executive is the human face of the corporation that she or he helps manage. If Mason and McNally are competent oral communicators, listeners will be better informed. Ideally, the listeners' good feelings about each company and its products and services are reinforced because of each speaker's effective communication manner, as well.

David Rockefeller, former chairman of Chase Manhattan Bank, outlined attributes he felt chief executives of United States businesses in the year 2000 should possess:

> [A corporate executive] must stand up for what he stands for. The CEO will be expected to represent articulately and coherently his company and industry to their critics. This will mean departing from

the serene seas of the boardroom and plunging into the rough and tumble waters of the hearing room and the press room.[1]

Opinions of successful business people like Rockefeller are corroborated by research studies that show that strong oral communication abilities are essential managerial skills. The Administrative Management Society asked a nation-wide group of middle managers to rate the importance of general and specific activities they performed on the job. Table 1–1 divides the top 20 responses into three levels of competency: super critical, highly critical, and critical. The ability to effectively communicate orally ranked eighth, and, of the remaining 19 management skills, ten (highlighted with an asterisk) are directly or indirectly related to oral communication.

Functional expertise in your job, whether your career is accounting, personnel relations, engineering, nursing, or architecture, is essential, of course, but competency in communications tends to be considered more important than technical skills. Promotable employees not only have a strong technical and educational base, but also the oral communication ability to explain their thinking to other people and to implement their plans through other people.

In addition to the communication functions they fulfil, your speaking opportunities become showcases of your thinking and organizational ability. Less experienced managers and staff members who are anxious about their speaking skills generally pass up, or mess up, chances to speak before a group, to conduct interviews, and to run meetings. On the other hand, people who excel at these communication tasks volunteer for them and in turn are noticed by superiors, who give them more opportunities to use these critical talents. Their visibility increases further, their contribution to the organization's success is greater, and these individuals are rewarded with more responsibility and higher pay.

Even if you are not pursuing a specific business career like accounting, management, sales, systems programming, or financial analysis, you will most likely be practicing your job skills in a business environment. A social worker, for example, uses competency in speech to interview clients, to speak before community groups, and to run staff meetings. An engineer must express project plans articulately and convincingly to other team members, superiors, and clients. People in such professions will ultimately manage people and resources to fulfill their objectives. Like

---

1. "Search is on for Executives of the Year 2000," *The Plain Dealer* Jan. 14, 1980: 9–C.

TABLE 1-1
20 Critical Managerial Competencies

Importance Rating	Rank	Competency
Super critical	1	*Listen actively
	2	*Give clear, effective instructions
	3	Accept your share of responsibility
	4	Identify real problem
Highly critical	5	Manage time and set priorities
	6	*Give recognition for excellent performance
	7	*Communicate decisions to employees
	8	*Communicate effectively orally
	9	Shift priorities if necessary
	10	*Explain work
	11	*Obtain and provide feedback in two-way communication sessions
Critical	12	Write effectively
	13	Prepare action plan
	14	Define job qualifications
	15	Effectively implement organizational change
	16	*Explain and use cost reduction methods
	17	Prepare and operate within a budget
	18	Develop written goals
	19	*Justify new personnel and capital equipment
	20	*Participate in seminars and read

*Directly or indirectly related to oral communication

Source: Harold T. Smith, "20 Critical Competencies for Managers," *Management World* Jan. 1978: 30–32.

business people, they have a critical need for above-average, even superior, oral communication competency.

Fortunately, you already possess many oral communication skills that you use successfully. You do not have to start from square one. Instead, you must evaluate your repertoire of oral communication skills, set realistic goals, and make small adjustments over time. In this way you will gradually improve. Remember, people are not *born* as naturally talented speakers. Good on-the-job speaking is actually a bundle of skills that must be practiced and developed.

Let's take on the challenge by first examining how you might use oral communication skills in the business and professional world, and then let's identify speaking situations in which you will need to perform well.

SPEAKING OPPORTUNITIES

Business and professional speaking is functional, goal-oriented, and practical; you are speaking to fulfil an organizational objective. The speaker recognizes a problem; in response to that problem, the speaker decides to communicate orally. Her immediate objective may be to inform, to analyze, to persuade, to motivate, or to inspire. If she communicates successfully and accomplishes the objective, the problem should be resolved; or at least lessened.

All business and professional people are managers of people, time, and resources; managers are paid to recognize and solve problems as well. Good communication skills are a part of the everyday interaction needed to perform such tasks. Therefore, you as a business or professional person will encounter many opportunities that will challenge your oral communication ability. Some of these speaking opportunities arise within the business organization itself, on company time and on company property—in your office, in a conference room, or in a small auditorium. In addition to the considerable time spent in informal speaking, which occurs in face-to-face or telephone conversations every day, oral communication takes the form of interviews, small-group meetings, and large-group conferences.

Interviews are planned, purposeful, structured conversations in which the interviewer and the interviewee exchange information, persuade each other, or solve a problem. Interviewing is a very common form of communication interaction in business environments. You are probably familiar with two common business interview situations: the job interview, an example of an informational interview, and the periodic job evaluation interview, an example of a problem-solving interview.

Small-group conferences are used extensively in organizations to gather and process information, to orient or train, to explore problems, and to make and implement decisions. They bring together five to ten people with an interest and/or expertise in the subject at hand. Staff meetings and committee meetings are the best examples of small-group communication. The speaking requirements may be very informal and spontaneous as conferees engage in focused discussion across the table. Or, the requirements may be more formal, calling for a standing presentation using a lectern and visual aids.

Large-group conferences and conventions occur less frequently, but demand a big investment of time and effort to plan and to manage. Examples of large-group conferences and conventions include meetings of employees, executives, sales representatives, stockholders, distributors, and current or prospective customers and clients. Such conferences may involve hundreds or more people meeting for several hours or even several days.

Speaking before small or large audiences is often termed **platform speaking** because the speaker may be using a lectern on a raised stage for better visibility, and a microphone for voice amplification. Platform speaking takes many forms: briefings to update listeners on new products, policies, or plans; question-and-answer sessions in which the speaker responds to questions after making short introductory remarks; lectures in which a single speaker develops a topic; and forums in which several experts make presentations followed by a question-and-answer period with the audience. Speakers may participate in person or may be taped or filmed for later viewing or broadcast. For example, a nurse might take part in an instructional videotape for diabetic patients on how to inject insulin correctly.

These on-the-job platform speaking opportunities are only the tip of the iceberg. Many off-the-job speaking opportunities also come up. Upwardly mobile business and professional people are active in the business, professional, and social community, often representing their organizations. The vice president of research and development, for instance, makes a presentation to the Rotary Club on Omega Foods' new non-caloric fat substitute, which is undergoing product-safety testing. You do now or will soon belong to professional, trade, civic, and social organizations that hold meetings and conferences. As an active member, you will have many chances to put your oral communication talents to the test—chairing a meeting, sharing in a group discussion on matters of administrative policy, or making a 15- or 30-minute speech followed by a question-and-answer period on a topic on which you have experience or which you have researched.

Mass communication opportunities arise, too. Professional people and executives, experts in their fields, are sought out by television and radio media for interviews for news programs or are invited to appear as guests on talk shows or public events programs. For example, the personnel director at Omega Foods may be interviewed by a reporter from a local radio station about plans to expand the local plant's labor force when Omega's fat substitute goes into production.

Opportunities for public speaking connected with your work never cease. But whether speaking on the job or off the job, for your organization or for yourself, you must select a preparation and delivery style—the style best suited to the speaking situation, and the style that lets you communicate in an interesting, forceful, interactive, and memorable fashion.

PRESENTATION MODES

Your presentation options are memorized, read, impromptu, and extemporaneous. The first two options have very little usefulness for the typical business or professional person. Let's see why this is so.

Memorized Presentations

Recall when you were in elementary school and took part in an assembly. You no doubt used the memorized mode to present your 25-word contribution on the health benefits of green vegetables in the eight-year-old's diet. Do you also remember how you feared forgetting your part, even though you practiced it dozens of times with your teacher and family? Do you remember saying it word by word without any emotion, much like the proverbial talking parrot? Weren't you more concerned with getting each word out in the correct order—before the whole word pyramid came crashing down around you—than you were with communicating? Fifteen or twenty years later, the memorized approach still holds these pitfalls in store for you.

In a memorized presentation, the speaker researches and structures material, writes out the entire speech, and then commits it verbatim to memory. Delivering the speech becomes simply recitation.

Business and professional people find little application for memorized presentations. Because, first of all, the speaker cannot adapt the subject matter to the audience; he knows exactly what to say and he cannot deviate from the memorized manuscript.

The content and organization cannot be modified to tailor the talk to specific audience needs. Even if a speaker works skillfully at studying the audience beforehand, audience analysis is still somewhat unpredictable. Because speaking is a dynamic, interactive process, the speaker cannot totally anticipate what the audience's reaction will be, nor should the speaker expect to. Therefore, memorized presentations will lack flexibility and adaptability. The speaker risks losing listener interest.

Secondly, the speaker may forget what to say next (as you might have done in that long-ago assembly). Because of the natural anxiety speakers have, their memory will quite likely fail them. Without back-up protection, such as a manuscript or notes to refer to in an emergency, you worry about forgetting what to say next, which in turn makes you more nervous, which in turn makes you worry even more. No wonder people forget.

Thirdly, a memorized speech will sound recited—words droned out automatically, without vocal color or personal involvement. The talk will resemble those lifeless, mechanical speeches given by tour guides or door-to-door sales people. Actors, through training, can take a script, memorize it, and deliver the words with realistic vocal inflection, facial expression, and body language. But most of us cannot do this. Lacking naturalness, our delivery will sound recited—because it *is*.

Read Presentations

Using the read presentation option, the speaker has researched, analyzed, outlined, and written out word for word the entire speech that she intends to read.

There are several disadvantages to a read presentation. For example, the speaker's eyes will be on the manuscript, not on the listeners, and important eye contact will be lost. The natural, spontaneous, interactive quality of face-to-face conversation will be lost, unless the speaker has mastered the art of reading aloud. Like memorized talks, the speaker cannot alter the planned presentation to suit the audience's needs better. Nor can she make the manuscript sound as conversational, interesting, or ad-libbed as desirable. Written communication simply sounds different from oral communication. When writing, our sentences are longer and more complex, our vocabulary more varied and studied.

Reading a presentation is not very compelling. If the speaker has written out the talk and plans to read the manuscript, why go to the considerable expense of assembling all the listeners in the same place at the same time when the content could be more cheaply and more conveniently distributed in written report format? The memo recipient can read just as well as the speaker. Besides, the memo reader can digest the information at her convenience and file the written document for later reference.

In defense of the read presentation, this mode has some usefulness. Suppose, for example, that a businessperson is dealing with highly complex, technical material. A read presentation may be the way to go. Through careful planning, the speaker has decided the ideal way to express each intricate concept. She may lose some spontaneity, but the precision of the finished product outweighs the benefits of improvisation.

Perhaps the subject is delicate or controversial, and the speaker wants to minimize misquoting. A read approach is warranted. In making a statement to the press, a firm's representative reads a carefully worded announcement describing an industrial accident that killed two plant employees. Ad-libbing is dangerous in this situation, leaving the speaker subject to unclear statements, ambiguous and incriminating remarks, or potentially damaging speculation.

A final reason to read a speech is tight time constraints. If the presentation will be broadcast, for instance, and the time limit is 60 seconds, the speaker should probably read from a prepared script to pack in all the essential information.

Where a read speech is called for, the speech maker will consciously have to strive for a conversational writing style and then practice delivering the content in a natural, relaxed style with frequent glances at the audience to avoid a mechanical, robotlike delivery.

While reciting or reading to an audience does not capitalize on the built-in advantages of face-to-face oral communication, two speaking modes do. The impromptu and extemporaneous speaking styles are more useful to business and professional people for this reason.

Impromptu Presentations

In the impromptu presentation style, the speaker talks without any formal preparation. This is the "say a few words" situation. In social conversation we speak impromptu all the time—

when you are introduced to three or four people at a business luncheon, when you strike up a conversation with the person next to you on the bus, and so on. In a business meeting, a topic comes up on which the chairperson thinks you are the best person to speak. You are asked to review the situation: "Sam, you've been investigating putting our employee shift scheduling on the computer. In a couple of minutes, update us on what you've done and what the picture looks like so far."

Because impromptu talk situations arise without notice, you cannot plan your presentation much, if at all. Your best preparation is your experience and a high level of awareness you have gained through reading and job involvement. Take consolation in the fact that a person is practically never asked to speak impromptu on a topic on which she or he knows nothing. Indeed, quite often people can anticipate impromptu talk situations. Sam, for example, might have foreseen that committee members might expect a status report on computer scheduling, so he could have come to the meeting prepared to discuss it. Professionals are expected to perform on the spot, to comply with requests, to have data and ideas at hand.

In impromptu situations, therefore, you will probably be quite conversant with the subject matter. And, if you have experience with the other types of planned presentations, you will be able to bring more organizational structure and natural delivery style to the talk situation. The challenge is to organize it quickly and deliver it comfortably. Speakers who are more experienced in public speaking can instantly analyze the speech request, marshal the supporting information from memory, choose a simple, logical, organizational pattern, and then speak clearly and confidently.

Extemporaneous Presentations

Most talk situations call for the extemporaneous speaking mode. The speech is prepared, outlined, and practiced. However, it is not written. The speaker delivers the talk from brief notes and the exact phraseology is chosen as the speaker interacts with the listeners. The talk outline should consist of just enough cues and supporting data to keep the speaker on the carefully planned organizational schedule. Because the main points and subpoints are presented in a predetermined order, the presentation has logic and unity. Also, because the speaker takes these brief notes and fleshes them out into sentences and paragraphs choosing words spontaneously, the presentation will quite likely be delivered naturally and conversationally. The speaker is responding to audience feedback, and the presentation is tailored to actual audience dynamics. For these reasons, extemporaneous speaking is the best approach to planning and delivering a speech.

Much preparation goes into an extemporaneous presentation. However, this does not mean that you should develop extremely detailed notes. If you do, you will take the easiest route and rely too extensively on your talk outline, reverting to the read style. This does not mean that you should over-practice, either. If you do, you will most likely fall into a set delivery pattern and revert to a recited style. The important factors in competent extemporaneous speaking of note design and practice techniques are presented in Chapter 3.

Extemporaneous speaking is spontaneous. That means it will not be perfect—every turn of phrase will not be flawless. The speaker will occasionally stumble or grope for a word, but the audience will be forgiving. The presenter will be focusing on them, and communicating to them, instead of concentrating on a bunch of memorized or read words. The audience appreciates that the speaker is really *talking* to them.

Extemporaneous speaking is therefore the most flexible, soundest, and safest speech mode. In fact, most of this text is directed at developing an effective extemporaneous speaking style. As we have discussed already, memorized and written presentations have very limited application for business and professional people. Impromptu speaking cannot be avoided, but experienced speakers often attempt to minimize impromptu speaking situations. They know that any preparation time, even a few minutes to organize thoughts, is better than none.

In fact, speakers may even try to convert an impromptu talk situation into an extemporaneous one. When asked to speak at the weekly planning committee meeting, the speaker legitimately says to the leader, "May I have ten minutes to fill you in on the progress of the Quantum Technology negotiations at next week's meeting? I'll bring the latest specs and preliminary bid figures that my people will be finishing up by then." Of course, without evading the talk opportunity altogether, the speaker has to decide quickly the best route: Either speak impromptu now and fulfil the communication need immediately or speak extemporaneously later at greater length, with greater detail, and no doubt more articulately. The postponed extemporaneous talk *does* keep the meeting members, and maybe the speaker's superiors, waiting. This risk itself may persuade the speaker to go the impromptu route.

What you are striving for as you begin refining your speaking skills is the spontaneous, relaxed, conversational, *talked* quality of extemporaneous or impromptu speaking. Be relaxed! Be conversational! That's easier to say, you may think, than to do. So, in the next section we will focus on speaking anxiety—we will define it and learn how it can be overcome.

SPEAKING ANXIETY

What is your greatest fear? When market researchers asked 3,000 people in the United States "What are you most afraid of?" 42 percent said "speaking before a group." This beat fear of heights (32 percent), insects and bugs (22 percent), sickness (19 percent), and even death (19 percent).[2] So, when you hear somebody say, "I'd rather die than make that presentation," that person may not be exaggerating as much as you think.

For many of us, speaking anxiety extends beyond formal speaking opportunities to simply asking questions or making comments in business meetings or in class. A group member has a thoughtful question to ask but cannot get the courage to raise his hand. Then 30 seconds later, he wants to kick himself because someone else pipes up with the same question and the group leader says, "That's a great question. I'm glad you asked it."

Accept fear of speaking in public as a common, almost universal, fear. It's perfectly normal to have stage fright. It will probably never completely disappear—in fact, you don't want it to. As we'll see later, *some* anxiety about a speaking opportunity is healthy and constructive.

Successful and rising professionals and executives are not immune to stage fright either. Imagine a successful executive, perhaps the president of a Fortune 500 company, perhaps having an MBA from a prestigious university, perhaps earning a yearly salary approaching seven figures. What makes her tick? What are her greatest strengths, fears, and insecurities? Would you guess public speaking? Corporate presidents, chief executive officers, and board chairs, often find it easier to direct a billion-dollar corporation than to speak in public. Put them before an audience, and their

---

2. David Wallechinshy, Irving Wallace, and Amy Wallace, *The Book of Lists* (New York: William Morrow and Company, Inc., 1977) 469–70.

Beattle Bailey © 1988. Reprinted by permission of King Features Syndicate, Inc.

You can overcome your anxiety about speaking in public, control it, and even use it to your advantage.

authority and confidence drain away. They are alone, and uncomfortable being judged as individuals.

Thomas A. Murphy, for example, retired chairman of General Motors, admitted that he was so nervous before a speech that he almost felt physically sick. But, like most top executives, he insists it was part of the job, and he made public appearances at least once a week during his six-year term as chairman.

When asked to speak before a group, maybe six or seven people, perhaps your job colleagues or classmates whom you've known for years, you may have physical sensations of nervousness—"butterflies in your stomach," increased perspiration, and dry, "cotton mouth." You may also have psychological problems. You may feel inferior to the audience: "What could I possibly tell my audience that is worthy of their time and attention?" Feeling insecure is another symptom: "Some of my listeners are my bosses; they may know more about the subject than I do." You might even want to avoid the situation altogether: "Maybe a big snowstorm will close the interstate and I won't have to give my talk to the accounting society tomorrow morning."

Anxious speakers attempt to physically withdraw. They hide behind the lectern. While the lectern is designed merely to hold the speaker's notes, some speakers use it defensively. It becomes a barrier, a fortress separating the speaker from the audience. The speaker may scrunch up behind the lectern to minimize his physical presence and interaction with the audience. Or, the speaker might withdraw by using a soft, hesitant voice, one that is difficult to hear and gradually fades away. Some speakers look away from listeners, trying to avoid eye contact. Instead, their eyes are glued to their notes or they look over their listeners' heads, stare out the window, or gaze at the ceiling. Ironically, they lose the vital and reassuring eye contact with their audience.

How many of these symptoms of speaking anxiety have you had? Understanding the problem and accepting it is the first step to overcoming your fear. Many successful people have overcome their anxiety about speaking in public and you can, too. The following suggestions on how to overcome speaking anxiety, or at least keep it to a manageable level, will help you reach that goal.

1. Approach public speaking with a new set of attitudes. Take the negative, destructive feelings, turn them around, and use them to your advantage. Channel your negative energy into positive outlets. Become excited about your subject matter and about conveying it to your audience in a personable, conversational manner. This is a bit of a mental trick you play on yourself, but it works nevertheless. Your fears about standing before your audience and talking will lessen if you focus more on your audience and on your content and less on yourself.

2. Realize that *some* anxiety is good. Your fears will probably never go away completely. There's always bound to be some apprehension; after all, you are putting yourself on the line when you speak publicly. If you have some anxiety, a nervous edge, you might call it, you obviously care about your presentation. You care about communicating clearly and convincingly to your listeners. You care about accomplishing your purpose and giving the listeners the information that they need. This attitude is important, and it is better than being too calm, too relaxed, or too psychologically removed from your communication responsibility.

3. Prepare well. By planning your talk systematically and thoroughly, you become an expert on your subject matter. You become more confident and secure. You will have more information than you really need or have time to convey. This information is not useless cargo: It comes in handy if you need to develop more content depth with your listeners, and you can use it during your question-and-answer period, too. Feeling like an expert will buoy your confidence.

4. Practice. Your talk is well planned and organized. You have developed good notes that guide you through your presentation and give you the verbal support you need. By working through your presentation several times, you gain a sense of success. You start to think: "My presentation has worked for me during practice sessions. I've accomplished my communication purpose interestingly and concretely. There's every reason to believe I'll do just as well before my audience."

5. Look for friendly faces in the audience. Concentrate your eye contact on especially receptive, friendly faces. Think of them as your support group. Your eye contact with these attentive, interested, sympathetic persons will add to your confidence. When you become more skilled and comfortable at public speaking, you can divert more attention to the more challenging members of the audience and work to win them over.

6. Relax. Take several deep breaths before you begin. This counteracts some of your body's physical symptoms of anxiety—your breathing rate and heart rate will slow. Standing straight helps, too. Your lung capacity will be greater, so you won't run out of breath in the middle of a sentence. Another relaxation tip is to keep your hands off the lectern. Clenching the podium is bound to tighten you up; with your hands free, you can gesture naturally, which helps you to relax.

Remain calm even if you make a blunder, skip a point, mispronounce a word, or grope for words. These things happen all the time, even to experienced speakers. Don't let these little delivery flaws throw you off balance. Instead, pause for a second, take a deep breath, gather your composure, and proceed with your material.

7. Share your fears with your listeners. This way you get your anxieties out in the open where you can deal with them, rather than having that extra burden of trying to hide them. Of course, this suggestion works best for beginners. Experienced speakers take the chance of losing credibility and respect by acknowledging their insecurities about public speaking. But if the circumstances are right, your audience will accept your confession of anxiety. In fact, this admission may heighten their rapport with you.

8. Get experience. Reading a book like this will acquaint you with the principles and techniques of good speaking, but ultimately you learn how to make a speech just as you learn how to swim, to ride a bike, or to play the piano: You learn to speak by speaking. Oral communication is a complex skill that improves gradually through focused practice. A feeling of control, ease, and comfort will develop as you practice your public speaking. Be patient, though. You cannot learn to play the piano in a week either. Building your repertoire of planning, organizational, and delivery skills is an investment of time and energy in professional development that pays handsome dividends.

Before you speak, look around at your audience of business colleagues, members of a social organization, or your fellow classmates. Don't they look understanding, sympathetic, and empathetic? Remember that the typical listener wants to have his or her time well used and to profit by this investment of time in hearing your talk. Especially in an instructional environment, your listeners will provide a supportive climate in which you can experiment, practice, learn, perhaps fail, and ultimately succeed as you work to improve your oral business communication skills.

SUMMING UP

For business and professional people, the ability to communicate clearly, persuasively, and confidently has always been one key to career success. Whether a manager, engineer, or scientist, people need strong speaking skills to carry out their job tasks, since oral communication is the primary means of communicating and working with people. Those wishing to strengthen their oral communication skills seek out speaking opportunities that allow them to demonstrate their thinking and organizational skills; thus they increase their visibility and promotability. Such speaking opportunities occur both on the job and off the job in the form of interviews, platform speaking before small and large groups, and participation in meetings.

Among the delivery modes available to business and professional speakers are memorizing and reading, both of which eliminate the speaker's ability to interact with the audience in a spontaneous, natural manner. Experienced presenters find that impromptu speaking—speaking without preparation—and extemporaneous speaking—speaking with preparation—produce a more relaxed, conversational, interactive delivery style. An impromptu speaker selects and organizes material on the spot and then delivers it comfortably. An extemporaneous speaker uses a talk outline to execute an organizational pattern carefully developed in advance, yet chooses the exact phraseology while reacting to the audience.

Regardless of presentation mode, speakers must address the universal fear of speaking in public. Employing such techniques as practicing thoroughly, focusing on supportive audience members, using relaxation techniques, and getting public speaking experience, you can overcome the symptoms of speaking anxiety and direct that nervous energy into positive channels. You become excited by the challenge of accomplishing both your communication objectives and your listener's by speaking confidently, dynamically, and authoritatively.

Application Exercises

1. Interview a successful person in your career area. Ask this person to answer the following questions, and share this information in a class discussion:
   a. What are the types and frequency of on-the-job public speaking in your career?
   b. What are the types and the frequency of public speaking opportunities that arise off the job in connection with professional, civic, and social organizations? Do you represent your organization on these occasions?
   c. What types of presentation modes do you use? What are the surrounding circumstances? What is your personal recommendation for a presentation mode?
   d. What is your degree of speaking anxiety, and how do you cope with it? Has public speaking become easier for you with experience?
2. Present a 30-second self-introduction. Tell your audience two or three things about yourself, other than your name: for example, your year in college, your major/minor, your goals for semester/quarter, your career plans, your current job, your favorite pastimes.
3. Pair up with a classmate and prepare a 30-second talk introducing this person to the class. Take three minutes to interview him/her and then develop two or three of the ideas in number 2 in your introduction.
4. Present a 30- to 60-second impromptu talk on one of the following topics:
   a. favorite hobby or recreation
   b. best movie seen recently
   c. pros and cons of your college or university
5. Present a 30- to 60-second impromptu talk on one of these food-related topics:
   a. favorite restaurant
   b. mom's best dish
   c. I don't see how anyone can eat . . .
   d. best fast food
   e. My comfort food is . . .
   f. About the only thing I can cook is . . .
6. Give a one- to two-minute extemporaneous talk. To prepare, take three minutes to develop a simple set of notes (a few key words to help you organize your points) on one of the following topics:
   a. If I were CEO of _____, I'd . . .
   b. I want a business career because _____.
   c. I chose _____ as my major because _____.
   d. If my career goes as I predict, in 15 years I will be . . .
   e. Why _____[name of your city]_____ is (or isn't) a great place to be a _____[your chosen profession]_____ .

Chapter 2

ORAL COMMUNICATION BASICS

You can spend your whole life communicating most of your waking hours and possibly never think about how communication actually works. On the job, at home, or at play, we take for granted the intricate and fragile communication process that we use to convey meaning to other people. Whether speaker or listener, understanding the building blocks of oral communication will allow you to communicate better. This chapter seeks to develop awareness of the tools we use as oral communicators. We will look at:

- how the process of communication operates and how you can make it work for you,
- how audience analysis can help you communicate better,
- how you can strengthen your listening abilities.

THE COMMUNICATION PROCESS

"You cannot not communicate." Think about the logic and meaning of those words. The grammar is strained, but the double negative serves to reinforce the point that human communication is an unavoidable and on-going process. We communicate all the time—we exchange meaningful messages with others through words and actions, whether we consciously plan to or not. Yet, it is this almost automatic, constant characteristic of communication that causes business and professional people to overestimate their communication ability. Most of us feel we communicate efficiently 95 percent of the time. The other 5 percent of the time, when we fail to make our point clearly, we blame the other person who "can't understand plain English!"

Redirecting the blame is common in failed communication attempts, but it is hardly justifiable. Communication is a complex process that is imperfect and malfunctions easily. Skilled oral communications must understand the mechanics and interactions of the communication process. Putting this knowledge to work, we can increase the effectiveness of our oral communication with superiors, subordinates, customers, clients, suppliers, and anyone with whom we speak.

Communication is a two-way process of exchanging information. Because communication is a two-way process, it can be diagrammed as a closed loop, such as Figure 2–1 shows. From the perspective of a business or professional person, we shall examine

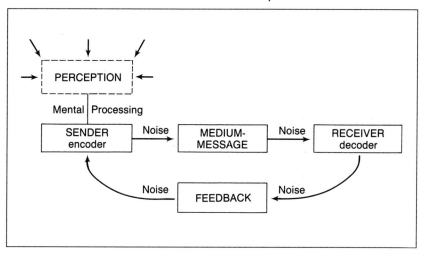

FIGURE 2-1
Communication Loop

The diagram illustrates the fact that communication is a two-way process.

each of the complex variables that make up the delicate communication process.

Perception and mental processing Perception is the act of using our senses to become aware of our environment. Perception is selective; naturally, we all have different perceptions of the world around us. Although we live in the same objective world, each one of us has a different subjective impression of the world.

Here is an illustration to make that point less abstract. You and two friends are studying for your accounting midterm in the student union lounge. Someone asks the three of you to describe your perceptions at that instant. Even though you all are in the same place, at the same time, engaged in the same activity, you will almost certainly have quite dissimilar perceptions of your environment. You might describe the physical environment in specific detail, concentrating on the shape and size of the room, the furniture, the colors of the floor and walls, and the room's temperature and lighting. One friend might concentrate her description on other people in the lounge, estimating the number of people, describing what they are wearing, and making guesses about their social and economic backgrounds. Your other friend might zero in on the activity in which the three of you are engaged, focusing on the studying you are doing, describing how you have decided to study only certain chapters from your textbook, how you have shared your class notes with one another, and how apprehensive you all are about doing well on the midterm.

Why do the three of you have such vastly different reactions to identical surroundings? We all have different mental filters that make us tune to different aspects of all the sensory information we are receiving. Because we are unique individuals with different backgrounds, likes, attitudes, and values, we react to only some of the millions of bits of data that flood our sensory organs. To avoid being overwhelmed—suffering "sensory overload"—we tune in to some of the data and tune out the rest.

Another complicating factor is at work. We each have different thinking styles, ways of processing all the incoming data with which we are bombarded. Are you a person who is very verbal, who can write or speak easily compared to others? Are you instead a numbers person, someone who takes to math? Are you good at spatial reasoning, dealing with objects in three-dimensional space like an engineer or architect must do? Over the years, each of us has developed a distinct thinking and behavior pattern that shapes our reaction to the concrete reality around us.

Going back to our example in the student union, you, being a product of your one-of-a-kind life experiences, are more sensitive to your physical surroundings, one friend more sensitive to the interpersonal workings of your study group, and your other friend, maybe because this subject is really tough for him, more sensitive to the quality of the study process.

Indeed, it is because of these differences in how we perceive our environment and how we process that sensory information in our brains that we are compelled to communicate. Can you imagine the kind of science-fiction world we would live in if we all perceived, thought, and acted the same way? In such a predictable world, perhaps we could say in such a dull existence, we would not need to communicate; what I would think would be what you would think. There is obviously no danger of this world coming about. Communication will always be a vital aspect of our lives. We perceive something, we think about it, we decide to share the result, and we form that concept into a message.

Sender In oral communication the sender is the speaker who formulates the message to be conveyed. The speaker *encodes* the message to be conveyed. The speaker encodes the message into words, other symbols, and actions—both conscious and unconscious.

Message What we communicate using verbal and nonverbal symbols is the message. For instance, a salesperson's self-introduction, discussion of a car buyer's needs, and pitch to fulfil those needs with a new car, is the message.

Medium The medium is the channel that is used. In oral communication, the verbal medium is speech supplemented by nonverbal symbols, including gestures and facial expressions.

Receiver The receiver is the audience, the listeners, who *decode* the sender's message. Ideally, the receiver will decode the message correctly and fully, without lost or added meaning. When this does not happen, we have miscommunicated. Often this miscommunication can be traced to faulty audience analysis on the sender's part. Often, miscommunication is caused by poor listening skills on the receiver's part. We will look into these causes later in this chapter.

Feedback Closing the communication loop is feedback from the receiver to the sender. Feedback is information that tells the speaker how well he or she has communicated. If the listeners' feedback indicates that the message was incomplete or jumbled in some way, the speaker often attempts to correct the miscommunication by repeating information or explaining in more detail, with better receiver-oriented examples. One advantage to oral communication is that feedback is instantaneous and constant; when communicating by writing, feedback is delayed and often too late to be useful to the sender.

A person listening to a lecture, engaging in an interview, or participating in a meeting provides feedback in a variety of ways. Feedback might be verbal. When an audience member asks questions of the speaker, that person is providing feedback that the speaker may use to determine whether the intended message was actually received correctly. Another form of feedback is paraphrasing; the listener, in his or her own words, will repeat the content and/or intent of the speaker's message. The sender uses the paraphrase to gauge if the message was accurately and completely transmitted. The sender can then correct any errors by re-explaining, elaborating, or clarifying.

Feedback from the receiver to the sender can also be nonverbal. Sharon, an observant and sensitive speaker, monitors her audience for signs of understanding, agreement, and interest. By keeping her eyes on the audience, she might see listeners nodding their heads, signifying their comprehension and approval. Of course, Sharon might sometimes notice puzzled expressions or scowls that may be evidence of confusion or disapproval. Worse, she might see listeners on the verge of dozing off or checking their watches—signs that she should enliven her delivery, end soon, or address the audience's interests more directly.

Noise At any of the junctions in the communication loop, noise can occur. Noise is anything that interferes with the accurate transfer of the message. Senders and receivers are affected by five categories of "noise":

1. Physical noise, actual sounds or distractions in the room that make speaking and listening difficult. A police car's siren may distract the speaker's and listeners' attention momentarily, or just make it more difficult for the listeners to hear. Being unable to make out slides because the room is too well lighted or being unable to see the small detail in the speaker's charts because the print is too small are also examples of physical "noise."

2. Physiological noise, distractions caused by the way one party feels physically. A speaker with a severe case of the flu or a listener with a painful headache is more likely to make encoding or decoding errors. They are concerned more with seeking relief from their bodily discomfort than with the communication process.

3. Psychological noise, distractions caused by the speaker and/or listener's mental states. Psychological noise acts like an emotional filter. If you were chewed out by your boss, you might have difficulty paying attention or participating in a staff meeting that begins five minutes later. Other causes of psychological noise are fear, boredom, discouragement, poor motivation, and alienation.

4. Perceptual noise, the conflicting factors of knowledge, values, attitudes, and backgrounds of the speaker and of the listeners. The unique mental filter mentioned earlier causes us to see and hear only what we *want* to see and hear.

For example at a meeting to update employees on changes to the company's retirement plans, Adam and Maria hear the same words, but they process and interpret them differently. Adam is 25, 40 years away from retirement. He just received his M.B.A. and started work as an assistant production manager. He has always had plenty of material comforts and is optimistic that the future will take care of itself. Maria is 63, 2 years from retirement. She worked her way up the organization from the production floor. She remembers the depression in the 1930s, and she is used to struggling hard for life's rewards. Adam is unconcerned and accepts the information without much thought. Maria is seriously and immediately affected. She begins to worry, adding psychological noise to her communications problems. Because of different mental filters, Adam and Maria react quite differently to the speaker's content.

5. Semantic noise, misunderstanding caused by the meaning of words. If you use the word "disintermediation" in a talk on investing and most of your listeners are not familiar with the word, you will likely confuse or annoy them. To avoid such reactions, train yourself to speak the language of your listeners. Avoid jargon and technical language unless your audience analysis indicates that you and your listeners share the same vocabulary. For the most part, use short, simple, conversational words. These come to your mind first anyway. Talking this way will also make your speech more powerful and emphatic. Say "end" instead of "terminate" and "carry out" instead of "implement." Remember, your audience wants to grasp and retain your content easily. Simplicity in word choice pays off in easier and more accurate comprehension by your listeners.

By now, you probably have developed a healthy respect for the miracle of human communication. In fact, you may now be thinking that it is a wonder that people communicate as well as they do. You, whether speaker or listener, have the responsibility to anticipate and minimize as many of the potential barriers to good oral communication as possible. Before looking at listener responsibilities in more detail, let's examine a major speaker responsibility—audience analysis.

AUDIENCE ANALYSIS

Audience analysis helps you put communication theory to work. How exactly do you go about researching the audience and using your acquired knowledge for mutual speaker-listener benefit? In this section, we will examine the special importance of audience analysis, the three kinds of data you research about your listeners, and a convenient classification for listener roles.

Value of Audience Analysis

In speech preparation, get your priorities in order. Look first at your audience. By knowing your audience's objectives and striving to fulfil them, you will more likely accomplish your objectives. In on-the-job, written communication, you develop the "you attitude," or emphasis on the reader's point of view. In public speaking you must cultivate this same understanding by analyzing the listener's perspective. You must appeal to that point of view to attract and maintain interest and, if necessary, motivate. The more you know about the audience, the more you will be able to organize the message to satisfy listener needs.

Fortunately, audience analysis for many professional and business speaking situations is uncomplicated. Your listener group is often **homogeneous,** meaning that they share many characteristics with each other and with you. When you are addressing a monthly staff meeting, your audience will be quite homogeneous since you all work in the same department, for the same company, and so on. You may have similar levels of responsibility, and share many organizational and personal career objectives. Also, because you work with these people daily, you probably know them well enough to know the level of their experience with your subject, their relative interest in it, and their probable acceptance or resistance to it.

Of course, even if your listeners are homogeneous, some important differences may still exist among audience members. Perhaps one person is new to your department and does not know the events leading up to the subject at hand. Maybe one of your business associates is stubborn and doggedly resists new ideas. One of your listeners may work in the field with clients and has a different orientation to the content than those who work in the office. Still, all things considered, in many business speaking situations you will have a pretty good understanding of your audience and what it expects.

Realistically speaking, not all audience analysis will be this easy. You may be presenting before an outside group about which little is known. Or, the audience may be a diverse group, one that is **heterogeneous** because it shows considerable variation in audience characteristics. For example, Deborah Browning's boss asked her to fill a speaking request by the Shaker Heights Professional Women's Club. This audience wants a 45-minute presentation on how to design a life insurance program. In talking with the program chairperson, Deborah discovers that her entire audience will be women with careers in business or the professions. About half the audience will be under 40. About half the audience are married. Over half of the women have children.

Deborah's task is challenging because of such diversity. Women with school-age children will be more interested in insurance that provides large amounts of protection at the lowest cost. The women without children or with grown children will want to maximize their retirement income through insurance with savings features. Married women in the audience will have greater incomes because they have two income sources, so they will probably want to integrate their insurance protection with their husbands' to achieve joint goals. The single women's perspectives will be much different. Understanding that she must meet the diverse needs of her listeners, Browning must present as comprehensive an overview of life insurance options as she can in 45 minutes.

Audience Analysis Factors

Like Deborah, you need to conduct some audience research to understand the people you will be speaking to. How can you get this information? You can rely on your memory to recall information about listeners if you have worked or spoken with them before. You can discuss the type of audience, their needs, and their expectations with the program chairperson or the person who requested you to speak. You can check the roster of meeting attendees to find out who will be attending. You can interview some of your prospective audience members. Regardless of your approach, you will need the following three types of information about listeners: demographic data, psychographic data, and knowledge-to-date.

Demographic Data   The hard information about your audience is termed demographic data. Common demographic factors that may influence the development of your content include:

1. Size of the audience. Some group interaction techniques work best with a certain audience size. A question-and-answer format may be fine for a 10-member audience, but it will probably be unworkable for 100 people. Audience size also dictates the choice of visual aids. A chalkboard presentation suits a small group, but a 500-plus audience will need and expect slides.

2. Age. As we illustrated before in Deborah's example, 22-year-olds have different expectations than do 60-year-olds.

3. Sex. Whether the audience is predominantly male or female, or if there is some other proportion of gender, it may affect your presentation. Women, since they generally live longer than men, may have different insurance needs.

4. Economic level. A speaker discussing financial matters would tailor her presentation differently for under $25,000-income listeners than for over $50,000-income listeners. The first audience is anxious to hear about money saving options, but the second audience may be more interested in higher-premium options.

5. Educational level. Have you ever heard a speaker who spoke over your head? To minimize semantic noise, good speakers take time to investigate their audience's education level, and develop their subject matter using an appropriate vocabulary. You will try to use words that are common to the listeners, or you will take special precautions to define unfamiliar words as they are introduced. Have you ever attended a program at which you lacked the background knowledge to follow the intricate concepts being presented? When you are dealing with complex subject matter, you must choose between a cursory explanation of the topic in a 30-minute presentation and a more thorough presentation of the topic, touching on more advanced concepts, in a 60-minute presentation.

6. Professional or organizational status. Speaking to people whom you perceive to have a higher position in your profession and in your organization is always delicate. You have to go outside your usual role relationship with those listeners. Instead of being the receiver of information or instructions, you will be the giver. You need to concentrate more on establishing credibility and maintaining a professional demeanor. When speaking with peers and subordinates, you may be more relaxed because you and your listeners are acting comfortably within accepted roles.

Other demographic factors that might be considered are racial or ethnic membership, political affiliation, social position, and marital status.

Granted, not all of these factors will be relevant in researching every audience. Our life insurance speaker will probably not need to consider racial, ethnic, and political composition in preparing her talk. In fact, reference to irrelevant demographic factors might be taken by some listeners as condescension, bias, or even discrimination.

Psychographic Data The soft data—psychological/motivational information—a speaker gleans about her audience is called psychographic data. Such data, like the following list, is more difficult to uncover and may require more skill to analyze and use.

1. Needs. Psychologist Abraham Maslow's need hierarchy is one way of partially accounting for human motivation. His basic concept of motivation is that people are driven to satisfy their needs. To apply Maslow's theory to audience analysis, begin by determining your listeners' strongest unsatisfied needs. Once you determine this, the information can be used to motivate your listeners. Aim to create an awareness of those needs in the listener, needs that many times are unfelt at a conscious level. Then present a solution to fulfil those now-recognized needs—the listener will be motivated to follow your advice by a desire to fulfil them. So, unsatisfied needs can be used as motivators, while satisfied needs (that is, non-motivating needs) can be ignored.

Physiological needs are at the base of Maslow's five-level pyramid (Figure 2–2). Examples are the desire for food or for comfortable surroundings. If a speech overlaps the lunch hour, the audience may be more interested in filling their stomachs than filling their heads. After lunch satisfies their hunger, listeners may be more susceptible to appeals to higher-level needs. Of course, they may also be so relaxed and refreshed that they are not inclined to pay attention to a heavy, serious speech. After-dinner speakers generally use a lighter, more humorous approach to the subject matter.

First-level needs are otherwise rarely significant for most public speakers, besides providing for the basic physical comfort of the audience. The higher-level needs are more important considerations—economic security, recognition, praise from others, prestige, and personal accomplishment. They are more likely to be unsatisfied and, because they are learned, more within the province of the speaker to use to his or her advantage.

Let's look at an example. Our life insurance speaker can paint a picture of an impoverished, unhappy family created by the loss of a wage earner's income. Many listeners fear that their family's standard of living could not be maintained after their death. They fear the financial consequences that their loved ones would face

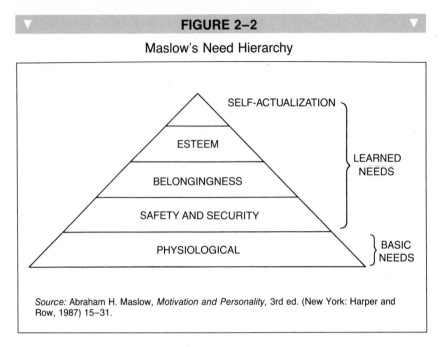

Maslow's need hierarchy seeks to explain and catalogue the forces that motivate individuals.

if they die suddenly. Deborah, by focusing on the economic security appeal, may be able to attract audience attention and motivate them to action by promoting life insurance as the best means of providing for one's family in the event of premature death. These audience members have a greater likelihood of buying life insurance if they see it as a way to fulfil the unsatisfied need for more economic security for their families.

Speakers, by successfully identifying their audience's strongest, most urgent needs, can devise effective persuasive appeals. Thus, the listener solves a problem—how to satisfy a need—and the speaker accomplishes her purpose—how to motivate the listeners to act in the desired way.

2. Values, attitudes, and beliefs. A speaker addresses the audience as a group, but each member of the audience listens individually. Using your new understanding of communication theory, you realize each person's mental filter affects what he or she hears and thinks. It has been shaped by distinct social, cultural, environmental, economic, and educational forces. To achieve your purpose as a speaker—especially if your purpose is to inform or to persuade—determine your listeners' attitudes and beliefs. Once you have this information—for instance, whether your audience's political beliefs are conservative or liberal—you can develop your talk's organizational pattern to move your listeners systematically and gradually from their point of view to your point of view.

Understanding your listeners' personalities and mindsets helps answer questions about your listeners: Are they interested in your subject matter? If not, how can you use their value systems, attitudes, and beliefs to capture and maintain their attention? What is your audience's relationship to you? Are the listeners co-workers, friends, or strangers? How can you bridge the gap or build on mutual lines of thinking to establish a common meeting ground between you and these listeners?

3. Knowledge-to-date. The last aspect of audience analysis is finding out what the audience already knows about the subject matter. The speaker needs to present the correct amount of information at the right level of sophistication for the audience. Failing to do this results in boring the listeners with information they already know or swamping them with more material than they can process. Our life insurance speaker would design one presentation for 25-year-olds with little knowledge of the basic concepts of life insurance and another, much different, presentation for middle-aged couples who already have experience with selecting life insurance coverage.

Audience Roles

Knowing your listeners' demographics, psychographics, and knowledge-to-date, you will now find it useful to classify the audience by the feeling-thinking roles that predominantly characterize the receivers.

Audiences fall into five categories (Figure 2–3). One or two receiver roles will normally dominate in the typical audience. With apathetic audiences, the speaker must work hard to attract and maintain attention by developing themes that will benefit the listener. With a sophisticated or hostile listener group, the speaker must establish credibility, develop areas of common agreement, and then attempt to persuade the listeners to alter their thinking. Faced with either of these three audience types, your goal is to change their receiver state to believing or critical. With believing or critical audiences, your objective is to preserve or intensify that receiver role.

FIGURE 2–3
Audience Receiver Roles

1. Apathetic	Receiver is psychologically numb and completely indifferent to speaker's communication. Audience is inattentive. Apathy is induced by forced attendance, previous negative experience with speaker, receiver saturation with speaker's subject matter, or poor physical environment (stuffy room, overcrowding, uncomfortable seats).
2. Sophisticated	Receiver assumes to know as much as or more than speaker and refuses to learn from speaker. Audience may be inattentive or "smart-alecky." Sophistication is induced by routine communication situations; flows of information from nonexpert to expert, subordinate to superior, peer to peer, or staff to line.
3. Hostile	Receiver opposes either speaker or speaker's ideas. Audience may be rude or heckle the speaker. Hostility is induced by same conditions causing apathy or sophistication, as well as by threatening situations, speakers with poor reputations, speakers with suspect motives, or cross-cultural reactions (manager to union steward or member of one ethnic group to member of another ethnic group).
4. Believing	Receiver accepts receiver and message. Believability is induced by speakers with good reputations, and flows of information from expert to nonexpert or superior to subordinate.
5. Critical	Receiver is willing to accept ideas based on facts and logical reasoning. Criticalness, with a bias either for or against the speaker and the speaker's ideas, is induced by open-mindedness, scientific thinking, substantiation of data.

Source: Adapted from George T. Vardaman, *Effective Communication of Ideas* (New York: Van Nostrand Reinhold Company, 1970) 102–16.

The believing audience is easiest to address. The speaker's main goal is to move the listeners to a stronger belief and/or to a commitment. Often the believing audience is *too* easy to speak to. These listeners willingly absorb the subject matter like a sponge, without necessarily intending to act or to respond. Most business and professional audiences are the critical type. This is a mixed blessing for the speaker. It is bad because it means more work since the critical audience may challenge the speaker more. The speaker must be very well prepared, needing a strong grasp of the subject matter. Content must be based on solid logic and facts that are substantiated. You cannot bluff this listener type with shallow material, gimmicky visual aids, or a slick, showy delivery style. The critical audience is good, on the other hand, because it is more likely to act if the speaker is persuasive. The listeners think: "I'll listen if your material is logically organized, thoroughly substantiated, and well delivered. And I'll follow through as you request because you've convinced me that doing so benefits me and the organization."

After completing your audience analysis, you will not be speaking to strangers. Your listeners are now familiar to you. You speak their language. You fulfil their need for information. You anticipate their reaction. The distance between the speaker and the audience has been shortened. Your speech communication will *probably* fulfil both speaker and listener goals—"probably" because you are only half the communication equation. Although the speaker has the responsibility to control and direct the oral communication process, the listener's job is equally important.

LISTENING

All the speaker's hard work and good intentions are ultimately at the mercy of the receiver's ability to listen well. Although communication consists of two distinct actions of sending and receiving, the notion, "you speak, they listen," is simplistic. The listener is not an empty jar into which the speaker pours information. The listener is an active part of the communication process—perceiving and processing verbal and nonverbal data. Assuming the speaker has done an effective job, the responsibility for successful communication now shifts to the listeners.

Barriers to Listening

Business and professional people spend about 80 percent of their time communicating. Communicating takes four forms: writing, speaking, reading, and listening. What percentage of time do you spend on each? Compare your answer to what communication experts say[1]:

        Writing   9%
        Reading   16%
        Speaking 30%
        Listening 45%

Were you close? If you're typical of most people, you spend almost half of your communicating time on the receiving end of speaking. Try another estimation: Rate these same four skills according to the amount of time schools devote to teaching each skill. Experts say that the actual order is: writing, reading, speaking, and listening. Note the inverse relationship. Listening, the communication skill we use 45 percent of the time, is the least taught skill. Consequently, the average person listens at 25 percent efficiency. After listening to a ten-minute presentation, the typical man or woman understands and remembers no more than half of what was said. One to two days later, he or she will remember less than one quarter. Most speakers at meetings and conferences speak longer than 10 minutes, meaning that listening efficiency is usually much less than 25 percent.

So, listening is the weakest link in the oral communication process. Contrast that fact with the importance of efficient listening skills for people in business and the professions—recall from Chapter 1 that listening actively was rated the number one managerial competency. Managers and professional people who do not listen cost organizations billions of dollars. Poor listening means orders are filled incorrectly, customers are lost, instructions are not followed, rumors are started, morale suffers. In a sense, managers and professionals are paid to listen. A major component of their jobs is decision making, and since decisions are made on information, we need to look at where much of that information comes from. It comes from listening.

Why are most people poor listeners? The lack of training and emphasis in schools is certainly one reason. Also, as children we learned bad habits from our adult role models, our parents and teachers, such as interrupting and faking attention. As grown-ups we continued to place more value on speaking than listening. To many people, the person at a meeting who does the most talking

---

1. George R. Bell, "Listen and You Shall Hear," *Association Management* March 1984: .

is seen as the most knowledgeable, assertive, and confident—even if what that person says has little value. Other meeting participants who are primarily listeners may be judged unfairly as timid, shy, or lacking in experience or knowledge. Yet these people are more likely to have a better understanding of what was said and a better insight into problems and their solution.

Another reason that listening is difficult is because we can think faster than we can listen. A normal speaking rate is 125 to 175 words a minute, but most of us process information at 300 to 400 words a minute. What do we do with the extra thinking time? Our thoughts jump ahead, our minds wander.

Six bad habits prevent listening according to Ralph Nichols and Leonard Steven, authors of the classic guide to effective listening[2]:

1. Faking attention. We assume that if we look like listeners we satisfy the expectations of the speaker. We only deceive ourselves with such thinking. We end up cheating ourselves out of learning from the communication opportunity—in effect wasting our time and the speaker's time.

2. "Overlistening." The listener becomes so busy memorizing the facts that he or she misses half the points, and eventually the main idea. Facts are only useful in constructing the ideas. Grasping ideas is the skill on which good listening rests. If you get the main idea, you will remember the supporting facts more effectively than the person who goes after facts alone.

3. Avoiding difficult listening. The terms "lecture" and "public address" frighten many people, who in turn stay away from them. Some people sit in front of their televisions switching from channel to channel with their remote controls trying to find something less challenging and more entertaining. Listening requires concentration, and many people are not willing to expend the energy to understand complex ideas.

4. Prematurely dismissing a subject as uninteresting. Poor listeners often rationalize that "uninteresting" means "not valuable" and they tune out the speaker. Uninteresting presentations often do contain information that is very much worth hearing and potentially quite useful. The English writer G. K. Chesterton once said that there is no such thing as an uninteresting subject, only uninterested people.

---

2. Ralph G. Nichols and Leonard A. Steven. *Are You Listening* (New York: McGraw-Hill Book Company, 1957) 104–12.

5. Criticizing delivery and physical appearance. An out-of-style haircut, too much make-up, a distracting, flamboyant suit, a shabby, untidy appearance, a foreign accent, or a speech impediment can all cause us to discount the value of a speaker, and thereby cause us to listen less intently. Physical appearance and delivery style, of course, do communicate valid information. Good listeners, though, never use them as alibis for not listening. The *content* of the message is almost always more important than the *form* of its delivery.

6. Yielding easily to distractions. True, people have short attention spans, but when motivated, we can overcome all sorts of distractions. When not motivated, we look for excuses not to listen. The room is too stuffy or the PA system whistles, screeches, and crackles. Rather than attempting to tune out the physical noise factors, they tune out the speaker.

Keys to Better Listening

Fortunately listening can be learned. Being able to improve your listening depends on whether you can develop a better attitude. Listening is a willful act; you must want to do it. Without a supportive attitude, you will not have the commitment to change your ineffective listening habits. And you must practice what you learn until the new skills become automatic. Listening requires mental conditioning. It's hard work—and we tend to avoid hard work. Good listeners listen actively, practicing the following listening techniques:

1. Prepare yourself on the subject to be discussed. If it is a new subject, find out about it. Some knowledge of the speaker's subject matter lets you evaluate him and his message better. At the same time, you increase the value of the conversation, presentation, interview, or meeting.

2. Limit distractions. Obviously, looking at the speaker rather than looking out the window helps you follow the speech better. Don't doodle, look at your watch, or drum your fingers during a sales meeting.

3. Stop talking. We must stop talking before we can start listening. Even when we are not talking during a meeting, we tend to be planning what we will say next rather than listening. Give the speaker time to deliver the message. Don't interrupt, rush for a response, show impatience, or fidget. Such behavior only creates barriers.

4. Focus primary attention on the verbal content of the presentation and secondary attention on the speaker's voice, appearance, and nonverbal message. Analyze the central theme. What are the speaker's main ideas? What is the pattern of reasoning?

5. Summarize material in your mind as you listen. That's a good way to use the extra mental processing time. Recap what has been said so far. Good speakers organize their content well, but with disorganized speakers you will need to fit the parts into the whole to complete the message from the isolated fragments. Think about the direction the speaker's topic is taking and follow the speaker's ideas to see if you are correct.

6. Take notes properly. Capture key words, phrases, and numbers. Be careful not to bog down in too many details or else you may miss the main points.

7. Be open minded. Do not make up your mind beforehand that the topic is uninteresting or not useful. Unlock your brain. Listen objectively; that is, avoid confusing the message with the source. Also, empathize with the speaker. See her point of view and withhold judgment until you have heard the entire message. Keep your emotions, like anger or jealousy, in check. Emotions are psychological noise that build barricades that block out the words of others. Hold criticism, or soften it, if you want to keep the communication channel open.

8. Be responsive. Ask questions. This provides feedback to the speaker and indicates you are interested. Respond in other ways. Nod in agreement, give a smile to encourage. In conversation and interviews, utter encouraging sounds or phrases ("Uh, huh," "Tell me more," "Go on"). Look and act interested. This helps create an attitude of information exchange.

9. Be selfish in your listening. Personalize what you hear by directing information toward your own benefit. This self-interest becomes your motivation. How can this information help me do my job better or accomplish my goals?

SUMMING UP

To accomplish their oral communication objectives well, business and professional people must understand the delicate process of communication and manipulate communication variables for both personal and listener benefit. The sender or speaker encodes a message into verbal and nonverbal symbols that the listener or receiver decodes. Successful speech communicators perform a thorough audience analysis of demographic, psychographic, and knowledge-to-date factors in order to shape the message to the listeners' needs. They also minimize noise factors and interpret feedback correctly.

Since everyone is a one-of-a-kind product of unique life influences and experiences, understanding the process of human perception is also critical to skillful oral communication. Our perceptions inevitably color the way we think, speak, and listen. Listening is the weak link in the communication process. Listeners cannot be passive; they must instead listen *actively*. Active listeners practice limiting distractions, focusing greater attention on verbal content than on speaker delivery, preparing mental summaries, taking notes, keeping an open mind, and providing feedback through questions.

Application Exercises

1. Attend a speech and analyze the communication process at work. The speech might be a business presentation at your job, a lecture at the public library or your school, an after-dinner speech sponsored by a professional organization in your field, or a political speech. (Try to avoid very specialized speaking situations like a professor's lecture or clergyperson's sermon.) In group discussion or in writing:
    a. Describe communication variables—sender, receiver, channel, message.
    b. Make inferences about the quality of the encoding/decoding process from the evidence you observed. Describe any examples of miscommunication you detected.
    c. Give several examples of feedback you observed or inferred.
    d. Describe and classify four examples of noise factors operating in the communication process you observed. (To give examples of some noise factors, such as perceptual noise, you will need to talk to audience members.)
2. Attend a speech, mingle with and observe the audience, and prepare an audience analysis for group discussion or extemporaneous speaking. (See Exercise 1 for examples of appropriate talk opportunities you might observe.) Cover the following content:
    a. As best as you can, state the speaker's purpose.
    b. Describe specifically the relevant demographic, psychographic, and knowledge-to-date factors that affected the speaker's presentation.

c. Was the speaker successful in adapting the content to achieve his purpose with this listener group?
d. Make any suggestions for the speaker that would have increased audience relevancy and interest.
3. Keep a listening log for two days. Hour by hour, record the following using a four-column format:
   a. Major activity in which you were engaged.
   b. Role, if any, listening played in the activity.
   c. What listening barriers or problems were you aware of?
   d. What effective listening techniques were you using? In retrospect, which techniques could you have used to strengthen your listening?

   As your instructor directs, present your findings in a written report, oral report, or small group discussion.
4. Divide your class into groups of five. Your instructor will read information to one representative from each group. (Two or three minutes of data might come from a *Wall Street Journal* article, an editorial in your local paper, a short story or anecdote from the *Reader's Digest*.) Now the first group member tells the information as accurately and completely as possible to the second group member, who then tells the third, and so on. The fifth group member then records the information on audio tape. Finally, your instructor will read the original data source again, and you can compare this to each of the final tape versions.

   Conduct a class discussion reacting to these concerns: What data is missing? What information was added? Using your knowledge of communication theory and effective listening, discuss causes of the omissions and additions. How could you increase the accuracy of the information exchange?
5. Present a one- to two-minute impromptu speech based on one of these topics:
   a. The ideal boss
   b. The best professor you ever had
   c. Your opinion of the president (governor, mayor)
   d. Your job—past, present, or future
   e. Changing gender roles in society
   f. Three wishes
6. Present a one- to two-minute impromptu speech finishing one of the following sentences:
   a. If I were dean of this school, I'd . . .
   b. If I were boss where I work, I'd . . .
   c. When I have a Sunday afternoon free, what I like to do is . . .
   d. Married women should (or shouldn't) work because . . .
   e. If I had the time and the money on my next vacation, I'd . . .
   f. The three things I'd want if I were ship-wrecked on a desert island are . . .

g. Last Friday night, I . . .
h. In ten years, I plan to be . . .
i. If I had a million dollars, I'd . . .
7. Present a two- to three-minute extemporaneous talk on one of these topics:
   a. Reactions to being an oldest, middle, youngest, or only child
   b. Reasons for choosing your major or occupation
   c. Advantages and/or disadvantages of your home town

   Develop a simple set of notes: Write out your opening sentence—devise an attention getter if you're especially creative, but be sure to state your subject clearly. Jot down three or four key phrases to jog your memory on points to develop. Write your closing sentence out—summarize your points or reinforce your main point for your listeners. Use these notes in your delivery. Maintain good eye contact with your listeners as you present.
8. Present a 30- to 60-second impromptu talk on one of the following topics that will be assigned to you:
   My favorite (or least favorite) . . .
       TV show
       Book
       Movie
       Sport

   Your instructor will determine speaker order by drawing names at random. Your topic will be assigned by random draw, too. Use your few seconds' planning time (the time it takes to go from your seat to the lectern) to select and organize two or three points to develop.

Chapter 3

BEFORE YOU SPEAK: PLANNING, PRESENTATION DESIGN, AND PREPARATION

Business and professional people who speak logically and forcefully have developed essential skills in planning and in presentation design. They proceed step by step, beginning with idea conception and audience analysis, organizing their talk's content into a smoothly flowing, unified presentation. They develop easy-to-use, supportive notes and practice them for a confident delivery.

The talk's design accomplishes both speaker and audience objectives in a concrete, interesting, and concise manner. Planning and presentation design skills, the focus of this chapter, enable speakers to present material confidently and naturally, as if conversing spontaneously one on one. We will see that this is an illusion; good speakers have in reality invested hours in planning, organizing, and practicing before facing the audience.

We will concentrate primarily on the extemporaneous style of speaking, but the planning and organizational principles in this chapter apply to impromptu speaking, too. Even in speaking impromptu, the speaker usually has a brief planning opportunity—seconds of time in which to make a decision on what points to present and in what order. People experienced in extemporaneous speaking can transfer good planning and presentation techniques to spur-of-the-moment speaking situations.

For most people, learning delivery skills, that is, how to speak, move, and express your personality, is easier than developing planning and presentation design skills. Beginning speakers find this difficult to believe; they think delivery is the tough part. However, so much of what is important in effective delivery comes with experience and patience. You will improve just by making presentations. But planning and presentation design skills do not come as naturally. If you are like most speakers, you will have to deliberately strive to replace weak planning and organizational skills with stronger ones. Therefore, we will concentrate first on planning and organizational aspects.

In this chapter you will learn how to apply:

- ▶ an easy-to-use, five-step planning procedure,
- ▶ organizational patterns business and professional people use most often,
- ▶ suggestions for devising and using notes,
- ▶ practice techniques.

Finally, by following a speaker from idea to the finished speech, you will gain an overview of how a professional presentation is developed.

ESCAP-E PLANNING FORMULA

Speakers often skimp on planning time or take short cuts. By trying to do several things simultaneously, they overtax their planning capabilities and frustrate themselves. Few speakers can read and analyze data sources, order the ideas appropriately, and develop notes at the same time—let alone do it *well!* Yet the total time involved is often greater because of the back-tracking and rethinking needed. The presentation is weaker, too, and shows the results of these time pressures and compromises.

To avoid the pitfalls associated with poor planning, use the ESCAP-E formula. Think of this five-step planning process as your ESCAP-E route from the anxieties and problems of anticipating and preparing a presentation. Proceeding methodically through each of the five steps in the ESCAP-E formula almost guarantees that you will consider all aspects of planning in a well-thought out, time-efficient fashion.

E = Examine the Speech Assignment

In the *examine* step, ask yourself these questions:

- What does my boss want me to do in my talk? (Or, what does the program chairperson or conference leader expect me to accomplish in my presentation?)
- What do I want to accomplish with my listeners? (What do my listeners want to gain from hearing my talk?)
- What content should I develop to fulfil these expectations?
- What is the talk setting?
- How much time will I have to speak?

Find the answers to these questions. Study the speech assignment to determine the background or context of the presentation, expected subject matter, audience (perform audience analysis discussed in Chapter 2), occasion, time limits, and setting. If you have any questions about what you are expected to do in a work situation, ask your boss or the person in charge of the meeting or program. In a public setting, discuss the actual specifics of your presentation with the program director. In a classroom setting, ask your instructor questions about the objectives of the talk assignment and how it will be evaluated. Knowing the parameters of your talk opportunity, you can proceed more accurately and confidently.

S = State Purpose of Presentation

Stating the communication goal is a challenge, especially for people who are just beginning to develop their planning skills. Just as if you were writing, when you prepare to speak you must determine precisely what your communication purpose is before you can go any farther. Answer the basic question: what are you going to talk about? Pin the subject down precisely. Determine specifically the purpose you want to accomplish. Obviously, if you don't know what you want to do, how can you do it—and how will you ever know when you *have* done it? If the speaker doesn't even know what she wants to say, imagine the confusion that her listeners will have.

Your goal is to develop your subject matter completely, concretely, and interestingly, staying within your time limit. Surprisingly, most speakers run overtime, not undertime. Limiting the scope of your purpose statement thus becomes important. If the speaker has too much to say, she will exceed the time limit. In turn, this creates time management problems for the other speakers and for the person in charge of the meeting or program. If this happens to you, be reassured. It is at least evident that you have something to say. Because you are enjoying the prospect of sharing the subject matter with your listeners, your time is getting away from you. Take solace in this sign of success and confidence, and then get out your red pen and decide what to cut.

Suppose Rebecca Foster has been requested to make a ten-minute talk at the monthly staff meeting. Her topic is choosing software for personal computers. It is budget time and several department heads are making decisions about what software to purchase in the next fiscal period. One way to get a variety of ideas and get outside her own personal frame of reference is to ask advice. She can brainstorm with some of her friends who use personal computers and with information processing staff members at work.

With an open mind, Rebecca explores approaches to her assigned topic. She devises this purpose statement: Ten factors must be considered when buying personal finance and word processing software for personal computers. She thinks it over. The purpose may be clear enough, but she would need 30 minutes to do justice to it. She certainly cannot develop it specifically in ten minutes—she would only have time to merely list them. The listeners would not absorb the information at such a rushed pace, nor would they remember it. She also fears that, without development of each point through examples, listeners would get little personal benefit from her list and probably lose interest. She would not satisfy her listeners' expectations and, therefore, she would not accomplish her own objectives as speaker.

Wisely, Rebecca decides to revise her purpose statement, limiting it considerably. Realizing from her audience analysis that her listeners' major software purchases will be word processors, she decides to consider only word processing software packages and present only three major buying factors. This is Rebecca's revised statement of purpose: Three key factors must be considered when purchasing word processing software for a personal computer. When her listeners hear her purpose statement, they will be oriented to her subject matter. She can develop this statement interestingly and specifically in ten minutes and she will give the department heads the information they need to make better buying decisions.

Rebecca recognizes that often it is better to "say more about less." That way, she will leave her listeners with a clear comprehension of three principles that they understand and can apply when shopping for word processing software, instead of six or seven vague generalities recalled from a recitation of a ten-item shopping list. Rebecca now moves to the third step in the ESCAP-E planning process.

C = Choose Ideas

What ideas must Rebecca deliver to accomplish her speaking purpose and her listeners' purposes? Dozens of ideas must be considered when selecting word processing software. Which are most important for her listeners to know, which are less important and beyond her scope in a short presentation? If this information is not in her memory, learned through day-to-day work and personal experience with word processing programs for PCs, she must research primary and secondary sources of data. Rebecca visited several computer and software stores to test several word processing packages. She talked to salespeople about the strengths of various word processors and solicited their opinions on the important features for the typical user. She interviewed several word processor users to widen her perspective on desirable operating features and the characteristics of good user manuals. She also studied secondary sources, such as articles in computer magazines.

Sorting through her material, Rebecca identifies the major and minor points she must develop if she is to execute her purpose statement well for her intended listeners. Her three main points will be features, ease of learning, and documentation. She will substantiate each of these three selection criteria with examples.

Take time with this step. If the presentation is ten days away, start working and thinking about it today. This minimizes pressure, and most people are less creative under pressure. With more planning time, you have more flexibility, more options. So, let your preliminary plans age and mature. Think about your talk assignment before you drift off to sleep, when you're in the shower, or as you drive to work or to school. At these relaxed times, your mind will be more fertile and sharper. Let several days go by. Then come back to your speaking plans and reexamine them from a fresher perspective. They may seem half-baked then; if so, scratch this approach and try again—you still have the time. Or, your ideas may look even better; if so, continue to refine your thinking after this confirmation.

Once the ideas start to gel in your mind, see how they look on paper. Jot them down. You'll probably want to revise: There might be some repetition and you'll want to drop an idea. One point may not seem convincing and you'll add another subpoint for substantiation.

After mulling her talk over for a few days, Rebecca decided that she should change "ease of learning" to "ease of operation" because she now thinks the long-term user-friendliness of a word processing package may compensate for some early learning demands. At this stage, she again brainstorms with friends, experts at work, and even a couple of potential audience members to solicit more points of view and feedback on her evolving subject matter.

A = Arrange Ideas

Put your ideas into a logical arrangement that your listeners will easily comprehend and remember. Impose order on your information. Step back from your ideas and see if some shape develops. (The next section surveys organizational patterns that business and professional speakers commonly use.)

Here's what Rebecca has done up to this point: She has chosen a workable framework for her presentation. She has discriminated between the main ideas and subideas; she has organized them appropriately, deciding on an order-of-importance organizational scheme. The talk flows smoothly from point to point. It builds; it doesn't ramble on or lack focus. She also, at this point, begins developing her notes.

P = Pick Verbal and Visual Support

At this junction, you should have the skeleton of the presentation in view. Now put some muscle and skin on the bones. You have your major and minor ideas in an organizational framework. In this last planning step, provide verbal and visual support, evidence to back up these ideas in a listener-related context. Without such support, you may fall into the trap of merely tossing out undeveloped ideas that the listeners will not remember nor be able to use.

Verbal support comes from your experience and your research conducted in the "*C* = choose ideas" step. Verbal support may be facts, statistics, examples, quotations, and comparisons.

You also choose your visual support now. For example, use mounted tables, charts, graphs, pictures, maps, or diagrams for display or transparencies for projection. (Techniques for using visual and other presentation aids to enliven your delivery and increase the impact of your data will be presented in Chapter 5.)

Rebecca enters the home stretch by studying each of her three major points and their subpoints. For each one, she lists two or three items of interest material—information that her listeners must comprehend to grasp the point and be able to apply it. Her verbal support consists of facts and statistics from her reading, several quotes from software vendors she talked with, and bits of practical advice gleaned from her conversations with more experienced word processor users.

She decides to use several simple visual aids. Three posters, one for each of the three major selection factors, will detail the three or four subpoints in each area to check when buying a word processing package. These will clarify her presentation structure for the audience and reinforce visually each point she makes verbally.

We have watched Rebecca Foster work through the five steps, the ESCAP-E formula. It obviously takes time to proceed this way, but good extemporaneous speaking requires thorough planning. Some experienced speakers say that one hour of preparation should be behind each minute of talk time. Thus, by this gauge Rebecca should prepare ten hours for a ten-minute talk. Actually, the preparation time will depend on the complexity and sophistication of the subject matter, the speaker's familiarity with it, the types of visual aids to be produced, and the speaker's skill in planning and delivering speeches.

One thing is certainly true: Extemporaneous presentations that are well organized, well developed, and delivered in a relaxed, conversational, seemingly impromptu manner are the results of hours of work and years of experience. Good speakers seem to be talking with the audience; they make it look easy. This success is *not* due to accident, luck, or natural organizational and speaking abilities. You will realize this as you develop your presentation skills. It takes time and effort to work through the ESCAP-E formula systematically, but the results will be evident in a tightly focused, interesting, and concrete presentation.

Remember that the ESCAP-E formula can help you during impromptu speaking as well as during extemporaneous speaking. When you must speak impromptu, you can use the ESCAP-E planning formula to make the most of the time between the speech request and the time you begin speaking. A few seconds of systematic planning are better than no planning at all—and it's definitely better than panicking. With enough practice applying the ESCAP-E formula for extemporaneous speaking, you can move through the ESCAP-E steps quickly, almost subconsciously, when speaking impromptu.

ORGANIZATIONAL PATTERNS

Recall that *A* in the ESCAP-E planning formula means arranging ideas. In this stage, the speech planner studies the material and looks for an organizational structure to emerge. If that does not happen, the speaker must rearrange the material until some logical order does appear. Basically, the speaker asks, "What is the best way to structure this information to accomplish my objectives and those of my listeners?" The answer to that important question can be found in the following overview of organizational patterns that business and professional people are most likely to use:

1. Chronological. Using the chronological pattern, sometimes called the story-telling or time-sequence approach, the speaker selects a point in time and moves forward. A variation is starting

Reprinted with permission of Tribune Media Services.

An effective presentation delivers the required content to the audience using the most logical and powerful organizational pattern.

at the present time and working backwards. For example, a progress report could be organized chronologically. When reporting background or historical information, you should use this pattern. Manufacturing or technical processes are done in a one-two-three sequence and can likewise be presented chronologically.

Let's assume you have spent a week in Chicago touring ten offices to update yourself on office automation. You arrived in Chicago on Monday morning and toured the corporate headquarters of Omega Corporation, Nova's corporate office on Tuesday, Omicron Enterprises' facilities on Wednesday, and so forth for the next seven work days. When you return to your office, you begin preparing an hour presentation. You will detail your findings, evaluate new office technologies you have seen relative to your firm's needs, and make a recommendation for the Long-Range Planning Committee. The chronological approach can be used to report your data, conclusions, and recommendations. Describe what you saw each day, developing any special comparisons or contrasts that are noteworthy, and drawing conclusions and making recommendations as you go along.

The chronological approach is quite easy to apply and is especially useful in impromptu speaking because the speaker has an easily remembered set of organizational cues—some period of time.

2. Cause and effect. The speaker presents a cause and then the resulting effect. This approach has an element of the chronological approach because causes obviously occur before their effects. Sometimes, the speaker will move on to solutions.

Suppose you are reviewing the events leading up to the current impasse in negotiations with your company's machine operators' union. You develop a cause-and-effect chain that takes you to the status of the bargaining. You review sequentially each of the following events: On November 15, after ten straight days of bargaining, negotiations broke down. This caused the union to call for a strike vote on November 19. To prevent a strike, management agreed to resume talks on November 18 using a federal mediator. After hearing both sides of the issues, the mediator proposed a contract calling for compromises by both sides. Management agreed to the contract, but the union representatives refused to endorse it or present it to the membership for a vote. The union has called another strike vote in two days, for November 23, which brings the situation up to date.

3. Categorical. What if no chronological or cause-and-effect pattern can be seen? Perhaps the data can be grouped into categories by common characteristics. To illustrate, a training director needs to describe 15 computer programs that the 25 executives in the audience can access from the central mainframe computer using their desk-top terminals. The speaker studies the data from all angles. No time factor or cause-and-effect relationship ties the data together. The programs can, however, be classified by five job tasks that they help the users perform (word processing programs for writing, spreadsheet programs for financial forecasting, graphics programs for chart and diagram generation, and so on).

The categorical organizational pattern will work well here. Instead of discussing 15 programs separately with no apparent inter-relationship, the training director sorts the data into five categories on the basis of a discriminating factor: program function. This structure increases the unity of the presentation and facilitates the listeners' retention of the programs that are available.

4. Problem-solution. In the problem-solution approach, the speaker goes through a logical problem-solving procedure with the audience. The problem-solution scheme is very useful to speakers in business and professional environments, for they often discuss problems that need to be solved or controlled, perhaps in a recommendation report.

For example, back-ups are occurring in the word processing department. Begin by orienting the listeners to the problem. Why, instead of a 24-hour turn-around time, must dictators wait 72 hours to receive finished documents? Company correspondence, memos, and reports are not being produced on time, causing costly internal and external communication delays. Describe the who, what, where, why, when, and how of the problem so the audience completely understands the situation. Then present solutions. In this example: "We could improve our input procedure for dictation, hire more word processing operators, or upgrade our word processing equipment." To choose among these solutions, the speaker examines the effect of each one and explains criteria that the solution must meet. After evaluating each of the three solutions, the presenter makes a recommendation and calls for action to implement it. More coverage of problem-solving techniques is presented in Chapter 8.

    5. Order of importance. Using the order-of-importance option, you look for priorities or qualitative differences in the information for presentation. Establish a "first, second, third," and so on, order. Present your strongest, most compelling point first. Your subsequent points will confirm or reinforce the initial argument, drawing your listeners even closer to your viewpoint. Or use a reverse order to build up to the major point. For instance, go from the least important to the most important reason for investing in new word processing equipment. This builds understanding and interest as you proceed to your capstone concept that, when finally revealed, should clinch your argument and sweep the listeners into your camp.

    6. Topical. Suppose a speaker mainly wants to inform the audience about something. The speaker may opt to use the topical or journalistic approach in which the information is logically developed topic by topic. As a newspaper reporter would, the speaker gathers and analyzes information by the 5W/1H plan (who, what, where, when, why, and how?). By providing answers to these six key questions as they are relevant to the subject matter and listener perspective, the speaker can be confident that the essential information has been presented.

    A topical approach might be recommended for educating staff members on proper dictation input procedures. The first topic might be "The value of efficient dictation techniques;" the second might be "Four things to do before dictating;" the third, "Tips for dictating the body of the document;" and so on through each of the topics.

    7. Spatial. The spatial pattern organizes content around locational relationships, where objects are in three-dimensional space—up, down, left, right, east, west, fifth floor, sixth floor, Ohio, New York, and so on. If you were reporting on the redesign of the main office layout, you might begin with the receptionist desk as you enter the office, move to the word processing area in the north quadrant, the records management area in the east quadrant, the telemarketing section in the south corner, and so on around the main office.

Occasionally, a speaker will use several organizational patterns in a talk. For example, a speaker may select the problem-solving approach for the main structure but, when proposing alternative solutions, present them by order of importance. You will develop experience in using these organizational patterns singly or in combination as you go along, developing a repertoire of organizational formats. You'll learn to choose the ones that ideally deliver your content and best accomplish your purposes.

Once you decide which organizational structure to use, you are near the end of your planning—but the job is not quite done. The preceding seven organizational patterns are used to develop the main ideas, the body of the presentation, but you just can't begin in the middle. You need a beginning and an ending. These segments are very important to the success of a business or professional person's presentation, as we shall see in the following section.

TALK STRUCTURE

Most presentations have a characteristic three-part structure. This section will give you a reliable and simple structural framework to use so each part of your talk does its job well for the listener and all parts fit together to produce an easy-to-follow presentation.

Effective speech communicators build their talks around a simple design: opener/body/close. Dale Carnegie, a famous speaker and speech trainer of the 20s, 30s, and 40s whose speech principles are still taught in workshops across the country, reduced presentation design to: Tell your audience what you are going to tell them, then tell them, and then tell them what you have told them.[1]

You might think this insults the audience. It may also seem repetitive, but it isn't. Carnegie's strategy takes into account the way people listen and process information. When reading a busi-

---

1. Dale Carnegie, *How to Develop Self-Confidence and Influence People by Public Speaking* (New York: Pocket Books, Simon and Shuster, 1956).

FIGURE 3–1
Attention-Getter Options

1. Make a shocking statement.
2. Ask one or more direct questions requiring visible audience response: "Who will volunteer to describe the factors you consider in deciding which brand of car to buy?"
3. Ask one or more rhetorical questions—thought-provoking questions you do not actually expect the listener to answer: "Did you ever get so fed up at work that you wanted to tell your boss off?"
4. Quote a well-known person or authority.
5. Announce your main point.
6. Tell an appropriate joke.
7. Present a story or an anecdote.
8. Refer to the occasion.
9. Present a hypothetical situation.
10. Relate a personal experience or make a self-disclosure.
11. Refer to the problem at hand, emphasizing its significance for all listeners.
12. Use a prop, visual aid, or demonstration.

If the attention-getter does not incorporate direct audience involvement, you must involve the audience as a separate opening element. One way is by explaining how the information is potentially important or useful for the listeners. Answer the listener's subconscious question, "Why should I listen to you? What's in it for me?" You might motivate listening by appealing to a personal benefit: for example, a speaker describing a new advertising campaign scheduled to begin running on local television stations in December might say to the audience of salespeople: "By becoming acquainted with these new television spots, you can anticipate what store items will be most in demand and what types of questions will be asked. This will mean better customer service, greater sales, and bigger commissions for each of you."

3. Self-involvement. Having involved the audience, you should focus some attention on yourself to further strengthen the developing communication channel between you and your listeners. This may be done simultaneously with the ice-breaker, for example, when you tell a personal story that shares a bit of yourself with the audience. Another device is to prove your credibility to talk on the topic. Using the same circumstances mentioned before, you might say, "Last year when we used television spots in the Boston stores before Christmas, my sales went up 25 percent, which certainly proved their value to me."

4. Purpose statement. The statement of purpose is the crucial part of your introduction, and in an impromptu talk, it may be the entire opener. State the purpose of your presentation explicitly. Do not bury it in your opening or imply it, forcing your listeners to infer what you will be speaking about. Make your purpose stand out so they cannot possibly miss it. For example: "Using a word processing program on a home computer has four advantages over composing on a typewriter. The first advantage is. . . ." If necessary for emphasis, label your purpose statement with something like "I will talk about. . . ." or "The subject of my presentation is. . . ." A few words of caution: do not introduce your purpose statement with worn-out, self-evident, vague cliches like "I'd like to say a few words about. . . ."

For a longer presentation—over ten minutes—a fifth element of the introduction, a **plan of presentation,** might be added. Indicate how the rest of the talk will be organized as you implement the talk's purpose: "I'll talk about . . . first, then . . . , and finish with. . . ."

Some don't's. Some approaches should be avoided because they hurt your credibility, fail to attract attention, or set an inappropriate theme. For example, do not begin apologetically or negatively. Such openers reduce the audience's desire to listen to you. "I'm sorry I'm a poor public speaker. I'll do my best." or "Please bear with me. I will try not to bore the more knowledgeable listeners with too many statistics and too much review," are ineffective openers. Speakers who make such statements make enemies of their listeners. Be positive in your outlook and well prepared so that you have no need to apologize for any real or imagined shortcomings.

Don't use the same opener for every audience, every subject, and every occasion. Using the same opener shows the speaker's lack of motivation to invest time and effort in communicating personally. Often these generic openers are trite, phony, and trivialize your entire presentation, anyway. Avoid such insincere openers as: "Ladies and gentlemen, it is my sincere pleasure to have the opportunity to talk to such an impressive audience on the subject of. . . ." Some attention-getters, like rhetorical or direct questions, are so easy to use that they have been overused and are no longer effective. Better speakers devise creative and appropriate openers matched to each speaking situation.

Don't use gimmicky or offensive openers. Unfortunately, creative energy may be wasted when people rely on openers that are irrelevant, distracting, or embarrassing to themselves and to the audience. Acting out a charade to begin your presentation attracts attention but in a silly manner. Flashing a slide of a scantily clad person on the screen and saying, "Now that I've gotten your attention," demeans both the speaker and the audience. Recovering from such beginnings is difficult, if not impossible.

To review, a good opener attracts attention, involves the audience and the speaker, and briefly but clearly states the purpose of the presentation. Check your own openers and evaluate how well they do these four jobs.

Body

The main part of the presentation is the body, maybe 75 percent of the talk. Here, you *tell them*. Carry out your statement of purpose using the organizational plan you chose from the possibilities in the previous section.

No matter what organizational pattern you picked, transition will be important in tying together the parts of the body and tying the body to your opener and close. Think of the mortar in a brick building as a metaphor for transitions. As mortar holds the bricks together, transition holds the structural elements of an oral presentation together, making it easier to follow. These linking transitional elements review briefly what you have just presented and suggest what comes next.

Transitional words, phrases, and sections help the audience navigate through your evolving organizational plan. Listeners appreciate these signposts. Some transitions indicate a time progression: now, later, meanwhile, next, finally. Some transitions lead your listeners from fact to conclusion or inference: therefore, as a result, thus, for this reason. Other transitions suggest reservation: however, possibly, yet; while others suggest certainty: obviously, surely, of course. Finally, transitions may suggest comparison: likewise, similarly; or contrast: conversely, on the other hand, just for argument's sake.

Transitions enhance the coherence and unity of your material, but be careful. Even skillful use of transition will not redeem a poorly organized talk. In this case, reapply the ESCAP-E formula to your content. Transition can be overused, too, when it points out obvious connections as though the material had no built-in logical flow of its own.

Close

In the close, the speaker "tells them what he has told them" by summarizing, concluding, or refocusing. Devote about 5 to 10 percent of your time to this part of your presentation.

The close is just as important as the opener. Audiences have a need for a wrap-up, or closure, as psychologists call it. Listeners want a presentation to come to a neat, tidy conclusion with all the loose ends tied up. Furthermore, people tend to remember most what they hear last. You can take advantage of this by hammering home the main point at the end. So, it is important, as you can see, to concentrate on constructing a powerful close for your talk. Don't waste your close by fading out—"I guess that's it"—or dissipating the power of your conclusion.

Just as listeners occasionally miss the statement of purpose, they may fail to detect the close. To some listeners, the talk ended abruptly with the body. They didn't see the seam between the body and the close, if there was one. Although forward progression through your plan of presentation, body language, and tone should let everyone know you are in the home stretch, labels help too. Use a transitional word or phrase to provide the clue that the body has been developed and the end of the presentation is near. Avoid trite expressions, such as "In closing, I'd like to say." Instead, "To summarize," "lastly," and "to review the main conclusions," are better signals.

Hagar © 1988 King Features Syndicate, Inc.

Develop a solid close, because your listeners will tend to remember more of what they hear last.

FIGURE 3–2
Closing Options

1. Summarize main points.
2. Draw conclusions from facts presented in the body and make recommendations.
3. Call for action or challenge the audience to act.
4. Relate an illustrative and clarifying story, anecdote, or personal application.
5. Tell an appropriate joke.
6. Use a quotation.
7. Make a prediction or forecast.
8. Use a prop, visual aid, or demonstration to emphasize the major point.

It's probably not necessary to thank your audience. It's too common, too anticlimatic. Rather, end your talk with a solid close. If you have a good talk, the "thank you" should come spontaneously from your audience.

Figure 3–2 shows eight ideas for closing a talk. (You'll notice similarities between suggested closings and the suggested openings in Figure 3–1.) A speaker may close by summarizing. Of course, a short presentation should not use a summary close because the content is probably too short and uncomplicated to require a review. In this case, a summary close might insult the listeners' intelligence. For a longer, more complex presentation, a summary highlighting major points of the body reinforces the talk's structure. Listeners will more likely retain the data.

An analytical presentation ends with conclusions and recommendations. The speaker evaluates the evidence presented in the body of the talk and then suggests a plan of action consistent with those conclusions. Most persuasive talks end with a call to action or a challenge.

Some speakers are comfortable in closing with illustrations, humorous statements, or anecdotes. These closes present the subject matter in an especially graphic manner, making the final point of the presentation unmistakably clear and memorable for the listeners.

Several more tips about closes: A speaker should add a refocusing element. This emphasizes, one last time, the subject matter's significance and potential usefulness for the listeners. To strengthen a talk's unity, a close can very effectively refer to the opener. For example, the speaker might answer the rhetorical questions posed in the ice-breaker. One thing the speaker should not do is incorporate new textual material into the close. This is like a *P.S.* in a letter, which is a sign of weak organization in most cases. The presenter should put this stray, leftover information back into the body where it belongs, or drop it altogether.

PERSUASIVE PRESENTATIONS

The structural plan presented so far has been direct. In such plans we use deductive logic, meaning the main idea/purpose statement was presented before the development. Most business and professional people and their audiences prefer the direct approach. The main idea is presented immediately, saving both speaker and listener time. However, just as writers sometimes choose an indirect plan, speakers will find occasions to use indirect organizational patterns. These patterns employ inductive logic. The development is presented before the main idea.

One situation in which indirectness might be preferred is when the listener cannot comprehend the main idea without first understanding the supporting details. Another situation calling for indirectness is when the speaker anticipates a negative listener reaction. For example, when the main idea is unpleasant or controversial. If stated immediately in the introduction, the listeners would reject it, perhaps not even listening for reasons and justification. In both situations, the speaker builds up to the main idea/ purpose statement after first developing the facts, details, and reasons. An additional speaking situation in which it is better to be indirect is the persuasive talk.

In a persuasive talk the speaker is promoting an idea, proposal, product, or service which, at first, seems contrary to listener beliefs, prejudices, or expectations. The direct approach usually will not work. Springing the main ideas on the nonreceptive, or even hostile, audience would result in disaster—immediate rejection of the idea. In a sales proposal presentation, saying "Kappa Corporation should purchase $19,000 of new word processing equipment" provokes the listeners to say "No, thanks" almost automatically. Their immediate reaction is to resist change, especially if it costs money.

On the other hand, the indirect persuasive approach is psychologically more effective and therefore more likely to get the positive reaction the speaker wants. The persuasive strategy leads listeners to accept a new point of view in gradual stages. The speaker establishes the need for change in the listener group and then presents evidence of the advantages to be gained from making that change. If the speaker can persuade the listeners that the benefits of the change exceed the risks and costs involved, the speaker usually succeeds in moving the listeners to agreement and action—buying new word processing equipment, switching from X advertising agency to Z advertising agency, building the new plant in Richmond instead of Boston, or whatever.

To be persuasive, a speaker must be trustworthy. The persuader must establish integrity and credibility. He must project goodwill toward the audience, not manipulation or self-interest. Also, a speaker must arouse emotions in the listener. Most persuasive presentations are more successful if the receivers' emotions are involved. Emotional appeals, though, must be blended with logical, rational appeals. One must reinforce the other. In this way, a speaker will more likely win over the critical audience, which business and professional audiences tend to be.

Persuasive presentations move smoothly through four stages called the AIDA pattern: A = attention, I = interest, D = desire, A = action.

A = Attention

Attract attention. Make the audience put aside other thoughts and concentrate on listening to you. Creatively pique their interest. Pose a question, offer a solution to a problem, make a startling statement. Make sure the attention-getter is relevant to the audience and your persuasive intent. The attention-getters and application techniques in the previous section are just as useful in persuasive situations. With attention drawn to you and your subject matter, you can move to the next step.

I = Interest

Build interest by explaining the situation, problem, or opportunity at hand. Your listeners are not persuaded to act or to think differently just because you asked them to do so. As we've said before, you need to convince them they will benefit *personally* if they change their beliefs and actions.

Using two techniques, put the receiver in the picture. First, if the listeners have something to visualize physically like a product, describe it now for them. Using vivid, concrete word pictures and presentation aids, describe its appearance, construction, or performance. Through examples, comparison, contrast, and cause and effect, picture your audience using and enjoying the product.

Second, develop rational and emotional appeals to promote your point of view and/or weaken the listeners' arguments. Psychographic data on your audience is used to especially good advantage in persuasive speaking. Recall the discussion in Chapter 2 of needs assessment by using Maslow's hierarchy and by understanding your listeners' attitudes, values, and beliefs. The ability to persuade employees, customers, clients, colleagues, and public groups depends on knowing your audience. Determine what needs and wants are unfulfilled in your listeners. To what appeals would your audience be susceptible? Once you identify these appeals, you may be able to use them as motivators.

Study Figure 3–3 and select benefits that you can develop to sell your idea, product, or proposal. For instance, what appeals could be made to sell a $19,000 word processor—efficiency (four-hour turnaround time, not 24-hour), increased profits (it will pay for itself in two years), solution to a problem (better document production).

D = Desire

Present the alternative(s) and build desire for a plan of action. Provide proof and convincing evidence. Few people are swayed by vague, unsubstantiated statements. If you have done your homework, you can present facts, statistics, testimonials from unbiased authorities, test data, samples, or guarantees. Use concrete, simple language your listeners will believe, not confidence-destroying exaggerations and unsupported claims.

You must not only stress appeals and listener benefit, but anticipate listener resistance to your arguments. Use the psychographic data from your audience analysis to identify potential barriers. Address and minimize these objections—before the negatives even form in your receivers' minds. If a receiver recognizes a point of resistance first, it is much tougher for you to overcome it.

Substantiate your belief that the benefits of acting or thinking in the desired way outweigh the disadvantages. Create a climate of agreement in which your listeners now think: "Yes, you've persuaded me. It's to my net benefit to change my way of acting or thinking." Or, "Yes, investing $19,000 in this word processing equipment will pay for itself in two years and increase efficiency by 10 percent."

FIGURE 3-3
Persuasive Appeals

Appreciation
Approval (by others)
Beauty, attractiveness
Cleanliness
Comfort
Convenience
Cooperation
Customer satisfaction
Distinctiveness
Efficiency
Entertainment
Fair treatment
Good reputation
Health
Improvement
Love of family, of others
Peace of mind
Pleasure
Popularity
Position of authority
Prestige
Pride
Profits
Protection for family, business, self, others
Provision for future
Recognition
Respect
Safety and security
Satisfaction of helping others
Savings
Solution to a problem
Success
Usefulness

Source: Herta A. Murphy, and Herbert W. Hildebrandt. *Effective Business Communications,* 5th ed. (New York: McGraw-Hill Book Company, 1988) 242–43.

A = Action

Review benefits the listeners will receive by embracing the desired attitude or taking the desired action. If some specific action is desired, state it clearly: "I propose we sign a sales contract to purchase four XXYYZZ Model 334455 word processors for

$19,000 with the North Coast Office Equipment Company for delivery the first of next month." The action close need not shout the message this way, though. The close may imply it, depending on your persuasive objective. If the action requires only forming an attitude, let your closing reinforce that message in the listeners' minds.

NOTE DEVELOPMENT

At this stage in your preparation, you have used a systematic planning procedure to devise a sound organizational scheme for your presentation. The next step is to develop notes.

For an extemporaneous talk, you will be working from simple notes. Notes keep you on the track as far as developing the intended organizational plan. They provide cues to the major ideas and verbal support needed to flesh out the talk's content. However, notes are not a script, written out word for word. A script would be relied on too much, and probably read.

Suggestions for Making Helpful Notes

The following tips provide guidance for constructing a helpful set of notes during the "A-for-arrange" and "P-for-pick" steps in the ESCAP-E formula and for using them skillfully when delivering a talk.

1. Use key phrases in your notes, not complete sentences. Your notes contain your organizational scheme and your verbal support. A brief phrase will jog your memory. You select the exact words to develop each point as you interact with the audience and process their feedback. Key-phrase notes are an essential element to achieving the spontaneous, conversational, interactive extemporaneous delivery style. Such notes produce *talked* presentations; detailed, sentence-for-sentence notes usually produce *read* presentations.

2. Provide more detail in your notes where needed. The opener and close, important for reasons already stressed, are often trouble spots for speakers. Have more note support here if it will give you that security to get started smoothly and finish strongly and confidently.

Other parts of the speech may require more detailed notes, too. For example, statistics, quotations, anecdotes, and punchlines to jokes may be written out fully. You will rely on your notes more here because of the type of material under development. The audience will understand and expect this.

3. Use either large sheets of paper or note cards. Some speakers prefer sheets of paper from a legal pad or notebook because they hold more information than the smaller note cards. The speaker will not have to turn the page as frequently as cards would require, and the notes appear less obvious to audience members. Larger note cards (4×6 inch or 3×5 inch) are a good compromise. Speakers who prefer note cards should remember to number them. If for some reason they are dropped or become unorganized, the speaker can easily rearrange them.

With either sheets of paper or note cards, avoid holding them or waving them about. Holding them reduces the options for gestures and waving notes around is distracting to the audience. Keep notes on the lectern or table.

4. Make notes easy to read. You should be able to glance down at your notes, instantly get that cue that will prompt your memory, and then reestablish eye contact with the audience. For easy reading, type or print notes. Avoid using all capital letters; most people find all caps more difficult to read. Have a lot of white space (wide margins, blank lines between body elements) so that the notes appear uncrowded and the information stands out in clearly discernible chunks. Using a numbering or outline system also contributes to more fluid note reference. Some people like to use highlighting pens to flag major or key elements. If used sparingly, this flash of color can make it easier to access data with little loss of eye contact.

5. Avoid making last-minute changes in note format. Do not add a point or marginal comment, cross something out, or draw an arrow to indicate a new order of presentation. With the normal amount of anxiety present in delivering the talk, these changes may be confusing. Don't compound delivery problems by booby-trapping your notes with potential stumbling blocks.

6. Rely on your notes as needed. As ironic as it may seem, some novice speakers use their notes too little, not too much. The audience understands why notes are necessary and they will expect a certain amount of reference to them. In fact, reference to notes, especially when citing statistics or explaining intricate or controversial subject matter, can increase speaker credibility and accuracy. Even the most confident, skilled speakers use notes. The presenter may not refer to them, the notes may be tucked away in an accessible pocket, but they are available and that gives the speaker security, knowing they are there if needed.

Note Format Guide

A sample note format guide is shown in Figure 3–4. This guide deliberately reduces talk structure and note format to the simplest form, making it basically a "fill-in-the-blanks" format. Using it, you are much more likely to include the four elements of a good introduction, to develop a body with logical structure and evident transition, and to finish with a close that summarizes or refocuses. Use it to help you internalize clear-cut talk structure and make that structure vividly apparent to your listeners.

Transfer the format to sheets of paper or note cards (without the part labels, of course.) Fill in the form with your key phrases

FIGURE 3–4
Note Format Model

```
                                    I. INTRODUCTION
Attention-getter:                   A.
Audience involvement:               B.
Self-involvement:                   C.
Purpose statement:                  D.
Plan of presentation                E.
  (optional):
Transition to body:
                                    II. BODY
Main point:                         A.
  Subpoint:                           1.
    Verbal support:                      a.
    Verbal support:                      b.
    Verbal support:                      c.
  Subpoint:                           2.
    Verbal support:                      a.
    Verbal support:                      b.
    Verbal support:                      c.
Transition to next point:
[Repeat and modify as needed for number of remaining main points,
subpoints, and verbal support items.]
Transition to close:
                                    III. CLOSE
Close:                              A.
Re-focus:                           B.
Transition to question-and-answer session (optional):
```

Source: Adapted from Jean H. Michulka, *Let's Talk Business,* 2nd ed. (Cincinnati: South-Western Publishing Company, 1983) 203.

for your main points and subpoints and add the verbal support (facts, statistics, quotations, and so on) you need to present these ideas concretely. Add the transitional words and phrases you need between the three major sections of your presentation and internally within the structural elements of the body.

Use these tips and experiment with note format until you develop techniques that are ideal for you. Perhaps at first, your notes will be too long. As you practice, though, you will change and shorten them until you devise a set of notes that are simple, well organized, and easy to access.

PRACTICING

Because extemporaneous speakers use notes, they must practice. Since key-phrase notes are relatively simple, the presenter practices to familiarize herself with them. Speakers also practice to increase their sense of control and to enhance their self-confidence. The speaker will be able to deliver the talk with all the major and minor points in the planned order, *talking* not *reciting* or *reading,* and with her eyes on the people in the audience, where they belong.

Practice with the following points in mind:

1. Do not *rehearse* your presentations, *practice* them. Rehearsing gives the impression of preparing to act out a role. Since you are striving to be your natural, relaxed self when you talk extemporaneously, you do not rehearse in the same sense an actor does. Don't practice voice inflection and body language. If your notes remind you to raise your voice to emphasize a phrase or to gesture to dramatize a point, your voice and movements will probably appear forced and unnatural. And, certainly *rehearsing* suggests memorizing, which is not the goal of an extemporaneous presenter.

2. Do not practice too much. Speakers who go over a talk ten times fix a prescribed delivery in their minds, robbing themselves of the spontaneity and interactive quality that good speakers demonstrate. Instead, their talks take on a mechanical, recited flavor. Practice only enough to become familiar with your notes and your ideas. Two or three run-throughs will be enough for most people to become comfortable, assuming they have developed workable notes. If it isn't enough, perhaps something is seriously wrong with the organization or note format, which must be resolved before resuming the practicing.

3. Practice in front of a mirror. This gives you a small audience—yourself—and makes the practice effort more formal. Evaluate your eye contact. Do you see your reflection most of the time? If you don't, your eyes must be elsewhere, probably glued to your notes. You can also gauge your body language at the same time. What are you doing with your hands and facial expressions to enhance the meaning of your content? (You'll find more about body language in Chapter 4.)

4. Use a tape recorder. Replay the tape and analyze how good it sounded. Be objective, as much as possible, listening from the perspective of an impartial bystander. Does your talk have evident three-part structure? Does it have good transition from point to point? Does it make sense? Does it have sufficient verbal support? Answer these questions and then make the necessary structural and note changes. Take this opportunity to evaluate your voice, too, on the vocal characteristics that will be discussed in Chapter 4.

With the rapidly growing popularity of home video recording, many speakers in business and professional occupations now combine the benefits of seeing and hearing their performances. If you have access to a videocassette recorder and television camera, you can videotape your presentation for in-depth self-evaluation of the structural, visual, and oral aspects of your speech.

5. Practice before a small audience, if possible. Your spouse, parents, co-workers, roommates, cat, and dog will oblige you for a few minutes. This adds a dimension of realism to your practice. You have an audience to talk to and with as you will when you actually deliver your talk. After the run-through, ask your audience members to critique your approach, organization, and delivery. Use this feedback to polish your next run-through.

6. Avoid becoming overly self-conscious. Especially when audio or video taping, recognize that this is the way you look, act, and sound to other people. These characteristics make you what you are to your friends and colleagues. They accept this as part of you and eventually you will, too. It may be surprising, jarring, even painful at first, but bear with it. It is a source of good feedback for most people.

Realize, too, that people tend to be their own harshest critics. You know what your internal goals are for your presentation and you compare your practice performance to those lofty goals. Your audience, fortunately, has more realistic goals for your presentation. The gap between *your* goals and reality will be larger than the gap between your *audience's* goals for you and reality. Take comfort in knowing that most of the time your audience's perception of your success will be higher than your own. This understanding should permit you to criticize yourself more objectively.

Some people, of course, cannot overcome this self-consciousness and tendency to tinker supercritically with all aspects of their delivery style. They become stilted and artificial. Their delivery suffers rather than improves. If you are one of these people, perhaps you should stick to practicing before a mirror or small audience.

7. Check and practice pronunciation of words you are unsure of. If you repeatedly stumble on a word or phrase, substitute something else. If you become tongue-tied, for example, saying "ten tank trucks filled with tar," make a change in your notes or your mind to say "ten truckloads of tar." Are you mispronouncing such words as "entrepreneur" or "genuine"? If so, substitute appropriate synonyms or master their correct pronunciation.

8. Work through the presentation completely, rather than section by section. This way you can judge the overall structural unity and timing more accurately. Force yourself through the entire presentation. It will be difficult at first. Your delivery will be halting and your eye contact weak. However, you will discover flaws faster in your organization, notes, and delivery this way. Little by little, your presentation will come together.

9. Check your timing. When practicing, keep your eye on the clock. Is your time management satisfactory? Have you developed your statement of purpose within your time period? If not, revise, cut, or add material. If the talk is too long, the solution is not talking faster. That will only multiply your problems. Instead, narrow down your purpose statement or delete some material in your introduction, body, or close (without harming your development).

It is common, too, for a talk to be precisely on time in practice but short or long on actual delivery. With experience you will learn if you are prone to this problem. During their actual presentations, some speakers may be overly anxious. Therefore, they omit items, skip points by mistake, skimp on development of material, or talk too fast. If this is the case, prepare for this contingency by practicing more, devising clearer notes, consciously slowing down your delivery rate, or having some extra material that can be developed if the presentation runs short.

Conversely, some speakers tend to go overtime during the actual talk. To their credit, they interact well with the audience and develop material in extra detail. These speakers need to have a back-up plan to delete material judiciously without the audience's knowing so that they still fully implement their purpose statements without exceeding the time limit.

10. Simulate as many of the actual speech conditions as possible in your last practice opportunity. Use your final, perfected set of notes, speak before a small audience, stand before a real or make-shift lectern, and incorporate any presentation aids into your run-through. In a sense you will already have delivered your presentation successfully and, therefore, your actual version will most likely go just as well or better. You have anticipated and worked out all the bugs. Your timing is fine, your notes are working, you know your material well, your eye contact is good. At this point, stop practicing and relax. You are ready to deliver your presentation. (We look at delivery in Chapter 4.)

PLANNING AND PREPARATION EXAMPLE

Before we go on to the specifics of delivery, let's take another look putting it all together—planning, organizing, developing notes, and practicing. We'll follow Paul Mitchell as he prepares a speech to see how he does it.

Paul is a staff accountant with a large national accounting firm. Oral communication is a skill that he is working hard to strengthen. He makes presentations to clients and participates in staff and committee meetings. He is also actively involved in several professional and special interest groups. Knowing that business speaking is a learned skill, not an inherited trait, Paul grabs every chance that comes his way to polish his planning, design, and delivery skills.

Paul has developed a strong off-the-job interest in personal home computing and belongs to a computer users group. Every month the group presents speakers on personal computer topics, and Paul has consented to make an eight-minute extemporaneous presentation on fundamentals of computer memory. To make a logical, concise, practical, and informative presentation, appearing confident, relaxed, and conversational, Paul invests several hours in careful planning using the ESCAP-E formula.

Audience Analysis

Being an active member of the computer users group, Paul is familiar with what audience members know, do not know, and want to know. He himself has only a year's experience with PCs, so he can relate quite easily to the confusion that inexperienced computer owners feel at first. This helped him to construct his purpose statement in terms of his audience's needs and expectations. He decides to discuss three basic concepts about computer memory: (1) importance of memory; (2) difference between RAM and ROM memory; and (3) typical user memory requirements. To supplement his personal experience, he researched his topic by studying several magazine articles.

Paul's audience analysis was relatively easy since he belongs to the computer users group himself. He knows most all of his audience will be either personal computer users with less than one year's experience or people contemplating their first personal computer purchase. His audience, therefore, has some basic knowledge of computers and an active interest in them. They know some computer terms, like software, hardware, program, spreadsheet, and so on. The audience will be approximately 50 members, mostly males aged 15 to 35. Two listener roles will predominate: About half the members will be believing listeners because Paul is a relative expert compared to themselves and they will lack any really critical basis on which to discredit his data. Furthermore, he is a fellow member. He's one of them; they know and respect him. The other half of the audience could be labeled critical listeners because they have as much or more computer experience than Paul does. They hope to profit from his presentation if he is well prepared, credible, and accurate.

Note Development and Practice

Using the planning, outline, and practice suggestions in this chapter, Paul gradually shaped his presentation to meet both his and his audience's high expectations. He is pleased with his approach and talk structure. The talk flows well and should capture and maintain audience interest. His notes went through three revisions—each time becoming shorter and simpler. He is now comfortable with his final set of notes shown in Figure 3–5. It

FIGURE 3-5
Sample Talk Outline

I. INTRODUCTION
   A. Groucho Marx: "Last night I shot an elephant in my pajamas. How he got into my pajamas I'll never know."
      Computers like elephants—famous for memory but smaller, weigh less
   B. Buying personal computer or own one?
      Uses: WP, budgeting, office work, recreation
   C. I have ABC for 1 year
      Uses: WP and computer games
      Greenhorn to confident user
   D. Share some imp. basics about computer memory so you get off to faster start
  TR. Specifically 3 things:
     1. Why memory is important
     2. How memory works
     3. How much memory you need

II. BODY
   A. Why memory is important
     1. Computers run on info., memory stores info.
        a. More memory = more info.
        b. More info. = more power
     2. Heard people talking about K—
        256K, 640K—what is it?
        a. K is how memory is measured
           K = kilobyte; K = 1000 bytes (spell)
        b. Byte = piece of info.
           Example: strike 1 character = 1 byte
        c. 256K memory stores 256,000 bytes
  TR. Memory really more complicated. Let's go to number two.
   B. How memory works
     1. Two kinds—RAM, ROM
        Not comedy team but heart and soul of computer
        a. RAM (spell) = random-access memory. User memory
        b. ROM (spell) = read-only memory. Permanent memory
     2. ROM built in at factory
        a. Has basic information to tell computer what to do
        b. Permanent—forever, even with computer off
        c. Can't change it = why it's called read-only memory
        d. ROM important,
           RAM star player
     3. Rest of memory is RAM
        a. Random access used many ways
        b. Read, store, copy, manipulate info.

FIGURE 3–5 *(continued)*

Sample Talk Outline

```
    4. How RAM works
       a. Load software = copy program into RAM
       b. WP example:
          Program takes up K
          Writing report puts words into RAM
          Turn off computer = you lose everything but ROM
          Need to save on floppy disk
   TR. That's how memory works—not so complicated
       On to number three
    C. How much memory do you need
       1. Simple answer—don't know
          a. Depends on your uses
          b. Wrong memory size can waste your money
       2. Some general guidelines
          a. Entertainment, education software—need less RAM
          b. Working software (WP or spreadsheet)—need more RAM
          c. Can add memory boards to some computers. Costs more
             money but cheaper than new computer
   TR. To wrap up, remember two things
III. CLOSE
    A. 1. More RAM = greater potential
       2. Make sure you can add more RAM
    B. These are basics of memory
       Don't really need to know about bits, bytes, and nibbles
       But to be comfortable, helps to have good overall understand-
       ing of what memory is, how it works
```

will keep him on track and ensure that he doesn't omit a section or important interest material.

Observe also that Paul's notes for the introduction and close are more detailed than those for the body. Having greater verbal support to begin and end confidently, he will more than likely be his usual personable, spontaneous self during his entire talk. Although he purposely provided greater note support in the opening and close, he uses key phrases throughout. He has timed his presentation, and it falls between seven and eight minutes. He has stayed within his time limit yet develops his talk's purpose effectively for his listeners.

Paul practiced a couple of times in front of a mirror, once with an audio tape recorder, and finished with a run-through in front of a small test audience (his girlfriend, a next-door neighbor, and a friend who belongs to the same users group). He feels confident. He is ready to face his audience and deliver his material, letting his personality shine forth.

Talk Structure

Figure 3–6 is the verbatim text of Paul's presentation. Compare his talk outline to his actual presentation. He has taken his brief key-phrase notes and fleshed them out, choosing his exact words conversationally as he interacted with his listeners.

FIGURE 3–6
Sample Speech

[INTRODUCTION] [Attention-getter] In the words of Groucho Marx, "Last night I shot an elephant in my pajamas. How he got into my pajamas I'll never know." Elephants aren't the only things famous for their memory. Computers are, too. But the great thing about computers is that they take up far less space, weigh less, and eat less.

[Audience involvement] Most of you are either considering buying a personal computer or already own one. You can use a personal home computer to do word processing, keep the family budget, do work you bring home from the office, or maybe just for recreation, to play games.

[Self-involvement] I purchased my ABC computer a year ago. I use mine to do two things mainly: word processing, because I do a lot of work-related writing at home, and playing computer games, especially simulations and adventure games. So in about a year, I've gone from a computer greenhorn to a confident computer user.

[Purpose statement] I will share a few important basics about computer memory with you so that you can get off to an even faster start that I did.

[Transition to body] We'll cover three things: why memory is important, how memory works, and how much memory you need.

[BODY] [Point A] Let's start with why memory is important. It's important because our computers run on information, and memory stores that information. The more memory you have, the more information your computer can hold. And the more it can hold, the more it can do. You've heard people throwing K around—256K, 640K—and you really don't know what it is. Well, I'm going to tell you.

K is how memory is measured. K means kilobyte. K equals a thousand, a thousand bytes, b–y–t–e–s. O.K., stay with me. A byte is a piece of information. For instance, if you strike any character on your computer keyboard, that character takes up one byte of memory. So a computer with 256K of memory means that computer can store 256,000 bytes.

FIGURE 3–6 (continued)

Sample Speech

[Transition] It's really quite simple, too simple, in fact. So I'm going to make it more complicated. Let's go to number two: **[Point B]** How memory works. There are two kinds of memory: RAM and ROM. That sounds like a comedy team, but RAM and ROM are really the heart and soul of your computer. RAM, r–a–m, stands for random-access-memory. RAM can be considered user memory. ROM, r–o–m, stands for read-only memory. ROM can be thought of as permanent memory.

Computers come from the factory with ROM memory built right in. It's in there because it contains all the basic information that tells your computer what to do. Now, it's in there forever even though you turn the computer off. And you can't change it. That's why it's called read-only. Obviously ROM is important, but RAM is the star player. Now the rest of space in the computer is RAM memory. You can use RAM many ways. Read it, store it, copy it, manipulate it.

Here's how it works: When you load software, you actually copy the program and store it in RAM. For example, a word processing program takes up so many K of RAM. Well now, you start writing your report and putting words into RAM. The more you write, the more RAM you use. Now you do all this work and turn off the computer. Yes, you lose everything you typed in—along with your temper, too. All that remains is ROM. That's why you have to save your work on a floppy disk before turning off the computer. When you load another program, the whole thing starts all over again. **[Transition]** So, essentially that's how memory works. It's really not that complicated, right? Now, on to number three:

[Point C] How much memory do you need? The answer is simple. I don't know. It really depends on what you will be doing with your computer. Oh, you can waste money by not buying enough *and* by buying memory you'll never ever use.

Here are some general guidelines: Entertainment and education software generally don't take up much RAM. But if you're using what is known as working software programs where you're moving around a lot of words and numbers, like a word processor or spreadsheet, and I have a hunch you will be eventually, you'll need more memory. And with some computers you'll be able to do this. You buy what are called memory boards. Install them and, presto, more memory. It costs you more money, but a whole lot less than buying a completely new computer.

[Transition to close] To wrap up, if you can't remember everything I've covered on memory, please remember these two things: **[CLOSE] [Summary]** One, more RAM memory equals greater potential. Two, make sure you can add more RAM. **[Refocus]** So that's pretty much the basics of memory. And it's the basics of memory that are important. I mean you really don't have to know about bits and bytes and nibbles. But if you are going to be comfortable in the world of computers, you should have a good overall understanding of what computer memory is and how it works.

How did Paul structure his talk? He used the direct, three-part organizational pattern. In the opener, his attention-getter uses humor, a famous Groucho Marx line, which should get a few smiles from the audience while relevantly bringing up the subject of memory. He then proceeds through his audience-involvement step, emphasizing the significance of his subject matter for the listeners, to the self-involvement step, at which time he establishes his expertise as the speaker and strengthens his rapport by identifying with the audience. Paul states his purpose emphatically. For a relatively short talk, he does not feel he needs a detailed plan of presentation. He does, however, provide a simple preview of his three-part development in his transition to the body.

Paul chose the topical organizational pattern for his body. He develops three computer memory topics in well thought-out, sequential order going from the general—what is memory?—to the specific—what is the difference between ROM and RAM memory, and how is this information important to the audience? Paul provides clear verbal signposts throughout his body. He uses transitional words and phrases frequently between and within sections and subsections: "Let's start with why memory is important" to introduce point one; "It's really quite simple, too simple, in fact. So I'm going to make it a bit more complicated" to bridge points one and two; and "Now, on to number three" to introduce the last section of the body. So, Paul's listeners know at all times where they are, where they are going, and how everything fits together into a unified whole.

He provides a transition to the close, a very brief summary of the most important things to remember. The talk is too short to require much more detail here. He finishes by refocusing on the value and usefulness of his information. His finish provides closure by summing up the body and reinforcing the personal significance of his material for every listener.

Paul aimed to present a professional quality speech, one that was practical, easy to follow, with concrete information for the listeners. Do you think he succeeded on both counts? Do you think you could have done just as well, or even better?

SUMMING UP

The secret of successful extemporaneous speaking is investing ample time in planning, structuring the talk, developing talk notes, and practicing. Do this conscientiously and you will be relaxed and natural when you face your audience to deliver your presentation.

Use a logical planning procedure like the ESCAP-E plan. *E* means *e*xamine the speech assignment from all angles so that you know what the parameters of the talk opportunity are and what the listeners' expectations are. *S* means *s*tate your purpose. Express what will be communicated to the listeners in a short, clear sentence. *C* means *c*hoose the major and minor ideas that must be developed to carry out the purpose statement. *A* means *a*rrange these ideas. To add shape and unity to their presentations business and professional people choose from direct organizational formats (chronological, cause and effect, categorical, problem-solution, order of importance, topical, and spatial) and indirect organizational formats like the persuasive approach, which uses the AIDA (attention, interest, desire, action) plan. *P* means *p*ick verbal and visual support. To add muscle to the skeletonal outline, select verbal support in the form of facts, statistics, examples, and other interest material and visual support, if desired, in the form of charts, posters, transparencies, and so on.

Business presentations using the deductive organizational format have three structural elements, each with an important task to perform. The opener attracts listener attention, involves the audience, establishes the speaker's self-involvement, and orients the audience to the speaker's subject matter. The longest part of the presentation is the body, which develops the purpose statement interestingly, concretely, and smoothly, using the appropriate organizational pattern. The close summarizes, concludes, recommends, or refocuses on the listeners to make the final meaning and value of the content clear to the members of the audience.

Extemporaneous speakers talk from brief, simple, key-phrase notes. Such notes keep the presenter on track and provide verbal support as the speaker chooses her exact wording while interacting with the audience. Because the talk outline is short, the speaker must practice to become familiar with the talk notes, polish and enliven delivery, and gain confidence. Practicing using a mirror, a small test audience, or taping equipment are excellent ways to polish a talk. You're now ready to learn how to face the audience—the actual delivery phase of speaking—in the next chapter.

Application Exercises

1. Begin preparing for an extemporaneous speech using the principles learned in Chapter 3. For the topic assigned to you or chosen by you, plan a presentation that meets the specifications given by your instructor—time, use of props and aids, audience expectations, speech

setting, and so on. Develop your talk's notes. Begin practicing your presentation, paying special attention to (1) strengthening your talk's organizational pattern, (2) managing your time well (you may need to narrow or broaden your purpose statement or develop more verbal support), and (3) improving and revising your notes as necessary.
Use the following list to chose a topic:
- a. Read a book or magazine article related to your managerial, business, or career interest, and present some of the author's major ideas.
- b. Investigate a Fortune 500 company or a major employer in your area. Subject matter might include corporate history, top managers' backgrounds, products and services, and recent management problems.
- c. Choose a controversial issue related to your career area. Explain and defend your position persuasively. For example, "Job responsibilities of nurses should be broadened to include diagnosis and prescription of drugs."

2. Present a one- to two-minute talk based on an article given to you by your instructor. The article might come from the local newspaper, *New York Times, The Wall Street Journal,* or a supermarket tabloid. Use five to ten minutes' planning time to read the article, determine the points to present and your organizational pattern, and develop a brief set of notes. Concentrate on a strong three-part organizational pattern: Write out your opening sentence containing your attention-getter and purpose statement, key phrases to develop that purpose, and your closing sentence.

Chapter 4

AS YOU SPEAK: DELIVERY TECHNIQUES

Having finished the *before you speak* preparation, you know how to prepare a well-organized talk, with easy-to-use, supportive notes. You have practiced your presentation so that it is listenable. You are more than halfway to your objective of making a logically organized, interesting, and worthwhile presentation. Now that you are ready to face the final hurdle, your audience, you must turn your attention to the *as you speak* dimension. In this chapter we focus on delivery techniques; we will work on refining your basic repertoire of delivery skills so that you can give a natural, conversational, and animated talk in your own personable, distinctive way.

Effective delivery skills make a major contribution to your presentation. When comparing the importance of words, tone of voice, and body and facial language, communication researchers have discovered that 55 percent of the believability and trustworthiness of human communication is conveyed through body language, 38 percent through tone of voice, and only 7 percent through actual words.[1] Studies also show that if body language contradicts the verbal language, the listener usually pays more attention to the body language. In other words, many times *how* you say something counts more than *what* you say, insofar as getting your listeners to accept and act on your subject matter goes.

For example, a salesperson—one who is quite clearly in the wrong line of work—is helping you select a new coat. He says to you, "This suit is made of the finest imported wool that has been specially treated to resist wrinkling but still maintain all the qualities for which wool is famous." You notice, however, that he does not look you in the eye when he speaks, his tone of voice is soft and hesitant, and he is twisting the ring on his hand back and forth. How likely are you to believe and trust him? Most people would doubt the truthfulness or knowledge of this salesperson because of the contradictory message his nonverbal language sends.

Don't assume, however, that you can emphasize style over substance. All the confidence and grace you can muster will not impress a critical business or professional audience very long if you have little of value to say or do not know how to organize and develop your ideas well. You must develop a delivery style

---

1. Albert Mehrabian, "Communicating Without Words," *Psychology Today* Sept. 1968: 53–5.

that complements and reinforces the impact of your content and organizational plan.

Bill Washington, a reporter for a morning newspaper, knows he must improve his delivery. Last week he made a 15-minute presentation at a high school's College Night. Being a young man who graduated from that high school himself just six years earlier, Bill's boss asked him to make the presentation, believing the students could probably identify with him. He did a thorough job of prepping for his talk that described a reporter's work day at a major city newspaper and offered career advice. Bill is a personable kind of guy, but when he got up to speak, he froze. He got through his presentation somehow, but he was very uncomfortable during his delivery. His voice was monotone, his eye contact with his audience minimal, and his body language stiff and colorless.

Can you identify with Bill's not-too-unusual experience? If so, you will profit from Chapter 4. This chapter explains how business and professional people use three aspects of a natural delivery style to enhance and reinforce their verbal language:

- voice,
- eye contact,
- body language.

Speech communicators use other devices to maintain a relaxed, open, sharing atmosphere with their listeners. Two audience-management factors important in delivering content comfortably and interacting well with listeners are presented next:

- humor,
- question-and-answer sessions.

Chapter 4 closes with advice on tying all these aspects of a natural, interactive delivery style together.

VOICE

Your primary delivery instrument in a talk is your voice. Ralph Proodian, a speech consultant who writes frequently on oral communication in *The Wall Street Journal* says: "Your tone of voice as an executive, not merely the literal meaning of your words, controls the way your staff and associates respond to you. . . . Precise vocabulary and a clear literary style are what you need on paper. But when you speak, you color your ideas with the way you sound. . . . an executive who is in command of his own voice is rarely misinterpreted by his staff and can avoid costly reexplanations of orders."[2] As a professional or business person, the sound of your voice is a powerful tool in creating the leadership image and the communication effectiveness you are striving for.

Everyone's voice has a natural timbre, those aspects that make your voice instantly recognizable when you telephone friends and relatives or when you call from one room to another. This one of a kind vocal quality is determined by the manner in which you use your vocal equipment. Your tongue, lips, teeth, jaw, throat, diaphragm, rib cage, and lungs all interact to create your special, distinctive vocal sound, rhythm, and texture. You probably have an adequate speaking voice that has served you rather well whether speaking face to face, on the telephone, or in front of a group.

Unfortunately, some people have insecurities about their voices. They deliberately try to change their voice qualities by manipulating how they use their vocal mechanism. They may try to imitate their favorite newscaster or television interviewer. They aim unrealistically to make their voices over; ending up sounding phony and uncomfortable. Plus, such effort misplaces a great deal of energy. So, don't try to *change* your voice. Channel your effort into *refining* the voice you already have. What you will want to do is maximize the vocal strengths you have by focusing on the four qualities of your voice that affect the meaning or impact of the words you choose to speak: pitch, rate, volume, and enunciation.

Pitch

Pitch is the highness or lowness of the voice. A pleasant voice has a varied pitch pattern. Vocal inflections rise and fall as the speaker's level of excitement changes. Your emotions are reflected in your voice's pitch. Fear and anger are reflected in a higher pitch and sadness in a lower pitch. High-pitched voices lend a frantic, anxious, or tentative quality to the words—maybe even a plead-

---

2. Ralph Proodian, "Executive Leader Needs an Expressive Voice," *The Wall Street Journal* April 22, 1985: 28.

ing or whining quality in the worst cases. The lower register of your voice, male or female, is generally more authoritative sounding. You can learn to cultivate this quality with practice.

Rate

Rate is the speed at which the words are spoken. Talented speakers, through experience and practice, have developed a sense of pacing. They adjust their speaking rate to the demands of the situation, considering the occasion, content, and audience's knowledge-to-date of the subject matter.

You can do this, too. Speak at a slower rate when presenting new, complicated, or challenging content. This permits the listeners to concentrate on the ideas. A slower rate, even a pause, also adds emphasis to key points and flags the audience's attention. Pausing strategically allows the speaker to phrase ideas and enhance transition as well. Pausing briefly between topics creates a boundary line, implying to the listeners, "I've finished one section and am going on to the next one."

Speeding up your delivery rate can serve your purpose also. Use a faster rate momentarily to present less significant content, perhaps when you are reviewing background or summarizing. The audience has less time to react and reflect, so this content has less impact. Toss off unimportant words. By saying articles—a, an, the—prepositions, and conjunctions quickly, the words that carry your real meaning are emphasized.

All in all, aim for a speaking rate that is varied and suits the situation. Guard against extremes. If your rate is too slow, your listeners' mental processing rate is not challenged. They may become distracted and remember less. On the other hand, never talk faster to cram in more material to finish on time. You may get all the words in, but your purpose will be not fulfilled. Fast talkers appear impersonal. They give the impression that they don't care if the audience comprehends the content. They suggest that time management is more important than communicating.

Recall from Chapter 2 that listening is difficult work for audience members. Just as you plan your presentation design to make listening and remembering easier, adjust your delivery rate for the same reasons. Test your pace by checking your speaking rate during your taped practice sessions. Help your listeners and yourself by speaking at a moderate rate with frequent variation to enhance your meaning.

The problem of verbal filler is related to speaking rate. Many speakers, beginning and well-seasoned alike, vocalize their pauses. Rather than have silence, they insert meaningless words and phrases such as "you know," "I mean," "like," "O.K.," "and daaaa," "ummmm," "errrr," "ahhhh," and so on. Overusing certain pet words or phrases, such as "basically," "actually," "as a matter of fact," and "what not" is equally annoying to listeners.

Many people use verbal fillers subconsciously—they don't even know it. Other speakers, because of their nervousness, vocalize gaps with such verbal garbage while they grope for the correct word or next idea. They mistakenly believe that they must keep flooding the air with words, even if the words are trite and meaningless, so their listeners will not think they are lost or confused. Whatever the reason, vocalized pauses are distracting and annoying to audience members. Have you ever detected a repeated filler word or phrase and begun to count the repetitions, ceasing to pay attention to the speaker's content?

Fortunately, using verbal filler is a habit that can be broken easily. If you are bothered by vocalized pauses and want to eliminate them from your vocabulary, start by raising your consciousness. Listen to yourself on tape and make a list of filler words and pet words you use, or ask your practice audience for feedback on this problem. Then, when you talk in public or even in conversation, you will begin to hear yourself saying "I mean" over and over again. You can gradually weed it out. With what do you replace verbal filler? Nothing—just silence. The pause will be only for a second or less, although in your mind it may seem like an eternity as you put together the next words to say. Use these pauses positively; they can help develop that sense of pacing recommended earlier.

By its very nature, extemporaneous or impromptu speaking has occasional pauses that are part of the conversationality of these delivery styles. You are choosing your precise words as you go along. Naturally, you will need to pause sometimes to search for the right words. The audience understands this, and furthermore, recognizes it as one of your speaking strengths, since you are evidently shaping the content to meet listener needs right on the spot.

Volume

Volume refers to the audibility of the voice. Again, pleasing voices have a variety of volumes ranging from soft to loud, depending on what suits the speaker's communication intent and other circumstances. Of course, the first rule is to speak loudly enough to be heard by every listener. But use variety to keep the audience's attention and to emphasize or de-emphasize words and ideas. Raise your voice's level to call special attention to a word or phrase. Gradually raise the level of your voice as you build to a climactic conclusion. Lower your voice to make your audience members listen more intently or perhaps to establish a more hushed, intimate atmosphere, drawing your listeners toward you.

Monitor your audience's nonverbal language to determine if your volume is adequate. If your listeners cannot hear you, they may have distant looks on their faces because they stopped paying attention. They may be leaning forward with their ears cocked toward you. They may be backing away from your booming voice. Read your audience's feedback. Their facial expressions and posture will tell whether you are speaking too softly or too loudly.

Enunciation

The fourth vocal attribute, enunciation, means the clarity with which the words are spoken. In casual conversation among friends, slurred, imprecise speaking may not damage understanding. You approach your co-workers at five minutes to noon and mumble, "Jeatyet?" Knowing your voice and using other cues, they decipher this to be "Did you eat yet?" Poor enunciation like this would not be acceptable for an audience of your professional colleagues, who might have difficulty comprehending the message completely and correctly.

Speakers with poor enunciation are often lax in the way they breathe and use their lips, tongue, and teeth to form individual sounds. Another cause of poor enunciation is speaking too quickly. Words are thus incompletely formed and run together. Regional dialects can cause poor enunciation or, at least, cause listeners to blame their difficulty in understanding on the speaker's strange or strong accent.

Most enunciation problems, fortunately, can be solved by improving the way you stand, sit, breathe, and move your tongue around to form sounds. We often think we breathe with our nose or mouth, but actually we breathe using our chest. The nose, mouth, or throat cannot pump air out or suck air in by themselves because they are just passageways. When you exhale and inhale, your diaphragm, ribs, and abdominal muscles do most of the work of moving air in or out of your lungs. If you have poor posture, the abdominal muscles do not function properly. Rounded shoulders and curvature of the lower back cause a constant downward pressure in both the chest and ribs, which prevents the diaphragm and lungs from moving air in and out efficiently.

The main goal to improving enunciation is to use the vocal mechanism fully and correctly. By shifting your breathing away from the nose and mouth and into your chest, you can use your mouth more precisely to support your speaking. The front of your mouth—the lips, tip of the tongue, and front upper teeth—produces most of the sounds making up our words. By breathing correctly, standing up straight with shoulders back, and concentrating your speaking in the front of your mouth, you improve your voice's clarity, reduce strain and voice distortions, lower your pitch, and increase your voice's expressiveness.

Putting these suggestions to work, you can gradually eliminate common enunciation flaws like these:

- Dropping word endings—saying "talkin'" for "talking."
- Running words together—saying "wanna" for "want to," "gonna" for "going to," "with 'em" for "with them," "kinda" for "kind of," or "lotta" for "lot of."
- Imprecise enunciation—saying "ta" for "to," "pitcher" for "picture," or "genwine" for "genuine."

In this discussion of voice qualities, the principle of variety came up often when describing a pleasant, effective speaking voice. An unpleasant voice lacks variety. Often called a monotone, such a voice is dull, flat, lifeless, and droning. Novice business and professional speakers often sound dull and lifeless.

During conversation with friends, Bill Washington's voice is colorful, animated, and relaxed, but in front of his audience these qualities slipped away. As he gets more experience, he will begin to feel successful; as he gains more control of the speaking situation, Bill's natural voice quality will return. This patient attitude, plus conscious attention to eliminating vocal flaws like sloppy enunciation or vocal filler, will soon make Bill's voice a powerful instrument that adds color, meaning, and nuance to the words he chooses.

EYE CONTACT

Bill's delivery needs more than correct voice usage. Speakers who care about communicating effectively establish and maintain eye contact with their listeners. Strong eye contact is one way speakers create that conversational, interactive rapport with everybody in the audience.

Think about a romantic interlude. Haven't there been many times when much was communicated by a longing look or a loving gaze? No doubt, too, you can remember talking with a person who refused to establish eye contact with you, refusing to look you directly in the eye. Didn't you feel uncomfortable? That person seemed distant, cold, or evasive. When conversing with someone who was wearing dark sunglasses, have you felt ill at ease? Part of the problem was lack of eye contact and the loss of information that eye contact contributes to the communication process.

In platform speaking, eye contact plays just as big a role. With eye-to-eye contact, every listener gets a strong impression that the speaker is talking directly and personally to her, rather than to a collection of people. Each listener feels included and listens more closely. A personal, caring quality is added to the communication exchange.

Eye contact benefits you as a speaker, too. First, it reminds you that your audience is human, thereby reducing your fears and defensiveness. You will recall that one of the techniques of handling speaking anxiety is drawing support and encouragement from friendly listeners in the audience. Making eye contact is a good way to gather support. Second, it is a valuable source of feedback. You can *see* if the audience members are listening, if they are interested, and if they are following the development of the subject matter. You are acting and reacting to the audience, and, when necessary, using the data from eye contact to make subtle adjustments in the presentation's format or delivery—speeding up, slowing down, going into more or less detail, or reinforcing the significance of the content with listener-oriented examples.

When speaking extemporaneously, you can maximize eye contact—you are working from basic notes and have practiced to develop a strong familiarity with your notes and subject matter, so you need only make minimal reference to notes and you can maintain maximum eye contact with the audience.

For improved eye contact, use these techniques:

1. Look at your audience. Don't stare out the window, at the ceiling, over the heads of the listeners, at the floor, or at your visual aids. These evasive tactics are signs of stage fright.

2. Distribute eye contact evenly over the entire audience. Don't concentrate only on your supporters in the first two rows or the members of a particular department on the right side. These audience members will think that your eye contact is great. Everyone else will feel neglected and outside your intended focus, both visually and otherwise.

3. Shift your gaze smoothly from one segment of the audience to another. Pick out a person to speak to, almost personally, and then after three or four seconds find another nearby person to talk to. This pattern is much more effective than the eye-dart style some inexperienced speakers use. By abruptly and frequently jumping their gaze from one section of the audience to another, they appear to be scared rabbits. Don't mimic a surveillance camera in a building lobby either, panning from one side of the audience to the other in a mechanical, sweeping motion. Using the extended eye contact pattern, you give everyone the feeling that sometime during the talk you were talking directly to him or her. Thus the audience feels more involved in the subject matter and complimented by your desire to fulfil their special communication expectations.

If Bill Washington develops stronger eye contact, he will have more of that conversational quality. He will be talking *with* his listeners, not talking *at* them.

BODY LANGUAGE

Bill not only uses his voice and eyes but his entire body when presenting. His body language is an essential nonverbal communication tool. In fact, he cannot avoid communicating with his body. For this reason, Bill must use positive, not negative, body language.

Your audience members, like Bill's, interpret your body language. The way you use your body will reinforce, weaken, even contradict your verbal message. Suppose you attend a campaign rally and hear a city council member's re-election speech. Several days after hearing the talk, you may remember little of the factual content, but you still have a solid opinion of this person's sincerity, motivation, and truthworthiness. Subconsciously—or even consciously, to some degree—you read that candidate's body language for signs of openness and honesty.

Let's examine the basic components of body language and learn how to make them contribute positively to your communication impact.

Personal Appearance

You may not be able to do anything about your height, weight, or surface attractiveness, but you can select clothing and groom yourself to create the strongest image of authority, knowledge, believability, and confidence possible. Meeting certain role expectations in the audience member's mind reinforces listener desire to pay attention to the speaker and accept and use the information.

Granted, this is a superficial motivation for listening. Nonetheless, most people do make judgments based on appearance. People commonly react first to the source of information and secondly to the content conveyed. First impressions are difficult to overcome. An inappropriately dressed and groomed speaker will have to work harder to establish his or her credentials just to counteract a negative or distracting physical appearance.

Test this premise by closing your eyes and picturing a successful executive with a Fortune 500 company. What is this person wearing? Blue jeans, a T-shirt, and worn-out sneakers? Corduroys, an ill-fitting, stained shirt, and loafers? Hardly! Most people would envision this talented and powerful person wearing a blue or gray pin-striped suit, a white or blue shirt or blouse, a quietly patterned tie or understated jewelry, and conservative shoes.

Looking the part makes your job much easier from your perspective, too. Dressing for the role increases your sense of self-confidence and strengthens your stage presence. You are more likely to act the role if you look the role.

You do not have to buy a large and expensive wardrobe and get your hair styled and your nails manicured every other week. Rather, groom yourself like a professional. Wear clothing that is appropriate for the occasion, consistent with the audience's expectations—your wardrobe should be well-fitting, properly coordinated, and neat and clean.

Speaking Position

If you do not have a lectern, assume a central position in relationship to your audience. Aim for the correct degree of physical and psychological closeness. Don't stand too close or you may appear too personal. Don't stand too far away, either, or you distance yourself and lessen potential involvement with your listeners. Suppose you are orienting a group of six new employees on your organization's personnel policies. They are sitting at the rear of a 20-by-30 foot room. Going back and standing three or four feet from the group—or having them move forward—is best. Speaking from the front of the room would separate your listeners from you with a 20-foot gulf, communicating aloofness both literally and figuratively.

If you have a lectern, your speaking position is predetermined. Think of your lectern as your home base. Feel free to move around occasionally to incorporate your presentation aids more naturally into your talk or to get closer to the audience to field questions. The lectern is designed to hold your notes, not to hide or to support you. Anxious speakers grip the lectern until their knuckles are white, hanging on to it for dear life. This is their ineffective way of minimizing contact with the listeners and of withdrawing from them.

Although moving around is fine in most speaking situations, a speaker should not pace from one side of the room or stage to the other. Such movement reveals as much anxiety as the white-knuckle approach. If you are using a microphone, your movements must be restricted. By necessity, stay close to the podium.

Posture

A relaxed speaker stands comfortably erect with body weight evenly distributed on both feet, with feet slightly apart. This stance signifies the in-control look the professional or business person wishes to project. As mentioned earlier, this posture will also strengthen the speaker's voice. Uncomfortable speakers often appear paralyzed and as stiff as fence posts. Equally distracting for the audience are other signs of nervousness, including foot tapping, shifting weight from one foot to the other constantly, and swaying from side to side.

How the speaker carries herself makes a statement, too. The audience makes subjective evaluations of your capability as a speaker from your bearing. An impressive speaker projects eagerness, control, alertness, authority, credibility, and quiet confidence in the way she walks, moves, and stands. The speaker must demonstrate these qualities while moving to the podium, through the entire presentation, and returning to her seat or leaving the stage.

Facial Expressions

According to an old saying, the face is the mirror of the emotions. Certainly this is true in good public speaking. Your facial expressions should reveal enthusiasm for the message and sincere warmth and rapport with the audience.

When you are presenting, how can you train your face to do this? You can't. Do you make a conscious effort to manipulate your facial expressions in normal conversation? As you become more relaxed before audiences, your spontaneous, animated facial expressions return. Your eyes will be wide and sparkling, revealing the excitement of communicating your talk's content well. You will smile occasionally, showing that you are enjoying the experience.

Gestures

A question speakers commonly ask is what to do with their arms and hands when speaking? Isn't it strange no one worries about that when chatting with co-workers at lunch or when conversing with friends over pizza and beer? In fact, people talk with their hands. Arms and hands communicate content and intent nonverbally. Just as in social interaction, let your hands respond naturally when presenting. People vary in the number of gestures they use in public speaking just as they do in conversation. Whether it is related to personality or habit is immaterial. You can and should cultivate gestures to enhance the meaning of your verbal content.

You can use gestures to: **Picture.** Outline a hexagonal shape in the air with your hands. This movement graphically suggests the geometric shape of your company's new logo. **Emphasize.** Hold up two fingers in front of you with about two inches of space between them and say, "We're still this far apart." Use this gesture to emphasize symbolically the small gap separating union and management in negotiations to renew the labor contract. **List.** Hold up five fingers and say, "Five reasons for reducing the price of the Model 9999 widget are. . . ." **Point.** Focus attention on a visual aid by pointing.

When evaluating your gestures, use the following criteria:

1. Gestures should fit the speaking situation. A platform speaker using a lectern does quite well with a few small gestures.

A workshop leader, moving around freely within the listening group and speaking without notes, will probably use more frequent, broader, and expressive gestures.

2. Gestures should involve the entire body. If the rest of your body is as stiff as a board, your hand movements will look forced and artificial to the audience. A relaxed quality of your whole body complements your hand gestures. When using a pointer to fix viewers' attention on a specific column of numbers on a chart, rotate your entire body about one-eighth of a turn toward the chart, turn your head briefly toward the chart to position your finger, and point at the relevant figures. Involving your whole body this way is more natural-looking than sticking your arm out toward the chart with your body and head facing forward stiffly.

3. Gestures should be varied. Repeated, single gestures are as irritating as vocalized pauses. Folding your arms in front of you may be perfectly all right at times. But if this is your only gesture, you look unnatural and frozen. Occasionally hooking your thumbs in your belt or holding your hands behind your back is acceptable, but alternating between these two gestures several times a minute would be interpreted as nervous fidgeting by your audience.

Your gestures are a logical, unthinking outgrowth of your interaction with the audience. Within reason, it really does not matter much what you do with your hands as long as you do not keep them in one position too long or resort to distracting repeated movements.

4. Gestures should be spontaneous. Let your gestures flow naturally from your feelings as you respond to the occasion, audience, and subject matter. This advice, of course, becomes easier with experience. Like vocal quality, your body language may desert you at first. Be patient and it will return. On the other hand, planned gestures look phony and stilted. For this reason, never specifically plan or practice gestures. Stage directions to yourself are complicating clutter in your notes. And in fact, they will probably only heighten your anxiety about what to do with your hands.

5. Gestures should make a positive, purposeful contribution to the communication process. Whether caused by habit or nervousness, eliminate negative and distracting gestures from your repertoire. Figure 4–1 shows ten frequently occurring gestures that you should consciously try to eliminate. Be on the lookout for these during practice in front of a mirror or ask your practice audience to watch for them.

FIGURE 4-1
Annoying Gestures Speakers Frequently Use

1. Hands and arms clasped in front of body (fig leaf position) or behind back (parade rest position).
2. Scratching.
3. Playing with hair or constantly brushing it away from face.
4. Rubbing hands together.
5. Twisting rings or jewelry.
6. Hands in pockets or jingling coins or keys in pocket.
7. Covering mouth.
8. Gripping lectern tightly.
9. Waving notes, pen, pencil, or pointer around.
10. Flighty, frantic, almost continuous hand movement.

USING HUMOR

Presentations need not be deadly serious. A joke or funny anecdote may be just the thing to open or close your presentation or make a point in a sure-fire way. Indeed, some presentations that professional and business people make are entirely entertainment. For example, at a retirement banquet for a colleague, each person's remarks may consist mainly of humor.

However, humor is more than joke-telling. Speakers often consciously strive for a lively, humorous turn of phrase or reference. Another kind of humor is unplanned humor. In developing the talk outline, the speaker says something in a comical way, makes a pun, or points out humor in the work surroundings, which gets a chuckle from the listeners. When this happens, the speaker just goes with it, sharing the light moment with the audience. No matter how it is classified, humor has several benefits: it provides comic relief, it reduces speaker and audience tension, it increases the audience's attention to and retention of content, and it strengthens speaker/listener rapport.

Whether humor will work for you or not depends on what type of person you are. Some people can tell jokes and amusing stories at parties with aplomb. They probably can use planned humor well in public speaking, too. You may have a good memory for jokes, funny stories, and humorous anecdotes. Do you always seem to have a joke or two to tell your friends and can you look at the humorous side of situations?

Many people don't have this ability. These people are just no good at telling jokes and funny stories. When they try to be deliberately funny, the audience does not get the joke or the speaker botches the joke by forgetting the punch line. They become self-conscious and inhibited. In any case, the speaker feels uncomfortable, and this uneasy feeling is communicated to the audience, who then becomes distracted from the talk's subject matter. If you are one of these people, you might be better off sticking to spontaneous humor. When it happens, be grateful and use it to your advantage.

When using humor in a professional or business setting, remember four things: First, make sure the light approach is appropriate. A speaker who is announcing that the company is going into a Chapter 11 reorganization to forestall bankruptcy should obviously avoid a humorous approach. Discretion is always advisable when using humor. Going for laughs calls for careful calculation on the speaker's part.

Second, make sure the humor is relevant and tasteful. Starting off with a stand-up comic's gag about your mother-in-law's personality as your attention-getter is a bad idea. The audience may roar with laughter and ignore the rest of the talk. You may not be able to provide smooth transition back to the rest of the opener. Besides, such humor is sexist. Humor based on sex, ethnic differences, or religion is usually a mistake. Even if listeners are not personally offended, they might be uncomfortable and embarrassed wondering how other people reacted.

Third, use humor sparingly. Your objective as a speaker is seldom merely to entertain. Perhaps two or three instances of humor at most is all an on-the-job presentation could justify. Irrelevant humor distances you and the audience from the talk content. You waste time and distract the audience. Of course, a joke or comical personal experience from which you can springboard into the subject matter is excellent. It attracts attention while relaxing the audience and you. When in doubt about the appropriateness of humor, test your humor on people who are not afraid to provide honest feedback. If you are the boss, your subordinates may hesitate to say you are not funny since they may be too eager to please.

Fourth, keep humor impersonal. (Or else, be sure the target of the humor will take it in the spirit intended.) Generally speaking, do not use humor at the expense of another person, especially an audience member. This is in poor taste. Avoid, too, humor that conveys personal antagonism or lack of feeling toward lower-level employees. You may be perceived as using your authority unfairly or being insensitive to those with less power. Poking fun at other people usually backfires because the audience will probably sympathize with the victim of the joke and become resistant or even hostile to your message.

Humor used with discrimination can be a powerful delivery tool. Take into consideration your personality, the image you wish to project, the occasion, the audience, and your communication objectives.

HANDLING QUESTION-AND-ANSWER SESSIONS

A major advantage of speaking over writing is the possibility of better two-way communication. Because the audience can talk back to the speaker, the relationship between the presenter and the listeners is stronger. Instead of being passive recipients, members of the audience can interact with the speaker by making comments and asking questions. For this reason, business and professional people allocate time for a question-and-answer period during many of their talks. In some cases, such as briefings and press conferences, the question-and-answer session may dominate the speaking opportunity. After a brief introduction, orientation, or statement, the balance of the speaker's time is devoted to fielding questions.

Bill Washington's shaky talk at College Night was capped off with a question-and-answer session. His delivery style was much better in this segment of his speech. One reason was because he relaxed more here. His talk was not really over, but he started to act like it was when he began answering students' and parents' questions. Being more at ease, he forgot he was speaking to 35 people and was more himself. Take heart from Bill's experience and look forward to interacting with your audience during a Q & A session. Your delivery might well be at its best here.

Handling questions skillfully is a valuable professional skill that reflects positively on your openness, credibility, and receptiveness. For these reasons, it should be part of your package of audience-management abilities. Aim to handle your audience's interrogation just as expertly as you did the planned, formal part of your presentation. Think of each response to a listener's query as a presentation in miniature. In this respect, good Q & A handling requires forethought.

Preparation

You are not a mind-reader and cannot prepare answers to questions before they are asked. Question-and-answer sessions clearly exercise your impromptu speaking talents. Still, expert handling of question-and-answer sessions is the result of experience and careful preparation. Do your homework. You can anticipate the kinds of questions that may arise and formulate potential responses. That way, you have the information at your disposal, and you will be more articulate responding.

Begin by studying your listeners. They offer clues on who will ask what: Accountants will be concerned with cost, production managers with production scheduling, sales representatives with customer response. Some speakers actually prepare notes for expected questions. They then have the facts—names, addresses, telephone numbers, technical data, and statistics—at hand.

Rely, too, on the fact that you probably ended up with twice as much material as you could use when working through the ESCAP-E formula to prepare for the formal part of your presentation. View this extra information as your data base from which you can answer questions concretely and specifically. This should increase your confidence level substantially.

Decide when during your presentation to field questions. Unless the group is very small and the atmosphere very informal, the break in at any time approach leads to frequent interruptions and disorganized presentations. For longer, more formal occasions, it is wiser to place a question-and-answer session after major sections of the presentation or at the end. You can thus control time and sequence of topic development better. Tell your audience at the beginning when and how you will respond to questions.

Provide for a transition to the question-and-answer period. Positively ask for questions and show your receptivity to audience involvement. Certainly, "You don't have any questions, do you?" is negative and discouraging. Likewise, "Are there any intelligent questions?" is intimidating to the listeners. A much better transition is: "I know you must all have specific worries on how this new early retirement program is going to affect each of you and I've saved ten minutes to respond to those special concerns. What are your questions?"

You might even prime the pump. If you don't get any response after your request for questions, you might coax your listeners to break the ice: "Determining early retirement benefits from that formula I presented looks quite complicated at first. Would one of you like me to go through those calculations again using your case as an example?" Speakers occasionally enlist the support of an audience member in advance to ask the first question to get the ball rolling.

Techniques

Use a plan for answering questions. This sequence works well:

1. Restate and clarify the question, either in your own words or the questioner's words. Make sure you, the interrogator, and the rest of the audience know what is being asked and answered.

2. Answer the question directly and briefly. Give an adequate response and move to the next question. The length of your response should depend on the significance of the question for the entire audience.

3. Ask if you have adequately answered the question. If you have, call on another questioner. If not, repeat the sequence.[3]

The following detailed suggestions should make you a more confident, knowledgeable respondent to listener questions.

▶ **Do** develop a positive attitude toward questioners and questions. We have all worked with teachers or supervisors who resent questions, who view questions as a negative reflection on their competence, authority, or integrity. They project a "I said it once and I won't say it again" attitude. Instead of being like such people, you should welcome questions as a compliment and an opportunity. They show audience interest, develop audience participation, bring confusion out into the open, and increase listener comprehension.

---

3. George T. Vardaman, *Effective Communication of Ideas* (New York: Van Nostrand Reinhold Company, 1970) 143–44.

Signal your receptiveness and give positive reinforcement to questions. Say something like "That's a good question," or "I'm glad you asked that." Of course, it is possible to overdo this, in which case you sound insincere and waste time.

▶ **Do** make sure the questioner speaks up so you and the rest of the listeners hear the question. Speakers often have a microphone, questioners seldom do. Some questioners are shy or reluctant, and speak in a soft voice. If necessary, politely ask the questioner to repeat the question more loudly. Repeat it yourself for the entire audience before responding. Few things are more annoying to listeners than listening to an answer to a question they could not hear.

▶ **Do** listen to the whole question. Cutting someone off in mid-question is rude. Interrupting the questioner is potentially embarrassing. You may end up answering the wrong question.

▶ **Do** paraphrase questions to make sure that you and the audience understood the question if the question is ambiguous or complicated. This, too, lessens the possibility of incorrect or imprecise responses. Additionally, rephrasing lets you defuse, soften, or broaden a question. The rephrased question is easier to answer, more relevant, and more interesting to the entire audience.

▶ **Do** go back to an appropriate visual aid if it will help you respond better or save time.

▶ **Do** be courteous. Even if the questioner is hostile to you or your ideas, don't take the bait. Be polite and objective in answering. By controlling your temper in these delicate situations, you gain respect and credibility from your audience.

▶ **Do** keep control of the Q & A session. You as the speaker are responsible for effective time management, even during this portion of your presentation. If the questioner starts making a speech or heckling you, interrupt the person tactfully, thank the person for the contribution, and perhaps suggest that you continue the discussion after the program. Avoid the impression that you are debating the questioner. Being drawn into an argument seldom works to your benefit.

▶ **Do** manage your time well. Keep one eye on the clock. Be brief in your responses—don't deliver the entire talk all over again. State a time limit, say, five minutes, or indicate you will take three more questions. Be careful because this approach can present problems. The answer to the last question is the real end to your talk. If the last question is weak, your final words may be trivial, and you lose some of the impact of the formal part of your talk. You might be better off having a shorter Q & A period. You can concentrate on the better, more broadly interesting queries that are usually asked first. In a long drawn-out Q & A session, the caliber of the questions usually deteriorates.

Another technique, if you can pull it off smoothly, is to be deliberately open-ended about the time limit. When you answer a particularly good question well, stop accepting questions. End your presentation and your Q & A session on a high point. Soften the abrupt ending by offering to answer more questions individually later.

Now for the other side of the coin. Consider these things *not* to do in a Q & A session:

▶ **Don't** play expert or bluff. Don't pass on incorrect information, guesses, or unwarranted opinion. If you don't know an answer, say so without apology or excuse. As Mark Twain once remarked, "I was gratified to be able to answer promptly and I did. I said I didn't know." Perhaps you can say you will investigate and follow through with an answer later. Such an approach will increase your believability. Try something like: "Gosh, Peter, that's an angle that goes beyond my research. Let me check my files and get back to you tomorrow." If a response is a guess or an opinion, label it so to prevent your listeners from acting on it as fact.

▶ **Don't** answer one question with another question. This is defensive and evasive. You put the questioner on the spot, and the audience is more interested in *your* answer anyway.

▶ **Don't** refer a question to someone else in the audience or room without prior approval. Maybe there is someone who is better prepared to answer a question than you are, but don't put that innocent person on the spot. You might get around this by asking, "Is there someone here who can answer that question?"

▶ **Don't** take questions from only one part of the audience (the people up front or the quality control department) or one individual (one of your supporters). Give everyone a fair shake at asking questions.

▶ **Don't** address your response exclusively to the questioner. If you do, you ignore the rest of the audience by engaging in private conversation. Respond to the entire group and state your answer in terms of broader audience understanding and significance. After answering, though, you may want to say something like "Does that answer your question?" in order to find out whether you addressed the question completely and clearly.

▶ **Don't** humiliate someone who asks a weak question. If you are maintaining a positive, receptive attitude, you realize that few people with honest motives ask dumb or stupid questions. Assume every question is well-intentioned and legitimate. Respond in good faith, minimizing any potential embarrassment that the question may provoke. Don't say "I guess that was tricky to understand. Let me try again." This remark is well-intentioned, but it might embarrass the questioner. Just try explaining it better the second time. And, as with ill-advised humor, dismissing a questioner for not paying attention or for displaying a lack of intelligence with an insulting or comical remark risks losing audience support.

PUTTING IT ALL TOGETHER

Bill Washington's problems with delivery at College Night were not unusual for an inexperienced speaker. He just wanted to be his own friendly, open, personable self. But he wasn't. You can probably sympathize with Bill. Your ultimate goal as a business or professional speaker is to be yourself. But, at this point, you may be thinking that being yourself is getting to be quite complicated. So much has to be integrated into an effective delivery style without becoming self-conscious and nervous. How can you do this?

In fact, you probably already do it! Most people separate public speaking from conversational speaking. Yet, you communicate successfully many hours each day with family, friends, and colleagues. You evidently have a firm foundation of delivery skills already or you would not have progressed as far as you have in your school or work career. You don't have to start from square one. You have an effective delivery style when conversing with two or three people; this same delivery style, with some fine tuning, will serve you just as well when presenting to eight or eighty people. You can take assurance from this. As you put this chapter's delivery techniques into practice, consider the following four points.

First, remember the goals of business and professional audiences you will be speaking to. They are listening to gain information they need to perform better in their occupational or personal

Reprinted with permission of Tribune Media Services.

You cannot make yourself have a relaxed, natural delivery style. It is the product of patience and experience.

roles. Your listeners do not want you to be a polished actor or a show-off. If that is what the audience wanted, they would probably go to a movie or a play. You need only be yourself.

Second, set your goals. Capitalize on the many strengths you already possess. Determine what changes you need to make in your delivery style to become a better speaker. Use feedback from your self-analysis, instructors, superiors, and audience members to target areas of strength and areas that need improvement.

Third, make your goals realistic. By setting too many goals, you put unnecessary pressure on yourself, which in turn increases your anxiety and decreases your chance of successfully achieving any of your goals. Instead, work on one goal at a time—for example, speaking more slowly. Then, once you have your delivery rate under control, you can shift attention to your next goal. Remember also that you cannot improve 100 percent on a goal from one talk opportunity to the next. If you say "you know" and "and daaaa" two or three times a minute, resolve to cut these instances of verbal filler in half. If you are successful, the next time you can reduce verbal filler even more. Happily, you will find that the other problem areas have improved, too, not by conscious effort, but just through practice.

And last, and maybe most importantly, relax and be patient as you focus on improving your delivery techniques. Delivery skills require time to develop. You can will yourself to design and prepare well before your presentation, for this effort will be substantially unaffected by the normal anxiety of speaking in public. Delivery is different—you cannot will yourself to be your comfortable, relaxed self. Paradoxically, attempting to force yourself to relax is counterproductive. It only increases the speaking anxiety that you have.

So how *can* you get out of this bind? Go back to Chapter 1 and review the suggestions for coping with speaking anxiety. Put these suggestions to work in your speech opportunities. Remember that a relaxed, natural delivery style is more the by-product of experience than of conscious mental effort. The more you present, the more experienced you will be, and therefore, the more natural and relaxed you will become. Your underlying speaking anxieties mask your natural, personable delivery style. As you gain more experience and become more comfortable with public speaking, these fears will slowly subside, revealing your true, expressive personality.

SUMMING UP

As you speak, your task is to present your content in a natural, relaxed, and personable manner. Your delivery style must be modified to fit the communication situation. Generally speaking, a good delivery style is characterized by these attributes: Your voice should exhibit expressiveness and variety in pitch, rate, and volume. To improve the clarity of your voice, actively use your vocal equipment to enunciate distinctly. Gradually replace verbal filler with strategic pauses.

Maintain strong eye contact to establish a conversational, two-way communication channel with your listeners. Use the extended eye contact method and distribute your eye contact over the entire audience. Use body language to enhance your verbal message and enliven your delivery. Groom yourself neatly, dress appropriately, and move confidently to project a believable, authoritative image.

When using a lectern, think of it as home base to hold your notes as you move around interacting with your listeners. Use good speaker posture, stand erect with feet slightly apart and weight evenly distributed on both feet. Make sure your facial expressions and gestures are a spontaneous outgrowth of your talk's content. Your face should show lively interest in your listeners and subject matter, and your gestures should be varied and positive.

The use of humor should be relevant and tasteful when delivering a presentation. Each speaker's approach to humor is dependent on his or her personality, the image the speaker wishes to project, the audience, the occasion, and the subject matter.

Question-and-answer sessions permit the audience to talk back to the speaker. Prepare for the question-and-answer session by studying your audience, by anticipating the types of questions likely to be asked, and by building the questioning opportunity into the presentation at the right point. In handling questions, restate the question, respond briefly and accurately, and ask the questioner whether the question was answered adequately. Welcome questions in a sharing mood, take questions from the entire audience, and be courteous in your responses.

In developing a seemingly effortless delivery style, realize you already have a good basis on which to build, set delivery goals that are realistic, and concentrate on achieving only one or two goals gradually. Most of all, be patient. Your relaxed, expressive self emerges as you practice and as you gain confidence.

Application Exercises

Note: **Please turn to the Appendix for an evaluation form and assessment scale that you and your instructor may wish to use.**

1. Deliver the presentation you began working on in Chapter 3, Application Exercise 1. Before you present, though, run through your talk once or twice more, concentrating on your delivery style. Now relax and deliver your speech to your audience.
2. Using one of the topics below, plan and present a talk. Your talk will be followed by a question-and-answer session. Follow your instructor's guidance on time, use of presentation aids, audience expectations, and speech setting.
   a. Research your career area and present career options and opportunities.
   b. Select a major metropolitan area and explain why it would be a good place to live and work.
   c. Select two competitive products or services and present a persuasive speech advocating one over the other.
3. Prepare and present an extemporaneous talk for videotaping to be followed by playback and *gentle* commentary. Implement these guidelines:
   a. Limit the talk to three minutes.
   b. Speak on a topic directly related to your area of professional or business interest.
   c. Use a prop if you wish.
   d. Prepare talk notes using the format presented in Chapter 3.
      After playing back your videotape, participate in a critical review

of your content, organizational structure, and delivery techniques with your audience and instructor. Use this feedback from your self-evaluation, peer evaluation, and instructor evaluation for setting achievable goals for your next talk.

4. Evaluate a videotape of an extemporaneous presentation you made. After studying the videotape of your talk several times, write a critical self-evaluation report for your instructor. Cover the following points concretely and specifically, substantiating your judgments of your strengths and weaknesses.
    a. Summarize your topic briefly.
    b. Analyze the audience. Describe and categorize your listeners. How well did you adapt your approach and content to their needs?
    c. Evaluate your presentation design (opener, organizational pattern of body, close, development, flow, transition of main ideas, clarity, time management).
    d. Evaluate your delivery technique (voice characteristics, poise, use of notes, eye contact, body language, and rapport with audience).
    e. Judge the effectiveness and usefulness of any humor used.
    f. If you had a question-answering session with your audience, criticize your question-and-answer technique.
    g. State an overall conclusion about your present level of speaking skill. Set several specific goals for your next talk—at least one presentation design goal and one delivery goal.

5. Observe a presentation by an experienced speaker and prepare a written evaluation. Select a business or professional person with whom you can identify—a person in the same career field or knowledge area you hope to be involved with in five years. The setting might be private (a presentation in a work environment or in front of a professional organization) or public (a lecture at the local library or part of a speaker series at a college or university). For leads on suitable speakers, check with family, friends, and employers. Check bulletin boards and newspaper listings. Make sure the talk will be at least 15 minutes long so you will have an adequate observation period. Cover this content specifically:
    a. Describe the nature of the event.
    b. Describe the physical surroundings (size of the room, seating arrangements, sound system, distracting noises, and so on).
    c. Analyze the audience (arrive early enough so you have time to mingle and obtain this information).
    d. Describe the speaker (identity, appearance, age, qualifications, demeanor).
    e. Summarize the presentation content briefly.
    f. Evaluate presentation design (opener, organizational pattern of body, close, development, flow, transition of main ideas, clarity, time management).

g. Evaluate delivery technique (voice characteristics, poise, use of notes, eye contact, body language, and rapport with the audience).
h. If the speaker fielded questions, critique the speaker's question-and-answer technique.
i. Comment on your speaker's use of humor, if any. Was humor planned or unplanned (in your opinion)? Was it appropriate?
j. State your overall impression. Was the speaker generally effective or ineffective in communicating the intended message? Why? Would you recommend the speaker to others? Why?
6. Share selected content from the report prepared for number 5 in an extemporaneous or impromptu presentation as directed.
7. This enthusiasm profile will help you develop a more dynamic speaking presence:

Pre-test

Have a friend rate you as you practice or present a talk. Using the rating form that follows, have your helper evaluate you on each of the six delivery variables that are described on the accompanying chart. Assign one point for behavior best characterized by the description in the low column, two points for the medium column, and three points for the high column. Total the points and discuss the evaluation with your helper for additional feedback and clarification.

Rating Form

Variable	Low = 1, Medium = 2, High = 3		
	Pre-test	Practice Tries	Post-test
1. Voice			
2. Eyes			
3. Gestures			
4. Body movement			
5. Facial expression			
6. Overall energy level			

Rating Scale

Variable	Low	Medium	High
1. Voice	Monotone voice, minimum vocal inflection, little variation in speech, droning quality, poor enunciation	Pleasant variations of pitch, volume, and speed; good enunciation	Varied, lilting, uplifting intonation. Many changes in pitch, volume, and speed. Precise enunciation.
2. Eyes	Looked dull or bored. Seldom opened eyes wide or raised eyebrows.	Appeared interested. Some changes in the eyes, lighting up, shining, opening wide.	Characterized as shining, lighting up frequently, opening wide, eyebrows raised occasionally.
3. Facial expression	Appeared impassive, did not denote feeling, or frowned frequently. Little smiling. Lips closed.	Agreeable, smiled frequently and longer. Looked pleased, happy, sad when obviously called for.	Appeared vibrant, demonstrative; showed surprise, sadness, joy, thoughtfulness, excitement as appropriate. Total smile—mouth opened wide. Quick and easy changes in expression.

Rating Scale (continued)

Variable	Low	Medium	High
4. Gestures	Seldom moved arms out toward person or object. No broad movement, kept arms at side or folded across body, appeared rigid.	Often pointed with hand, using total arm. Occasionally used sweeping motion using body, head, arms, and hands. Steady pace of gesturing.	Fluid and demonstrative movements of body, head, arms, and hands.
5. Body movements	Seldom moved from one spot.	Moved freely, slowly, and steadily.	Used broad body movements, frequent changes of pace, enthusiastic, energetic quality.
6. Overall energy level	Lethargic; appeared inactive, dull, or sluggish	Some variations in appearing energetic, demonstrative, but mostly an even level maintained.	Exuberant. Maintained high degree of energy and vitality. Highly demonstrative.

Practice

Repeat the evaluation several times during the next two or three months. Through practice and conscious effort, aim to achieve at least the medium level on each variable. Your ultimate goal should be to reach the high performance level in as many areas as possible.

Watch good speakers—professionals like television news personalities or popular lecturers—for examples of animated, enthusiastic delivery skills. They are excellent models from which to learn.

Post-Test

Have your friend repeat the evaluation procedure a last time. How much have you improved? Continue to work on your weakest areas to become a relaxed, animated, and expressive speaker, one to whom your associates, clients, and customers will want to listen.

Source: Exercise adapted from "Developing Delivery Skills in Oral Business Communications" Kenneth R. Mayer, *The ABCA Bulletin* Sept. 1980; 21–24.

Chapter 5

PRESENTATION AIDS

Business and professional people have discovered the value of putting on a good show. Speakers in the United States invested over $14 billion in visual presentations in 1985, producing more than 600 million original slides and at least that many overhead projector transparencies.[1]

Presentation aids are more than just *visual* aids. Many aids use the other senses. Some encourage audience involvement even more directly. For example, you could have audience members smell a new perfume or taste a new, improved chocolate chip cookie your company is about to market. Some presentations include demonstrations using props and equipment that not only *tell* but *show*.

The term **presentation aids** is used in the broad sense in this chapter to include visual aids, audio aids, and demonstrations and audience participation that require sensory involvement and movement.

Remember Paul, the computer buff who gave a presentation to his computer users group? Paul could easily have used presentation aids to provide visual support to reinforce his verbal content. He might have displayed samples of floppy disks or showed a mounted, enlarged photograph of a memory board. He might have listed his three major points on a poster to fix in the listeners' minds, not only a "road map" of the presentation, but also new vocabulary, like RAM, ROM, K, and kilobyte.

Paul might even have used computer graphics. Instead of low-tech posters, he could have used a personal computer and monitor or large-screen projection to display his plan of presentation. Paul might have cleverly demonstrated the difference between the functions of RAM and ROM. For example, he could have filled a glass bowl with yellow jellybeans to indicate ROM memory and then poured in red jellybeans to represent RAM, the rest of a computer's memory space. By dumping out the red jellybeans from the bowl, he would have visualized the abstract idea of "dumping" RAM to disk; thereby creating a vivid, easily remembered picture of losing RAM memory when a computer's power is turned off.

Chapter 5 concentrates on the selection, design, and use of the growing variety of presentation aids that professional and business people use. To help you harness the communication power of presentation aids, we will examine:

---

1. Christopher O'Malley, "Graphics," *Personal Computing,* Oct. 1986: 105.

- benefits of presentation aids,
- selection criteria and design factors,
- media options,
- computer-generated presentation graphics,
- techniques for use.

Speech communicators who have logged hours and hours of presentation time in front of small and large audiences have discovered the contribution that presentation aids make to an effective talk. You will too, because they offer many advantages that you will quickly come to appreciate.

BENEFITS OF PRESENTATION AIDS

Presentation aids are the counterpart to graphic aids in business writing. Just as a skilled writer will add charts, tables, pictures, and so forth, to a report to supplement the written words, so the skilled presenter uses presentation aids to supplement the spoken word. We will examine the major incentives for using presentation aids next.

Meet Audience Expectations

We live in a visually and aurally exciting world. Interest-grabbing colors, textures, shapes, and sounds surround us in nature, at home, and even at work and school. We have come to expect the movies we attend to be shown in true-to-life color on wide screens with flawless four-channel soundtracks. In our homes, we take for granted wide-screen, color, stereo television. We demand concert-hall realism in the music we recreate using state-of-the-art stereo systems.

Remember that people with such sophisticated expectations make up your audience, whether you speak on or off the job. Although the need for presentation aids depends on the precise speaking situation, your audience often expects you to do more than just talk. They frequently expect you to use audio, visual, and other forms of presentation technology to open up the conference room or auditorium. Making your presentation more exciting in this way is a challenge, of course, but a real opportunity to put today's technology to work in your job-related oral communication.

Maximize Audience Retention

More sensory involvement generally means more interest and retention on the audience's part. Hearing is not a human being's most effective way to receive information; seeing is. Of information that is remembered, 85 percent is perceived through seeing, 11 percent from hearing, and the other 4 percent from touching, smelling, and tasting. Communication researchers have also found that only 10 percent of an average lecture is remembered. The percentage jumps to 50 percent if visual aids are used and 70 percent with both visual aids and audience participation.[2]

You can increase the success quotient of a presentation by appealing to several senses. Hearing words has its limits. Search for ways to develop content through other senses. To present an idea visually, use a picture, graph, or diagram. To demonstrate the sensory appeal of one product over another, conduct a product comparison test where audience members taste, smell, or touch. To prove product quality or operating ease, demonstrate product use. Better yet, let audience members take part in the demonstration. Doing is even better than seeing. Good speakers appeal to as many senses as appropriate to maximize audience involvement and, consequently, retention. This old Chinese saying illustrates the idea well:

> I hear and I forget,
> I see and I remember,
> I do and I understand.

Increase Comprehension

Complex, technical, and statistical data is difficult to present without presentation aids. With complex content, the speaker tries to paint a word picture in each listener's brain. You might describe spatial relationships, changes and trends over time, or construction and operation. Instead, why not present the data visually in the first place? This would lessen the possibility of encoding and decoding errors and reduce the listening strain on audience members.

Suppose Lydia Gerski is presenting data on changes in Omicron Corporation's financial condition over the past five years. She

---

2. Robert L. Montgomery, *A Master Guide to Public Speaking* (New York: Harper & Row, 1979). 36.

will compare revenues, net income, and return on assets for each of the company's seven divisions and for the company as a whole. Without presentation aids, Lydia must use mind-numbing, number-laden sentences to present over a dozen figures in the million-dollar range or percentages expressed to one decimal place. From these statistics she expects her audience to absorb the main point—that is, while Omicron's revenues have been increasing, its net income has been falling, and its return on assets has been flat. It is highly doubtful that anyone in the audience, except for a few accountants and financial types who are already familiar with the numbers, will grasp this information because it will be floating in a sea of indigestible statistics.

Using visuals, maybe posterboard charts or overhead transparencies, Lydia could communicate her main points more easily to the audience and, more importantly, they would understand and recall more financial data with more accuracy. She would thus be wise to develop several line and bar graphs showing trends over the five-year period. Both seeing and hearing the data would reduce the concentration and mental processing that each member of the audience must do. The verbal clutter of her presentation would be cut, too.

Increase Persuasiveness and General Effectiveness

Besides increasing audience comprehension and recall, presentation aids help the speaker in other ways. The persuasive power of using visual support in presentations has been proven in two research studies. The Wharton School of Business of the University of Pennsylvania examined the impact of overhead transparencies on business meetings that involved marketing an imaginary product. Delivering the same content, one group of presenters used only verbal communication and handouts, and another group used overhead transparencies as well.

The Wharton study's findings were revealing. Presenters who used graphics persuaded their group successfully 67 percent of the time versus a 50 percent success rate for the nongraphics group. In addition, audience members perceived the presenter using visuals to be better prepared and more professional, credible, and interesting.[3]

---

3. Wharton Applied Research Center, The Wharton School, "A Study of the Effects of the Use of Overhead Transparencies on Business Meetings, Final Report," University of Pennsylvania, Sept. 14, 1981. (Sponsored by 3M Corporation, St. Paul, Minnesota.)

In the second study, presentations with visual support were 43 percent more persuasive than presentations without visual aids in getting test subjects to commit time and money to a seminar. According to the study done by the University of Minnesota measuring the effects of both transparencies and slides, presenters using visuals were judged to be clearer and better able to support their positions. Another finding was very encouraging for beginning speakers: A "typical" presenter using transparencies or slides could be just as effective as a better-than-typical presenter using no visuals.[4]

Both studies document what experienced speakers in business and the professions have always known: Presentation aids increase your persuasive powers, make you appear more believable, and enhance the listeners' perceptions of your preparation and professionalism

Save Time

The old cliché, "A picture is worth a thousand words," may be worn-out, but it's true. Charts, graphs, pictures, and other presentation aids enable you to be more concise. You can deliver more substance in less time without sacrificing audience comprehension. Both the Wharton and Minnesota studies verified that meetings were generally shorter when visuals were used—28 percent shorter, in fact, according to the Wharton researchers.

Think how many workdays a year you could save and how much more productive you could be at that rate. For instance, you might use 1000 words and 7 minutes of presentation time to explain the changes in the company's management structure. With organizational charts showing the structure before and after the change, you could present this information in 3 or 4 minutes. The 500 words used this way will be better understood and remembered longer and with more accuracy.

Improve Speaker Delivery

Presentation aids will benefit speaker delivery technique in several ways. Eye contact improves. The speaker relies on presentation aids for visual cues and verbal support and less on notes.

---

4. Douglas R. Vogel, Gary W. Dickson, and John A. Lehman, "Persuasion and the Role of Visual Presentation Support: The UM/3M Study," 3M Corporation, St. Paul, Minnesota, undated.

With some types of aids, like charts and posters, the presenter can place brief, lightly penciled notes on the aid itself. Being a foot or two away from the aid, the speaker can see these notes, but the audience cannot.

Aids improve talk continuity. Speakers often put a plan of presentation on a poster, projection screen, or handout that the audience can refer to during the presentation. This strategy makes the presenter's organizational plan apparent, and the listener stays oriented at all times. The listener sees the pieces fitting together one by one to create the whole.

Body language improves when using presentation aids, also. When you move away from the lectern to use some aids, you might use hand gestures to focus attention on the aids or to demonstrate. And, usually this greater amount of body movement relaxes you, helping you be your own natural, personable self—and you are, after all, really the best presentation aid there is.

If you are like most business and professional people, once you begin using presentation aids and reaping the benefits, you will employ them in more of your presentation opportunities.

CRITERIA FOR DEVELOPMENT AND DESIGN

Presentation aids can make the difference in whether or not you present your content clearly, vividly, concisely, persuasively, and memorably. However, the results of aids are not guaranteed. The four criteria that follow will help you develop presentation aids that make the greatest contribution to your talks.

First Criterion: Relevancy

Keep in mind that presentation aids are a carrier device for presenting your content better; your ideas remain the starting point and focus. As we've just seen, your presentation aids must accomplish one or more specific purposes with your audience. They must also justify their existence and be smoothly integrated into a talk. *You* must remain the master of your aids, and not the other way around.

It is easy for beginning speakers to break the relevancy rule. They often use presentation aids for the wrong reasons: to show they are prepared, to make their presentation appear more professional, or to be like everyone else. Presenters also let the technology and presentation options tempt them to use too many presentation aids.

Calvin and Hobbes   by Bill Watterson

Calvin and Hobbes © 1987 Universal Press Syndicate. Reprinted with permission. All rights reserved.

Flashy presentation aids should not be substituted for substance.

Aids take time and effort to create and to practice with, time that might be better invested in other aspects of talk preparation. Furthermore, using too many aids dilutes their impact. If a speaker drags out every conceivable gimmick, most of the time the audience will label such a performance a "dog and pony show." The audience can be assaulted with too many sensory-involvement devices, just as they can be bombarded with too much verbal support.

Recognize the situational need for presentation aids. Many informational speaking opportunities, such as a staff meeting, do not require presentation aids. Basic, straight-forward content does not need them either. You must ask yourself: Why am I using this aid? How does it help me accomplish my statement of purpose? In other words, if your presentation aid is relevant, use it; if it isn't, omit it.

Second Criterion: Simplicity

If someone says your presentation aids are simple, take it as a compliment, not a disparaging remark. Appealing to too many senses may overload the audience's processing capabilities. You are already using your audience's sense of hearing when you speak. By adding presentation aids, you compel audience members to use other sensory input at the same time. Although this can be advantageous, you have to be careful not to overdo it.

As a reader, you have control over how fast you read—you can slow down, speed up, or reread a passage. As a listener, however, you have a limited amount of time to absorb the content of a talk. Falling behind in a group setting, you can't always say,

"Whoa, slow down!" or "Wait, can you run that by me again?" You're clearly at the mercy of the presenter, who must consciously adjust the rate of information flow to the audience.

When designing presentation aids, remember the simpler the better. If you have several points to make, use a series of aids. You can only develop one point at a time, and the audience members can only comprehend one point at a time, so why put multiple distractions before the audience? If a chart has eight rows and six columns of data and demands much time-consuming explanation and discussion, you are probably trying to do too much with one visual. You should instead use a couple of charts that build up sequentially.

This simpler-is-better rationale also means that what works on the printed page of a written report will probably not be as digestible in an oral report. The differences between reading and listening/seeing require that a table or chart in a written report be adapted for a poster or for projection. Simplify charts and graphs using your audience analysis as a guide. You can use more intricate multiple-line graphs, for example, when speaking to senior managers with college degrees. A series of less sophisticated single-line graphs is better for a lay audience without college degrees and professional experience.

Third Criterion: Visibility

This is almost too obvious, but lack of visibility is the most common flaw of presentation aids. How many times have you heard a speaker say, "I know you can't see this but. . . ." The content of a visual aid must be large and legible enough to be seen by everyone in the audience, even those viewers in the back and side rows. Aren't those people just as important as those in the first ten rows? A visual aid that cannot be comfortably and clearly seen immediately becomes a visual distraction. The viewer soon loses interest and feels left out. Worse, the audience member may be confused because he does not have all the information necessary for complete understanding. Because of size limitations, some presentation aids are suitable only for smaller audiences, as we shall see later.

To avoid this problem, look at your visual aids yourself from the location of the most distant audience member to make sure they are readable. Can you see them well? If you can't, your audience members won't be able to either.

Fourth Criterion: Appropriate Production Quality

Good presentation aids are well produced physically. Those that are sloppy and have misspellings and smudges because they were hurriedly made are a negative reflection on the seriousness and credibility of the presenter. To a viewer, a messy chart might appear to be the product of a sloppy, careless thinker.

Speakers in large organizations have access to equipment and talent in the graphics or art departments and perhaps outside professionals. These experts can provide the guidance and preparation skills for producing high-quality presentation aids. Small organizations will have experts you can call on also, like secretaries or more experienced speakers.

Regardless of the size of business or professional organization in which you work, you will find that responsibility and control over presentation aids is gradually shifting to the individual presenter because it saves production time and money. This transfer of responsibility means you will be expected to have more production know-how. Being able to do it yourself as both speaker and designer gives you the flexibility to tailor presentation aids for a specific audience and topic, as well. You can also make last-minute changes and corrections cheaply and quickly.

Staying within the scope of the time, talent, and equipment that is available, your presentation aids should show several production qualities.

Neat, Readable Printing and Art Work Use press type (prepared stick-on letters) or a lettering machine, if possible. If you must handwrite, use a wide-tip marker to make well-formed, well-proportioned, easy-to-see letters. If you use stencils, fill in the gaps of the letter framework to improve visibility and readability. Use a ruler to provide even, well-spaced lines of print.

Follow these additional guidelines for the sake of simplicity, clarity, and visibility in using printing and art work on presentation aids[5]:

- ▶ Don't use more than four or five words on each line.
- ▶ Don't use more than three vertical columns.
- ▶ Do condense information.

---

5. Adapted from Lee Pitre and Larry Smeltzer, "Graphic Reinforcement for an Oral Presentation," *The ABCA Bulletin,* Dec. 1982: 7.

FIGURE 5-1
Recommendations for Printing Size

Viewing Distance	Height of lettering used on screen or display board
8 feet	¼ inch
16 feet	½ inch
32 feet	1 inch
64 feet	2 inch
128 feet	4 inch

Source: Lee Pitre and Larry Smeltzer, "Graphic Reinforcement for an Oral Presentation," *The ABCA Bulletin*, Dec. 1982: 6.

- ▶ Do eliminate unnecessary words or figures.
- ▶ Do use large symbols, art, and abbreviations.
- ▶ Do make sure all printing and art work is large enough to be seen by everyone in the meeting place. (Check Figure 5–1 for recommended minimum print sizes.)

Appropriate Use of Color Color can be used to attract attention to specific detail, to represent a concept, and to make the visual more interesting. But color is a powerful and easily misused tool. First of all, color must support your meaning. Red is considered a *stop* or danger signal and green a *go* cue. Therefore, you should show the correct way in green and the wrong way in red. Stay away from a lot of green and red unless you want a Christmas theme. Traditionally profits are shown in black and losses in red. Common sense tells us that pink and lavendar work well with women's cosmetics but not with bulldozers. Consider the following messages that colors convey.

- ▶ Red is warm or stimulating.
- ▶ Blue is cool, calming, or depressing.
- ▶ Yellow carries warm, sunny overtones.
- ▶ Green is pleasant and healthy.
- ▶ Orange stimulates.
- ▶ Purple suggests dignity and reserve.

Secondly, use color conservatively. Color loses impact when too many hues appear at once. Clarity suffers. Too many colors

FIGURE 5–2
Visibility of Color Combinations

Poor	Better
Blue on orange	Black on yellow
Yellow on black	Black on orange
Red on yellow	Orange on navy blue
Yellow on navy blue	Green on white
Purple on yellow	Red on white

Source: Lee Pitre and Larry Smeltzer, "Graphic Reinforcement for an Oral Presentation," *The ABCA Bulletin,* Dec. 1982: 8.

distract from the message and lead to the gum ball machine effect. Three or four basic colors will make your point without distracting from your information.

Thirdly, select colors and color combinations that are bold and bright enough to make an impact. Some greens and yellows are difficult to see from far away, for example. Figure 5–2 contrasts some of the best color combinations with some of the poorest. Choose colors for the printing and art work that will have maximum visibility on your background color. Room lighting and audience size make a difference, too. Light colors are fine in darkened rooms, but use bolder colors in more brightly lighted settings. Small audiences are more tuned in to slight variations in color because of the more intimate atmosphere; larger groups require sharper contrasts in color.

Don't add color and graphics to increase the visual interest of words and numbers at the expense of clarity. Use color, art work— such as drawings, cartoons, logos, and symbols—and variations in printing styles to make the visual aid truly visual, but not cluttered. Spice up a well-organized table of statistics by putting the title in red italics, using black printing for the data, and adding the company's trademark in an upper corner in color to relieve the plainness of rows and columns of words and numbers.[6]

Ample White Space   Visuals should have a border of white space all around the perimeter of the poster or projected image.

---

6. Adapted from "Graphic Reinforcement for an Oral Presentation," Lee Pitre and Larry Smeltzer, *The ABCA Bulletin,* Dec. 1982: 7.

Within the aid itself, plenty of blank space should set off titles, headings, or parts of the visual. Without white space, visuals look crowded, less appealing, and are more difficult to read.

Titles and Labels   Visual aids need printed explanations like titles, labels for columns and rows, legends and keys to colors and other symbols, sometimes footnotes and source lines. Viewers who forget your oral explanations can refresh their memories with your clear labeling.

Correct Spelling   When speaking, you are spared from the distracting, embarrassing, and credibility-destroying effects of misspelled words, except when using visual aids. "Reciepts—1985 though 1989" as the title of a bar graph cancels much of the effort and careful thinking that may have otherwise gone into your presentation.

No Smudges or Obvious Corrections   Such flaws call attention to your shortcuts, time pressures, or low standards.

Refer to Figures 5–3, 5–4, and 5–5 to see how many of these principles apply to constructing professional-looking, easy-to-understand, attractive visuals.

PRESENTATION AID MEDIA

So far, we have examined advantages of using presentation aids and standards to apply in developing them. Now, we need to select the presentation aid medium that will ideally serve our communication purposes and suit the audience, occasion, and speaking environment. Speakers can choose from three categories of presentation aids: direct, projected, and audio.

Audio aids alone have limited application value for business and professional people. Sound sources such as audiotape recorders, record players, and compact disc players, are in this category. Cassette tape recorders that are readily available have the most potential. They are easy to use, and ideal for capturing interviews, sound effects, or music. The sound can be played back through the tape deck's own speaker for a small group or through the meeting room's sound system for a large group of listeners.

FIGURE 5–3

HELP EMPLOYEES SET GOALS

✓ Negotiate job agreement

✓ Select goal-setting areas

✓ Agree how to measure performance

✓ Set the actual goal

This word chart has a simple, neat appearance. Note the perimeter of white space and the check marks to focus attention on each of the four briefly worded points.

PRESENTATION AID MEDIA **123**

FIGURE 5–4

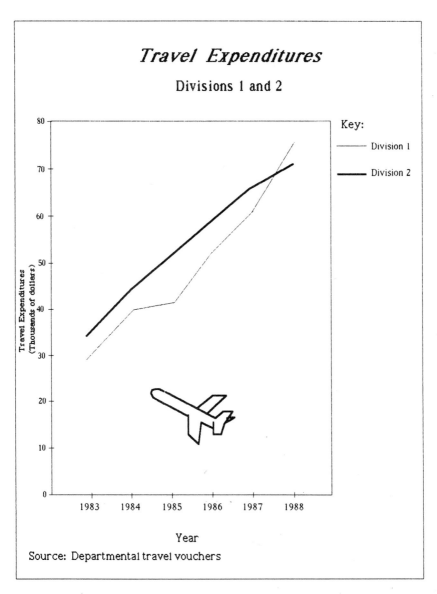

An airplane drawing in this multiple-line graph serves as visual relief. The explanations in the title, subtitle, labels and scales for both axes, key, and source line make the chart easy to understand.

FIGURE 5-5

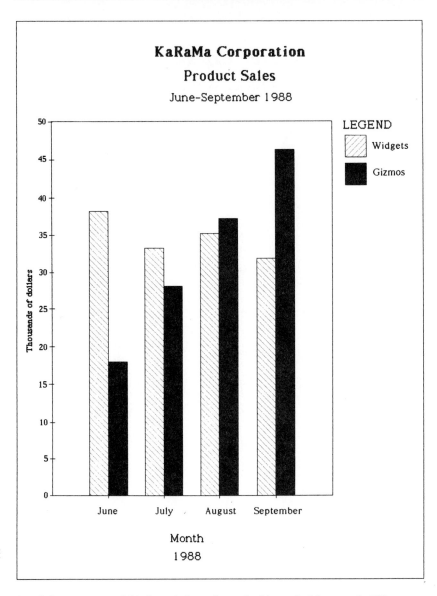

Carefully using several kinds and sizes of type in this vertical bar graph differentiates information and adds visual interest yet does not distract.

Direct Aids

Direct aids that are used directly with the audience and do not require projection equipment are covered in the following discussion.

Three-Dimensional Objects For greater realism, professional and business people can use props in their presentations. For example, a marketing executive might describe the newly designed, easy-to-close cereal box that just completed consumer acceptance tests by showing off the container itself. Samples can be used as pass-arounds for each audience member to touch, smell, or otherwise examine if the object is small enough and if audience attention will not be lost.

Often, the actual object cannot be used. It may be too small for the presenter to handle or the entire audience to see. It may be too big and unwieldy to bring into the meeting room. It may be too costly or fragile. In such situations, models or replicas can be used.

For example, in presenting the mechanics of telecommunication satellite networks, a communications consultant could not use an actual sample of a $10 million, one-ton satellite, but this speaker could use a more manageable 1-to-12 scale model of the satellite. Conversely, in discussing the advantages of a redesigned hearing aid a sales representative may use a model of the device that has been enlarged 20 times. Working with such full-scale or reduced models of devices is a technique frequently used to demonstrate equipment operation. Cut-away sections may permit viewers to see internal workings that are normally hidden. Such might be the case with a videocassette recorder specially built so the speaker can describe its internal construction and operation.

Mounted Visuals Charts, graphs, tables, illustrations, pictures, diagrams, and maps drawn or mounted on posterboard are in this category. These can be displayed on an easel or thumbtacked or taped to a surface. Smaller-size versions of these aids (8½ by 11 inches or so) are called desk charts. These visuals are used for very small presentations of three or four people who are seated just across the desk from the speaker. The presenter holds them up or flips through them as needed.

Tables and charts need not be restricted to numerical data. Especially useful are word charts, rows and columns of text information that might, for example, list the major points of your presentation in your introduction or review the major benefits in your summary.

Mounted visuals are relatively easy to make and simple to use. They are suitable for smaller groups and can be saved for later use. However, their size often makes them bulky to store and awkward to transport. They cannot be added to or revised impromptu like chalkboard visuals.

Handouts A talk outline, a copy of a table or graph, or supporting material that everyone should have during the presentation for reference are examples of materials handed out to the audience.

Use handouts judiciously. Passing items around during a presentation inevitably complicates the speaker's job and distracts the audience. Furthermore, listeners have a tendency to divert their interest to the handouts instead of paying attention to the speaker. If the handout will be needed throughout the entire presentation, a talk outline, for example, perhaps the speaker can distribute it before the presentation. Each listener can refer to the handout throughout the presentation as the presenter directs. If a handout will be needed only in the midst of a presentation, like a detailed chart, distribute it then (the task may be delegated to an assistant). If a handout is needed for later review, follow-up, or filing by the listeners, distribute it at the end of the presentation.

Chalkboards and Markerboards A very familiar form of direct aid is the green, black, or white chalkboard. Business meeting rooms usually are equipped with permanently mounted or portable chalkboards. Markerboards—sometimes called writeboards—are newer. The user writes or draws on their white surface using black or colored ink markers that can be easily wiped off.

Losing eye contact is a problem with this medium. Speakers have to turn their backs on the audience as they write. They can end up talking to the writing surface instead of their listeners. This problem can be eliminated by preparing the visuals first and concealing them until needed, maybe with a pull-down projection screen that is often mounted above the board.

Chalkboard and markerboard visuals cannot be kept for later use, which is another disadvantage. An electronic copyboard eliminates this problem. This expensive, free-standing or wall-mounted writing surface can be written on or drawn on like a regular chalkboard or markerboard. By pressing a button, the user can produce a copy of whatever appears on its surface. Some copyboards can even transmit images over telecommunication lines to another copyboard at another meeting location.

Flip Charts Some speakers, by preference or lack of another large writing surface, write or draw using a broad-tipped marker on an oversized tablet of paper called a flip chart, supported by an easel stand. As the large pages are filled, the speaker flips to the next page and continues. If necessary, the speaker can flip back to earlier pages. In contrast to a chalkboard or markerboard, this approach has the advantage of keeping only the most current and relevant material on view. The material can also be prepared in advance, and the speaker can leaf through the visuals one page at a time as needed.

Chalkboards, markerboards, and flip charts should be used sparingly. They are good media when you want to be spontaneous and involve audience participation directly into your visuals; when the talk is informal and you want to create a climate of openness, avoiding the appearance of delivering a too well-planned and anticipated presentation; and when you want to be economical.

However, these media are best thought of as a last resort when preparing a professional-caliber presentation. The speaker inevitably looks less prepared and less professional than if using already prepared visuals. Furthermore, flip charts, chalkboards, and markerboards do *not* save time. Much preparation and practice time is needed to use them well. Because drawing or writing neatly takes considerable time, the speaker must be able to speak and draw or write at the same time—a difficult task without practice. In the end, chalkboards, markerboards, and flipcharts may not be any more time-efficient than posters, charts, and some types of presentation aids that require projection.

Projected Aids

Projected aids require a projector and viewing screen. Therefore, they require more forethought and preparation than direct aids. The user must decide if the benefits of using projected aids outweigh the hassle and risk involved.

Overhead Projector Overhead projectors have become probably the most commonly used projection device (and perhaps the most frequently used presentation aid of any type) because of availability and ease of operation. They project an image onto a screen from a piece of acetate film called a transparency. Most overhead projectors have only two main controls—an on-off switch for the projector's bulb and a knob for focusing the image on the screen—so anyone can operate one.

The overhead projector operates in normal room lighting so transparencies do not require any room darkening as most projected aids do. You can face the audience while using the overhead. What you see on the transparency is what the viewers see on the screen. You can maintain excellent eye contact, the audience can take notes if necessary, and can observe your body language.

You can use commercially prepared transparencies or make them from a copy of a word chart, graph, diagram or other material to be projected. The transparency is placed on top of the copy and run through a thermal copier. Special markers may be used to prepare a visual on a blank transparency beforehand, or you can write or draw on the transparency directly on the overhead.

The ease of making transparencies tempts some people to overuse them. Using them incorrectly, for example, making transparencies from typewritten or printed documents, is even worse. Such source copy is almost never suitable for large-group viewing unless simplified or enlarged substantially.

Transparencies that will be used, stored, or transported repeatedly should be mounted. Frames block light around the edge of visuals, increasing their professional appearance, adding rigidity for handling and storage, and providing a convenient border on which to place notes visible only to the presenter. Like transparencies, frames are available in bookstores, stationery stores, and office supply outlets.

As with a chalkboard or markerboard, the presenter can develop a visual bit by bit. Overlays with differently colored text and art work let the presenter build up a concept sequentially. Overlays are hinged to the frame on one side with tape to allow the base transparency to be presented first. Then one or two overlays can be flipped over adding more content to the visual. For example, the base transparency could show a single-line graph plotting 1986–1988 production data for the Richmond plant in red. After discussion, the speaker could flip down the first overlay, adding a green line revealing the Houston plant's figures, and finally the second overlay with the Sacramento plant's trend line in blue.

To highlight a particular part of the visual, you have two choices, depending on the projection screen's placement. You can point on the transparency itself, focusing attention on the specific part of the visual with your silhouetted hand, pencil, or pointer. Alternatively, you may use a pointer or your hand on the projected image. Masking is a another simple but effective technique to focus attention on specific parts of a transparency as you discuss it. Place a blank sheet of paper on top of the transparency. Slide this mask down, gradually revealing your message point by point.

Although the overhead projector is easy to use, speakers often have problems because of misplacement of the projection screen. With proper placement of the screen, the speaker avoids blocking the audience's view when changing transparencies or writing on them. Figure 5–6 shows the ideal screen position—to the side, not directly behind the user. The overhead's projected image on the screen should be a square or rectangle, not the more common keystone shape where the top of the image is wider than the bottom. Keystoning causes distortion and focusing problems. To eliminate keystoning, tilt the top of the screen forward toward the projector head, as Figure 5–7 illustrates.

Opaque Projector. An opaque projector projects a visual without any special preparation. The original, a letter, contract, map, or picture, for instance, is placed on a conveyor belt or drawer and inserted into the machine that then projects it onto the screen. The opaque projector is not widely available and is used infrequently for several reasons. The projector is large, cumbersome, and noisy. For a readable image, the meeting area must be as dark as possible.

Slide, Filmstrip, and Film Projectors These projectors project slides, filmstrips, and films onto a screen. Unless commercially prepared materials are purchased or rented, their production requires photography and technical skills that the typical business or professional person may not have or wish to pay for. The projected image, however, is larger and clearer than the image an overhead or opaque projector can deliver.

One drawback is that for a bright, detailed image the room must be darkened. In cases where the speaker is talking while

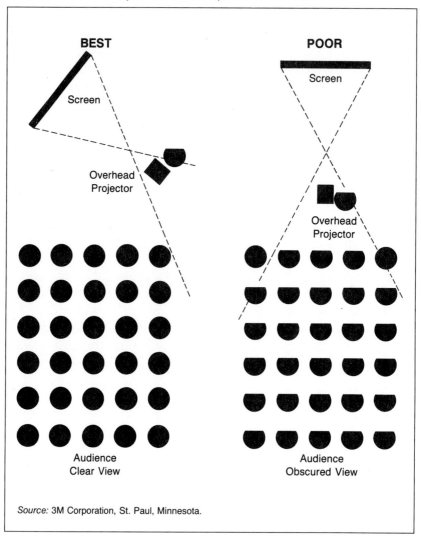

FIGURE 5–6

Proper Overhead Screen Placement

Source: 3M Corporation, St. Paul, Minnesota.

using these projected aids, narrating a slide show, for example, body language is lost. Also, the audience cannot take notes. Additionally, because these media require more technical skill, preparation time, and expense, they are usually saved for larger, more important, or more formal presentations.

Video Commercially marketed or speaker-prepared videotapes played back through a videocassette recorder can be shown

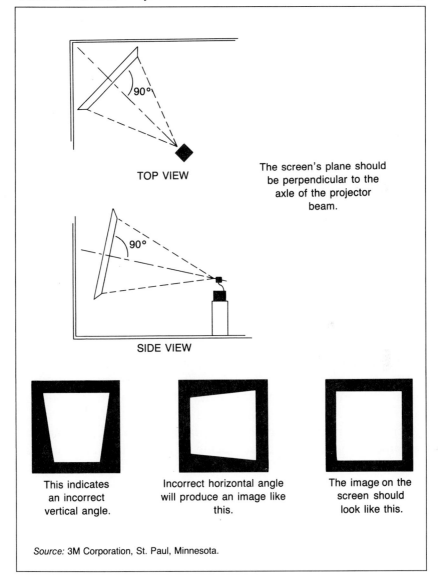

FIGURE 5-7

Correct Overhead Projector Screen Placement To Prevent Keystoning

Source: 3M Corporation, St. Paul, Minnesota.

to a small audience on a regular television monitor. For a larger group of viewers, the speak must use a large projection screen. Miniaturization, increased ease of operation, and falling costs of cameras, videocassette recorders, and large-screen monitors and projectors have greatly increased television's potential for presentation purposes.

Increasingly, business and professional people are using personal computers to create direct aids, transparencies, slides, demonstrations from computer keyboards, and video presentations.

PRESENTATION GRAPHICS

Every picture tells a story, but some pictures tell it better than others. A major factor in bringing the best response from your audience is the professional polish of sharp, lively, high-quality presentation aids. Within the last five years, personal computers using presentation graphics software (computer instructions or programs) and output hardware (computer attachments that produce the presentation aid) have made it possible for anyone to create first-class visual aids that approach the standards of commercial artists, without the high costs and the time delays.

Using presentation graphics, you, as the speaker and designer, exercise greater control over form and content. With the right software and accessory hardware, you can develop excellent visuals even if you have little artistic talent. For example, to create a graph, you select a chart type—say, a vertical bar graph printed in blue—plug in the required numbers, titles, and labels, and the software does the drawing on a printer or plotter.

Computers will have a hand in creating 25 percent or more of the presentations given in 1990.[7] Personal computers and presentation graphics software will evidently have a tremendous impact on how visual presentations are created.

The following overview of some of the techniques and equipment possibilities for producing all four of the major presentation graphic formats will orient you to the exciting possibilities. See Figure 5–8 for a sampling of the software options that you can explore to accomplish your oral reporting needs more quickly, less expensively, and more professionally using a personal computer.

Direct Aids

Graphic images such as bar and pie graphs (produced by software like Chart-Master or PFS:Graph), flow charts (Freelance), and maps (Map-Master) produced by printer or plotter can be used

---

7. Christopher O'Malley, "Graphics," *Personal Computing;* Oct. 1986: 106.

FIGURE 5-8

Sampling of Presentation Graphics Software*

Media Category	Software Title and Publisher
Business graphics:	Chart-Master (Ashton-Tate Corporation)
	Freelance Plus (Lotus Development Corporation)
	Harvard Presentation Graphics (Software Publishing Corporation)
	Microsoft Chart (Microsoft Corporation)
	Graphwriter (Graphic Communications, Inc.)
	PFS:Graph (Software Publishing Corporation)
Word charts	Sign-Master (Ashton-Tate Corporation)
	WordChart (Digital Research, Inc.)
Maps	Map-Master (Ashton-Tate Corporation)
Transparencies	Overhead Express (Business & Professional Software)
	Sign-Master (Ashton-Tate Corporation)
Slides	35mm Express (Business & Professional Software)
Video slide shows	PC Storyboard (IBM Corporation)
	Show Partner (Brightbill-Roberts & Co.)

*Most business presentation software listed here works only with properly equipped IBM personal computers and 100 percent IBM compatibles. Similar software is also available for other computers.

Sources: Adapted from Christopher O'Malley, "Driving Your Point Home," *Personal Computing,* Aug. 1986: 103; and Robin Baskin, "A Better Way to Sell Your Ideas," *Family & Home Office Computing,* April 1988: 43.

directly as handouts. These images can be enlarged from their standard 8½ by 11-inch printout size by office photocopiers, typically increasing their size by 15 to 50 percent. The enlargement can then be mounted on posterboard to produce a desk chart or bound into a flip chart for a presentation to a small group.

It might be better to use special printers or plotters that make super-size printouts from 11 by 17 inches up to as big as 36 by 48 inches. Although costly, another option would be commercial art and photography shops that can enlarge the printout for you (up to four by twelve feet) and even mount the visuals on sturdy illustration board.

Transparencies

Replacing markers, lettering machines, and typewriters, you can produce transparencies with a printer or plotter and special software. Any printer capable of printing out the visual can be used, but you need a photocopier that can transfer the images from paper to transparency sheet. Some color printers and plotters can draw directly on the transparency film eliminating that step. Graphics packages like Chart-Master or Graphwriter will produce the lettering and symbols for transparencies, but more specific software expedites the job. Such programs as Overhead Express and Sign-Master are ideal for producing word charts with an appealing and clarifying variety of page layouts, type styles and sizes, and graphic symbols like bullets, arrows, and check marks.

Slides

While you can easily develop photographs into slides for projection, the process of converting computer-generated graphics onto photographic film is lengthy and costly. That is changing, however, because of new graphics software (like 35mm Express) and special computer accessories.

Photographic equipment, either screen cameras or film recorders, can be connected to your personal computer to transfer graphic images and text onto film, which can then be developed into color slides. Screen cameras shroud your computer monitor with a fitted hood so a 35-millimeter camera can snap a picture of the display. What you see on the screen is what you get on the film, meaning that often the image is slightly sketchy and distorted, especially when enlarged on the projection screen. On the other hand, film recorders process your computer's video output electronically and record it on 35mm film. Thus, the detail and color of the projected slide is actually better than the monitor's display.

Video

Video productions—lights, cameras, action—can have great impact on an audience, but they usually go beyond the scheduling and budgetary reach of most business and professional people. Again, a personal computer with the proper accessories can quickly and inexpensively create moving images for on-screen video projection. PC Storyboard and Show Partner are two programs that specialize in creating right at your desk video presentations.

With these programs, you can draw original images or capture screen images from other programs, edit these images into a simulated slide show, and run the show from your computer. Using a graphics-creating program like Chart-Master, you can create business graphs to include in your video show. In the editing process, your visuals (ones you draw yourself, those from other programs, or those selected from an image library of "clip art") are animated. You can move text or graphics around the screen. You can use dissolve or fade techniques for moving from one screen to another.

You can even program the electronic slide show to run automatically, showing each visual for perhaps eight seconds before going on to the next, while you narrate. Or, you can manually advance to each visual when ready by pressing a key on the keyboard. Depending on software and hardware, some video presentations may be recorded for later viewing on videotape with a videocassette recorder.

You have several options on how to display these productions for your audience. A normal computer monitor is large enough to display video slide shows for two or three people. A large-screen monitor will work for 10 to 20 people. Larger gatherings will need a screen the same size as used with overhead and slide projectors. A standard projection television or special computer projection equipment like the Sony Videoscope can beam the images onto a large screen.[8]

Another device for large-group viewing is an electronic transparency system for displaying computer images through an overhead projector. It consists of a flat projection pad that you place over the transparency stage of an ordinary overhead projector. The pad is then plugged into the personal computer's video output port. The electronic transparency system is especially attractive for training sessions. An instructor can work with an entire class of students instead of only two or three who could peer over his shoulder at a computer monitor. Presenting from the keyboard, the trainer could present word processing instruction or use special educational programs quite efficiently.[9]

---

8. Material for this section was adapted from Christopher O'Malley, "Driving Your Point Home," *Personal Computing,* Aug. 1986: 86–105.
9. "Slideless Slide Show for Groups," *Personal Computing,* March 1987: 162.

USING PRESENTATION AIDS IN DELIVERY

Being blessed with all these presentation aid options forces us to make some tough decisions. Ultimately, you—the designer, user, and presenter—must decide upon the best aid or combination of aids to help you deliver your content. As you make your decision, consider your purpose, audience size, preparation time, and speaking environment. Generally speaking, follow this rule: For a smaller audience and less important occasion, use the more informal aids, such as the chalkboard or mounted visuals displayed on an easel. For a larger audience and more important event, use projected aids, such as transparencies or slide projection.

Figure 5–9 highlights the major advantages and disadvantages of the most commonly used presentation aids, to help you decide which visual aids to use.

Presentation aids will inject more complexity into the actual presentation, so you must learn to use them properly in your delivery. The following tips will help you use presentation aids more competently and with greater confidence.

General Advice on Using Presentation Aids

Some delivery advice applies to all presentation aids. Whether using direct or projected aids, remember these six suggestions:

1. Adequately explain the presentation aid before making your point. The amount of explanation depends on the complexity of the presentation aid and the audience members' sophistication. Your discussion reinforces the significant points that the audience members should grasp and integrates the aid into the context of the developing subject matter.

For example, with a multiple-line graph, saying "This line graph shows that return on investment peaked in 1985 while return on sales peaked in 1986" is too abrupt since the viewer may have a hard time digesting the graph data. With a bar or line graph, the speaker will usually need to explain what the axes represent and their units of measurement. This explanation is much better: "Figure 2 is a line graph showing return on investment, indicated in green, and return on sales, indicated in red, for Monolithic Enterprises for the period 1985 to 1989. Note that Monolithic's return on sales increased gradually from 1985 to 1987,

FIGURE 5-9
Summary of Presentation Aids

Media	Audience Size	Pros	Cons
Three-dimensional objects, demonstration items	Depending on size of object, up to 30	Realistic, involves audience, easy to use	May take time to construct and set up, limited size
Flip charts, posters, charts, graphs, pictures	Depending on size, up to 30 Desk charts, up to 5	Inexpensive; easy to prepare, set up, and use; can be prepared in advance; can be reused; notes can be placed on visual	Limits audience size, may be difficult to transport and store
Chalkboards, markerboards	Up to 30	Readily available, adds spontaneity, ideas can be added, almost no expense	Less audience involvement, eye contact jeopardized, easy to block view, less professional and credible, less detail possible, content not easily saved
Transparencies	Up to 60	Uses normal room lighting, speaker faces audience, easy to prepare and use, inexpensive, professional, notes can be placed on frames, easy to transport and store, content can be slowly revealed	Screen often poorly placed (keystone effect, speaker blocks view), equipment may fail

FIGURE 5-9 (continued)
Summary of Presentation Aids

35mm slides	Limited only by room and screen size	Suggests professionalism and preparation; easily updated, transported and stored; shows pictorial realism; can be operated by remote control	Costly and time-consuming to produce, room darkening required, equipment may fail, slides may get out of order, speaker's role diminished
16mm films	Limited only by room and screen size	Shows motion, very realistic	Requires professional production skills; requires long production lead-time; expensive to produce, buy, or rent; projector needs more skill to operate; requires more set-up time
Video	Large-screen monitor, up to 20; large-screen projection, depends on screen size	Same as film at lower cost, computer-generated video output can be used	High equipment investment (VCR, projection equipment, monitors, and/or computer hardware and software), special preparation and operation skills, complex equipment more failure-prone

reaching its highest level of 5.9 percent. However, return on investment did not peak until 1988 at 3.7 percent. . . ." Some viewers will need more explanation than others. Be careful not to explain the obvious or talk down to them.

2. If possible, only show a presentation aid when you are actually using it in your presentation. If displayed too soon, some members of the audience will stop paying attention to you and concentrate on the aid, losing your verbal content. Keep a posterboard-mounted picture turned over on the easel stand until needed. Then flip it over to develop your concept. Similarly, turn an overhead projector on only when the audience needs to refer to the projected transparency. Conversely, when through with an aid, remove it from audience sight. This eliminates a potential source of distraction and pulls attention back to you.

3. Maintain eye contact as you use your aids. Do not talk to the overhead projector, the chalkboard, or screen. Although you must make some eye references to the aid to orient yourself or to point, maintain eye contact with the audience as much as possible. Speakers who rivet their eyes on their presentation aids are just as annoying to audience members as speakers who keep their heads buried in their notes.

4. Provide an unobstructed view as much as possible. Staying out of the viewer's line of sight is often a problem with many aids, especially the chalkboard, markerboard, and overhead projector. If you are using these visual aids, review the techniques presented earlier. As you practice, concentrate on eliminating this common audience annoyance. During your presentation, read your audience feedback for viewing problems or ask outright if your visuals are easy to see.

5. If necessary, use a pointer to focus attention on the relevant part of your aid. Although a pen, pencil, or finger does the job, a regular or collapsible pointer looks more professional and guarantees that you do not block the audience's view of the visual. Move the pointer slowly and purposefully as you point on a chart, model, or screen. Use it *only* to point—do not use it as a plaything with which you nervously fiddle. Put it down when you're done so your hands are free for constructive body language.

6. Speak more loudly when using presentation aids. Since each audience member's attention is divided, additional volume is sometimes necessary to maintain attention on the spoken content.

Projected Aids

Projected aids require extra precautions. Although Murphy's Law was probably not formulated with projected aids in mind, it definitely applies: "If something can go wrong, it probably will at the worst possible time." To minimize embarrassing failures with projected aids that compromise your effectiveness and believability, consider these aspects in their preparation and use:

1. Know how to operate the specific equipment yourself or use a skilled operator. When you are in front of an audience of 50 colleagues, it is no time to learn how to focus a slide projector.

2. Check the suitability of the room for use of a projected aid. Go through this check list:

- Is an electrical outlet available?
- Will extension cords be needed? (While you're at it, ask yourself if an extension cord will be long enough and whether you will need a three-prong plug adapter.)
- Can the screen be properly positioned for maximum viewing ease?
- If darkening the room is necessary, can lighting be dimmed easily or outside light blocked by shades or drapes?
- Are loudspeakers well placed, and sound quality adjusted for good hearing?

3. Check that equipment is ready. Has it been set up properly? Has it been tested? Are the projection media all set? For instance, are the slides inserted into the carousel holder in the correct position and order? Make a dry run with the equipment—in the speaking room, if possible—when you practice. Then double-check just before the presentation begins.

4. Be prepared for emergencies. What would you do if, heaven forbid, the film on management practices in Japan didn't arrive for your workshop? How could you still accomplish your objectives? Or must you modify your presentation objectives? What if the overhead projector's bulb blows? Have a spare or know where to get one. What if the slide projector breaks down in the middle of the slide show? In the event you cannot repair it or get another projector, what can you do to salvage the rest of the presentation?

These catastrophes seem to happen to inexperienced speakers. Perhaps on the way to becoming a better user of presentation aids, experienced speakers have learned the hard way. Smart beginners avoid as many pitfalls as possible and devise a "Plan B"—just to be on the safe side.

Chalkboards, Markerboards, and Flip Charts

Even relatively uncomplicated direct aids, such as the chalkboard, markerboard, or flip chart, can be misused. To use these relatively informal aids correctly:

1. Plan your use of the writing surface as much as possible. Develop a readily apparent organizational and locational logic as you build up your visual. Move from left to right or top to bottom, for example, to avoid a haphazard placement of words, figures, and illustrations.
2. Use only the top two thirds of the writing surface. Information near the bottom may be difficult to see because of viewers' heads, and writing clearly on the bottom third is challenging unless you stand on your knees.
3. Write or draw clearly and largely enough. Visibility and legibility are big problems with these aids. Make heavy lines, not faint strokes. With complex visuals, use contrasting chalk and marker color.
4. Erase the board or flip to a clean page when your presentation is over. This action shows courtesy to the next speaker who may wish to use the aid and removes distracting information from the audience's view for the next presenter.

These tips, suggestions, and reminders may seem complicated, but all of them are common sense, at least after you think about them a little. Take the time and effort to learn to use presentations aids well. This investment pays dividends steadily throughout your business and professional career. And, your audience will never hear you say, "I know you can't see this but. . . ."

SUMMING UP

Professional and business people select, design, and use presentation aids to add to their oral communication effectiveness. The benefits of using presentation aids are many—meeting audience expectations, maximizing audience retention, increasing listener comprehension, adding to the speaker's persuasiveness and credibility, increasing conciseness, and improving the speaker's delivery style. To obtain these positive outcomes, though, presentation aids must be relevant, simple, visible, and well produced.

Presentation aids fall into two main categories. Direct aids are relatively simple to use and better suited to smaller audiences in informal settings. Examples of direct aids are demonstration items and models, mounted visuals, handouts, chalkboards and markerboards, and flip charts. Projected aids require a projector and screen, but they are ideal for larger audiences and lend an air of polish and professionalism to presentations. The overhead projector is the most frequently used projected aid. Other projected aids are the opaque, slide, filmstrip, and film projectors and television.

Computer-generated visuals called presentation graphics have had the greatest impact on presentation aids in the last five years. Using a properly equipped personal computer, a presenter can produce high-quality, low-cost direct aids, transparencies, slides, and video slide shows.

The best-chosen, best-designed presentation aids quickly lose their effectiveness unless used competently by the presenter. Good delivery suggestions include: (1) smoothly integrating and adequately explaining presentation aids, (2) focusing attention on aids with a pointer, (3) keeping aids out of view until needed to eliminate distractions, (4) maintaining eye contact with the audience, not the aid, (5) being doubly cautious and prepared when using the more complicated projected aids, and (6) using good techniques even with such a deceptively simple presentation aid as the chalkboard.

Application Exercises

1. Using the resources available at your school or workplace, develop a direct presentation aid (model, chart, graph, table, map, pictures) or projected aid (transparency, slide series, videotape). The aid must be suitable for a presentation to 20 people. Your instructor will give you any other special expectations or restrictions. Attach a note to your presentation aid describing: overall objective of the presentation, specific objectives of the presentation aid, when it will used, and suggestions for successfully incorporating it into your delivery.
2. Compare two similar, competitive products or services using at least one presentation aid. Be creative and try to appeal to as many senses

as appropriate. Leads: You might compare Kellogg's Corn Flakes to Post Raisin Bran using a nutrition analysis chart and a taste test performed with audience members. Using transparencies displaying specifications, options, and cost data, you could compare the Chevrolet Cavalier to the Ford Escort. Other ideas: designer perfumes versus generic recreations, Nikes versus Reeboks, U.S. Postal Service parcel post versus United Parcel Service, McDonald's versus Burger King.
3. Present a talk about a Fortune 500 company, preferably one located in your area, using presentation aids. Data sources include company publications (like annual reports, product brochures), interviews with company representatives, newspaper and magazine articles, and business reference sources like those published by Moody's and Standard and Poor. Build your presentation aids into your presentation so they are an integral, vital part, not just a gimmick. Two approaches suggest themselves:
   a. Specialist: Cover one area in depth. For example: Company history—using a time line or mounted pictures; Products—using models, samples, demonstration; Marketing—using diagram of distribution channels; Production—using a flow chart to describe a manufacturing process; Financial/economic—using graphs and charts to analyze profitability and investment potential.
   b. Generalist: Cover several areas in less detail, being careful to adequately develop them and tie them together smoothly.
4. Deliver a talk with presentation aids based on information researched about a non-profit organization in your area (social service agency, library, school, cultural organization, hospital, government agency, for instance). Possibilities: Describe the planning, implementation, or operation of a newly installed on-line card catalogue at your public library. Discuss the sources of funding for a local symphony orchestra or ballet company. Take your audience on a guided tour via 35mm slides of the physical therapy department of the local hospital.
5. Present a talk with presentation aids built around a topic related to your major and career plans. A journalism major might detail the process involved in printing the local newspaper, following a reporter's story from word processor to its final location on page 3 of the evening edition. If you are an engineering student, you could discuss what CAD/CAM (computer–aided design/computer–aided manufacturing) is and how it is changing the engineering profession. A marketing major might describe the steps a local food manufacturer goes through to design and test packages for frozen food entrees.
6. Using presentation aids, demonstrate a process. You might want to relate your demonstration to your career interest. Examples: how to load and operate a carousel slide projector, take a blood pressure reading, develop color film, replace a faucet washer, use an electronic spreadsheet to calculate financial ratios, or give a newborn baby a bath.

7. Prepare a report, oral or written as directed, on how a particular business or professional person you know uses presentation graphics. Collect data by observation and interview. What software is used and how? What computer hardware and accessories are used? Relate several experiences this expert has had with presentation graphics. What tricks of the trade did you pick up?
8. With the computer software and hardware available at your school or place of employment, complete Exercise 5 using presentation graphics.

Chapter 6

INTERVIEWING

Interviewing is an oral communication skill that is a component of all business- and professional-level positions. Almost everyone is familiar with the most common type of interview, the job interview, but many of us do not realize that we are involved almost daily in many other face-to-face communication encounters that are interviews, also. No doubt, you have used interviewing techniques many times to gather information, identify and solve problems, or complete some other personal task or job task without being consciously aware of it.

In Chapter 6, our goals will be to:

- ▶ define interviewing,
- ▶ explore how professional and business people use interviewing,
- ▶ differentiate between directive and non-directive interviewing styles,
- ▶ discover how to prepare for a productive interview,
- ▶ examine effective questioning and responding strategies,
- ▶ survey other skills a capable interviewer or interviewee needs, including perceptivity, listening, and responsiveness,
- ▶ analyze good interview organization.

WHAT IS INTERVIEWING?

Communication theorists define interviewing as "the process of dyadic communication with a pre-determined and serious purpose designed to interchange behavior and involving the asking and answering of questions."[1] To define interviewing in less abstract terms, think of interviewing as a *conversation with a purpose*. An interview is little more than a planned and purposeful dialogue. The word *planned* is important. People come to an interview with a pre-determined purpose to accomplish. This aspect distinguishes an interview from a friendly conversation, which is unplanned and serves no purpose other than sociability. If you consider interviews as structured conversations, they are less foreign, less intimidating. Interviewing becomes a more approachable and pleasant task, too.

Going back to our theoretical definition, interviewing is indeed dyadic communication. Two parties are involved, alternating in the roles of speaker and listener. In an interview dyad, one

---

1. Charles J. Stewart and William B. Cash, Jr., *Interviewing Principles and Practices,* 3rd. ed. (Dubuque, Iowa: Wm. C. Brown Company Publishers, 1982) 7.

party is termed the interviewer, and the other is called the interviewee or respondent. Because interviewing is a highly interactive, dynamic type of communication, sometimes it is hard to tell who is the interviewer and who is the interviewee. Often those involved will change roles, sometimes acting as interviewer, sometimes sliding into the role of interviewee.

In some situations, the interview parties consist of more than one person. If you are a fan of television talk shows, you frequently see the host interviewing two or three respondents at the same time. As a supervisor in a work situation, you may interview two staff members to resolve an interpersonal conflict. Or, as a job candidate and interviewee, you may be interviewed simultaneously by three interviewers—your prospective boss, that person's boss, and a member of the department in which you would work.

WHAT ARE THE PURPOSES OF INTERVIEWING?

Business and professional people use interviewing on the job for four major purposes:

1. To get information. For this purpose, the information flows from the interviewee to the interviewer. The interviewer tries to increase his store of knowledge by asking the respondent appropriate questions. For example, the vice-president of management information says to the manager of office services: "I'm building my budget and I need to get a run-down on personnel requirements in each department for the next fiscal year. What is the staffing situation in your department for the next twelve months?" This question should lead to a response about any major plans for increasing or decreasing department staff during the new budget year, and thus the interviewer obtains the necessary information from the interviewee.

2. To give information. Here the flow of information is reversed. The direction is from interviewer to interviewee. For instance, at the beginning of an interview, the marketing director says to the two sales representatives in the Lake County sales territory: "Let me fill you in on our pre-Christmas advertising campaign that will run from November 1 to December 31 for the Flying Fingers Model 8008 electronic typewriter." The interviewer, the marketing director, then shows examples of newspaper and magazine ads and television and radio commercials. The marketing director explains several promotional gimmicks that office equipment suppliers will use. Through an exchange of questions and answers like this, the interviewees, the sales reps, receive the information to improve customer contact and sell more aggressively.

3. To persuade. In a persuasive interview, more than just exchanging information, one party tries to convince the other party to alter beliefs or behavior. As a persuasive speaker carefully analyzes the audience before a talk, a persuasive interviewer analyzes an interviewee before the interview. Then the interviewer can appeal to the interviewee's needs, wants, values, and emotions as convincingly as possible. For example, asking your boss for a raise in a persuasive interview. (We'll develop this in more depth later.)

4. To solve problems. Here the interviewer and interviewee work through a problem-solving procedure to resolve a troublesome situation. An example: Poor morale is seriously affecting production of data entry clerks in the data processing department. Sylvia Brand, data processing manager, calls in her three data entry supervisors. She says, "I've asked you to meet with me to iron out the morale problems in our department caused, I believe, by the changeover to the new TX10 terminals." Through a question-and-answer process led by Brand, the problems need to be fully identified, explored, and accepted by the participants. Then solutions must be proposed and evaluated, and corrective action recommended and implemented. An effective problem-solving procedure that can be applied in this type of interview will be discussed in Chapter 8.

Interviews, of course, are not necessarily single-purposed. In many interview settings, the participants will have multiple goals, although one of these four purposes may predominate. In the persuasive interview requesting a pay raise, your boss, no doubt, will have information-seeking questions to ask (how long since your last raise, what evidence can you present to prove your increased worth to the company, and so on).

WHAT ARE COMMON KINDS OF INTERVIEWS?

It's easy to underestimate how important interviewing skills are. To many people, interviewing is just one step in the job hunt. Actually, job interviewing is only the tip of the iceberg. As a social worker, teacher, accountant, systems analyst, nurse supervisor, sales representative, whatever your current or future business or profession, you will use interviewing skills almost daily as you carry out your job responsibilities. Here is an overview of the types of interviews business people and professionals will be most often involved in, either as the interviewer or the interviewee.

1. Employment interview. This is the familiar interview between the personnel director or other company representative and the job applicant. During an employment interview, each person is interviewing the other. Both participants are trying to give and get information—the interviewer about the skills and talents of the job seeker and the respondent about the strengths and weaknesses of the prospective employer.

2. Training interview. Sometimes called an induction interview, this informational interview occurs after the job candidate has been hired. It orients the new employee to company policies, organizational structure, job responsibilities, and the overall company environment. A training interview might be done one-to-one or in a small group of five or six beginning workers. Presentation aids, maybe a videotape or slide program, might be used to convey information more efficiently and interestingly.

3. Appraisal interview. Periodically, every six or twelve months in most organizations, an employee's immediate supervisor will discuss the results of a performance review with each subordinate. In most cases, the supervisor first completes a written report form, which is reviewed with the employee and then signed by him or her to show that the interview took place. The purposes of an appraisal interview are to recognize job strengths and discuss ways to improve job performance in weaker areas. Often, goals to be achieved during the next evaluation period will be mutually agreed upon now. Written results of the employee appraisal interview are frequently used to determine pay raises, make promotions, or give the company concrete, documented grounds for dismissing an employee.

4. Exit interview. When an employee leaves a job, an interview may be conducted to obtain data on reasons for leaving, pros and cons of working for the organization, and other candid information that supervisors and the personnel department can use to improve the employee/employer relationship.

5. Informational interview. Obviously, the objective of an informational interview is either to get or give information—or a combination of these objectives. Information-getting interviews occur, for instance, when a stockbroker asks about a new client's financial status and probes to discover long- and short-term investment goals. A lawyer conducts an information-getting interview when interrogating a client, victim, or witness in the office or courtroom. Information-giving interviews occur when a physician instructs a diabetic patient on how to alter his diet and when a sales representative explains the facsimile machine's warranty, how to obtain service under warranty, and owner-maintenance responsibilities.

6. Persuasive interview. This interview's major goal is to convince the other party to buy a product or service or support an idea or position. An example of a persuasive interview: An executive calls a production supervisor into the office. This young manager has been transferred two times in five years and will be urged to transfer yet another time to the new Atlanta plant. The boss says, "I want to talk to you about a possible transfer to our new Atlanta facility." The boss must convince the production supervisor that this third transfer is best for both the supervisor's career and the company's management needs. Salespeople, of course, use persuasive techniques all the time on sales calls and in sales meeting. For this reason, persuasive interviews are sometimes called sales interviews.

7. Counseling interview. The goal of this problem-solving interview is to help the interviewee recognize a problem and work toward resolving it. To illustrate, a supervisor might counsel a subordinate on tardiness. The supervisor will substantiate the tardiness claim, review company policy on job tardiness, try to get the employee to recognize the consequences of repeated lateness, explore reasons for the problem, and motivate the employee to solve the problem by catching an earlier bus or replacing a failing car battery.

In this example, the boss brought a problem to the attention of a subordinate. The situation could be the reverse, the subordinate asking the superior for assistance. For example, one of your staff comes to you with a complaint. Mary claims that Craig, one desk over, smokes during coffee breaks at his desk. Not only does this violate the office smoking rules, but it irritates Mary's eyes and throat, lowering her productivity and job satisfaction. You, as Mary and Craig's boss, must use your interviewing skills to settle the grievance.

Other conflict-resolution interview situations involve teacher and student, salesperson and customer, or production supervisor and union steward. Emotions run high in this type of interview, making it especially important for the interviewer to be a good listener and problem solver.

These seven common management-level interactions are interviews because they involve the structured asking and answering of questions as the primary technique to fulfil a pre-determined purpose—getting or giving information, persuading, or problem solving. You, therefore, will encounter many communication situations like these on the job.

ARE THERE DIFFERENT INTERVIEW STYLES?

Your interview objectives will be accomplished using either the directive approach or the non-directive approach (also called unstructured or open-ended). In the directive style of interviewing, at least at the beginning, the interviewer is in control and the interviewee merely cooperates. Such interviews are quite efficient. The interviewer primarily asks specific questions and wants to-the-point, concrete responses.

You are probably most familiar with the directive interview because the typical job interview is a directive one. The prospective employer makes all the major decisions about the interview interaction from meeting place to time length to the questioning pattern. The job candidate has a passive role and exerts little influence on these planning or organizational factors. The candidate accepts the interviewer's decisions and mainly answers questions. Although she can certainly prepare well and anticipate the interview and questioning format, the interviewee will have considerably less responsibility for shaping the interview process than the interviewer. Training, informational, and persuasive interviews are also conducted primarily using the directive approach.

In a non-directive interview, usually by the decision of the interviewer, the participants jointly share the responsibilities of planning and conducting the interview. The interviewee assists in setting up the interview, determining its expected outcomes, and selecting the interview procedures and structure. Certainly, this added control and responsibility makes for a more advanced and challenging interview from the interviewee's perspective.

Not having the opportunity to follow the interviewer's lead, the respondent must be prepared to participate actively throughout the non-directive interview. The interviewer more frequently asks open, broad questions to which the interviewee is expected to respond with careful thinking and creativity, such as "What are your thoughts about . . .?" Further information is pursued with neutral questions like "Could you tell me a little more about that?" Rather than saying "I agree" or "You were right in acting that way," the interviewer non-judgmentally remarks "I see" or "I understand." Demonstrating an attitude of respect, interest, and appreciation, the interviewer is ready to listen to whatever is said without disapproval or approval. Using questions like this, the interviewer often obtains much information, some of which is usually not relevant. For this reason, non-directive interviews are generally longer than directive interviews.

The interviewer and interviewee roles blur in the non-directive style. It may be difficult to label one party the interviewer and the other party the interviewee. The participants share control of the interview; the asking and answering roles shift back and forth between the parties. However, each party's greater involvement strengthens the communication interchange. Each has a better understanding of the other's intentions and goals and, therefore, feels more commitment to accomplishing the mutually agreed-upon interview objectives.

The non-directive interview style adapts well to the problem-solving needs of business and professional people and is used in appraisal, exit, and counseling interview situations. You may have heard, too, that job interviews sometimes use the non-directive style. The job applicant is given broadly focused, open-ended questions, such as "Tell us about yourself and why you should be hired as executive director of the West Side Community Service Agency."

An interview like this means that the job candidate must be extremely well prepared about his credentials, the position, and the organization or department with the job opening. The candidate must show maturity, accept responsibility, and demonstrate problem-solving and decision-making talents while presenting relevant job qualifications confidently, concretely, and articulately. Being on the spot like this, the applicant can demonstrate some of the managerial competencies an executive director must have. Such an interview is stressful. It deliberately puts the job-seeker on the spot to see how he handles difficult, free-form situations.

In many cases, a combination of the directive and non-directive approaches is used. One of the interviewer's tasks is deciding which style is better and when to switch from one approach to the other to accomplish the purposes of the interview. An employment counselor, for instance, may use the non-directive style when assessing a client's personality type and career goals and the directive style when determining the client's educational and work credentials.

HOW DO YOU PREPARE FOR AN INTERVIEW?

Some inexperienced interviewers *don't* prepare for interviews. After all, they think, interviewing is a dynamic process. As an interviewee, I don't know what questions will be asked. Or, as an interviewer, I don't know what questions to ask until I meet the interviewee. Of course, this kind of thinking violates the very essence of what interviewing is—a planned, purposeful conversation. For a productive interview, both parties must be well prepared or they court disaster, or at best, inefficiency.

Never go into an interview situation cold, whether you are the interviewer or the interviewee. Being well prepared means, first of all, that you know your purpose. Give careful forethought to defining your goals. What do you want to accomplish in the next 15 or 45 minutes of interview time? Do you want to exchange information, persuade, or solve a problem? Without a precise statement of interview goals, the interview interaction will be loosely structured, repetitive, and, quite likely, without a goal. Both the interviewer and the interviewee must be able to briefly define in a clear sentence or two what their purposes are.

Secondly, learn as much about the other person as possible. Research the interviewer or interviewee's preferences, dislikes, thinking style, and management orientation as much as possible.

John Darling © 1988 King Features Syndiate, Inc.

Careful preparation helps insure that embarrassing mistakes don't occur that waste time or affect interview rapport.

This investigation, depending on the interview situation, may involve examining personnel files and other company records, talking to other people who know the interviewer/interviewee, or studying the job applicant's resume and contacting their references. Similar to the objectives of audience analysis, the more you know about the other person, the easier you can communicate. Remember to phrase questions or answer questions with the other person's background and objectives in mind.

Thirdly, if you are the interviewer *plan,* or if you are the interviewee *anticipate* the interview format and questioning plan. This increases the likelihood of asking or answering questions in an articulate, specific, and appropriate manner that will help move the interview along toward its objective. An interviewer in an information-seeking encounter formulates questions to get the desired data, considers potential interviewee responses, and plans alternative questioning tactics to use. An interviewee with a grievance would come prepared to describe the problem clearly and present supporting evidence. More advice on formulating questions and sequencing them will follow in the next section.

Fourth, make the interview arrangements. The interviewer will inform the interviewee of the time, length, place, and purpose of the interview—or make these arrangements jointly in the non-directive style. The interviewee will need enough time to prepare for the interview and to assemble and review any background information or documentation. You might say: "Roger, I've arranged for us to meet with Bill to iron out the disagreement on his vacation time request. We'll meet in my office between 10:30 and 11:00 Thursday morning."

Any special requests should be made now, such as recording the interview, having someone else present, or making special use of information. Asking permission for such requests shows consideration and allows the other party to plan with this irregularity in mind or to object to it.

Choose the location carefully because the physical surroundings can influence the interview interaction. For a formal interview, select a formal environment like an office, a meeting space that is free from distractions and private. To avoid giving one participant a power advantage by conducting an interview on home turf in her office, a neutral locale like a conference room would be preferable. Neutral territory may relax the participants and put them on a more equal standing. For more informal and relaxed communication, the company cafeteria or a restaurant may be appropriate.

To illustrate these planning suggestions, let's follow someone preparing for an information-gathering interview. John Newberg is responsible for planning a new flex-time schedule for the six employees in his department. Peak work loads occur between 10:00 and 2:00 each day, so he must have all six of his staff members on duty then. Twenty-five percent of the work load occurs between 6:00 and 10:00 A.M. and ten percent between 2:00 and 6:00 P.M. Although he could ask questions over the telephone or in a questionnaire, Newberg decides interviewing his employees is the best way to get the information to design a work schedule that will please his staff and meet department needs.

Newberg's purpose in each ten-minute interview will be to ascertain individual preferences as to starting and quitting time. Next, he assesses what he already knows about the work habits and personality of each subordinate. He knows, for instance, that Martha and Paul commute long distances to work, that Phyllis's husband works the night shift, and that Harvey likes to jog every day, before work if possible. Now he can think about the questions he must ask to obtain the data he needs to design a fair flex-time schedule. He decides to ask three or four questions:

1. What personal factors would you like considered when the new flex-time schedule is set up?
2. Do you prefer to work 6:00 to 3:00 or 9:00 to 6:00?
3. Would you prefer the same time slot each day?
4. If no, on what days would you prefer the alternate work schedule?

Newberg next creates a simple interview guide. He writes these questions down on a sheet of paper, leaving a blank space after each question. Here he can jot down notes on each employee's responses. By sticking to this questioning plan, John will get the standardized information from each staff member he needs to devise a fair work schedule. Finally, he decides to conduct each interview in his office—for privacy—in the late afternoon—when work load is less and he can call each person away easily—and notifies each staff member of this brief meeting.

This example shows how to plan for a simple interview. If the interview were longer, if the subject matter were more complex or delicate, if the interviewees were more sensitive, if the interviewer had no prior relationship with the interviewees, or if the interview had more than one purpose, Newberg's preparation would have been considerably more complex, time consuming, and yet all the more essential.

Newberg wisely performed the groundwork for his interview. He's half done. Now he must conduct his interview. Interviewing is an exciting challenge for both the interviewer and the respondent because a variety of communication skills must be successfully woven together.

WHAT QUESTIONING AND RESPONDING SKILLS ARE NEEDED IN AN INTERVIEW?

The back-and-forth questioning and responding pattern is the major method of interviewer-interviewee interaction. Asking the right questions in the right order and responding fully and clearly are hallmarks of a productive, high-quality interview. We will look first at question options, then at some questioning and responding suggestions.

Open versus Direct Questions

Questions are either open or direct. Open questions force the respondent to provide longer, more detailed answers. Answers to open questions are less likely to be suggested or shaped by the questioner. By encouraging the answerer to respond at length, open questions provide information (facts, attitudes, and beliefs) that the questioner could not know otherwise. Direct questions can be answered "yes," "no," or with two- or three-word responses.

"Is your budget growing?" is a direct question to which the respondent may merely say "yes" or "no." The problem, of course, is that that response is too vague and incomplete to be of much value to the questioner. For more depth and detail, the questioner should ask an open question like, "How much has your department's budget increased during the last two years?" The response will be longer and more specific. Other examples of open questions:

- ▶ Tell me how your previous work experience as a branch bank manager can be helpful to you as our credit account manager.
- ▶ What's your complaint with Mrs. Murphy's supervisory abilities?
- ▶ Describe the driving and weather conditions when the accident occurred.

Direct questions do have their uses as well. They are time-efficient. When an interviewer simply wants a specific fact, then a direct question is appropriate: "You were born in 1969, weren't you?" "Do you have a working knowledge of Lotus 1-2-3?" Direct questions are usually easier and less stressful for the interviewee to answer. However, interviewers must often work harder if they ask many direct questions. They may need to ask repeated, rapid-fire questions to get the desired information, almost seeming to pry the data out of the respondent in small chunks. Constantly probing and rephrasing questions puts more stress on the interviewer.

Open questions may cause problems, too. Responses to open-ended questions are sometimes time consuming. The content of responses may be only somewhat related to the questioner's intent or even irrelevant. In such cases, the interviewer can begin to lose control of the interview.

Generally speaking, though, when planning the questioning format and developing an interview guide, emphasize open-ended questions.

Primary versus Secondary Questions

Questions are also classified as primary or secondary. The interviewer has a formal, written guide, or at least an informal, mental guide, on the sequence and type of questions to be asked. Primary questions are these planned questions.

But good interviewers remain flexible. During the interview, the perceptive questioner will be alert for clues in the respondent's verbal responses and body language in order to make adjustments in the planned questioning strategy. As interviewer, you have prepared carefully, but you cannot anticipate everything. The respondent seems uncomfortable, for example, in dealing with certain information. So you adjust your questioning approach accordingly. Or, certain information may be divulged that raises your curiosity or jogs your memory about additional fruitful questioning areas. Secondary questions are these unplanned questions that arise spontaneously out of the planned questioning. Maintain enough freedom to sneak in these follow-up questions to pursue alternate paths to desired information or to go after additional relevant data.

Experienced interviewers use both kinds of questions—planned, primary questions to get the essential information and unplanned, on-the-spot, secondary questions to be adaptable and sensitive to changes in the interview interaction.

Mirror Questions

Another useful question option is the mirror question, which restates and probes. In a mirror question, the interviewer summarizes previous responses in such a way that the respondent is invited to expand on previous answers. It might be done this way: "I gather you dislike completing travel reimbursement forms, especially after returning to the office from a long sales trip. Can you explain what exactly bothers you about the travel reimbursement form?" This type of question also indicates that the questioner is paying attention and provides feedback to the respondent. It brings any misinterpretation out into the open and permits the correction or clarification of information.

Question Format to Avoid

Some kinds of questions should be avoided altogether, or used very carefully in specialized situations.

1. Closed questions. Queries that restrict the respondent's range of answers are closed questions, like "Who is easier to work with—Jóse or Margaret?" or "Would you say your greatest communication skill is interviewing or writing?" Such questions increase interviewer control by leading the respondent to a limited range of answers. They save time also. The problem is that the choices given may or may not contain the respondent's preferred choice. The interviewee feels frustrated, and the interviewer may receive misleading information.

2. Loaded questions. With questions such as "Are you still using drugs?" or "Do you lose your temper as much as you did when we were in college?" any answer to the question will be unflattering, and in fact it may be difficult to obtain a truthful answer.

Faced with such possibly incriminating and misleading response options, the question's only effect will be to antagonize you. Interview rapport will deteriorate. You will begin to suspect the interviewer's motives and your responses will become more guarded. Even an expert interviewer whose objective is to determine how the respondent handles stress or difficult situations would be taking a risk posing a loaded question.

3. Leading questions. A leading question implies the correct or anticipated answer: "We fired the last director because he couldn't control the agency's budget. You have successful budgeting experience, don't you?" It's clear what the acceptable answer is, so the interviewer gets the desired answer, but not necessarily the truthful answer. A direct question would be a little better: "Do you have experience with building and living within budgets?" Much better would be an open question: "In your last position with the United Fund, what budgeting responsibilities did you have?"

Questioning and Responding Tips

The following suggestions will help you improve the caliber of the questioning process:

1. Group questions together logically. Organizing questions by topic or category so that they fit together smoothly provides structure to the questioning process. It helps the interviewer and interviewee's thinking process, too. Jumping from topic to topic makes it difficult for the interviewee to answer questions. She cannot focus on the questioner's objective or springboard off previous related responses. The interviewer appears to be unprepared, and the interview becomes fragmented and confusing.

An experienced personnel recruiter does not ask a job applicant questions in this crazy-quilt order: a question about the interviewee's related-work experience, then one on college extra-curricular activities, followed by why the candidate wants to work for the firm, then two questions on previous part-time jobs, followed by a question on five-year goals within the company if hired, then an inquiry about in which department the applicant is most interested in beginning, and finally questions about the applicant's college major. Instead, the recruiter explores the applicant's qualifications using a questioning pattern that has logic and forward movement:

- ▶ In what department is the candidate interested?
- ▶ What was the candidate's college major?
- ▶ What were her extra-curricular involvements?
- ▶ What is her related-work experience?
- ▶ What are her reasons for wishing to join the organization?
- ▶ What are her five-year goals with the organization?

Grouping questions logically does not mean you avoid unplanned questions. Avoiding unplanned questions would prevent you from realizing the value of secondary questions. Instead it is important to learn to integrate secondary questions into your questioning pattern smoothly. Jot down additional questions you are reminded of as you go along and insert them at the next appropriate place. Veer off the planned questioning path to ask a follow-up question, but gradually work back to the main questioning strategy. Make transitional comments to do this like "Can we get back to what we were discussing earlier, the issue of . . . ?"

Questioning follows one of two broad patterns. In the funnel sequence, questions move from general (open questions) to specific (direct questions). Starting with open-ended questions eliminates many primary questions later because the respondent has volunteered the desired information. It often relaxes the interviewee. It gives the interviewer an opportunity to listen, gather information, and then respond with follow-up questions.

In the inverted funnel sequence, questions go from specific (direct questions) to general (open questions). The beginning short direct questions will encourage a reluctant, shy, or unmotivated person to respond. Further into the interview, open questions will meet with more success.

The effective questioner is flexible. The interview's entire question/response segment may be characterized by either the funnel sequence or the inverted funnel sequence, or the interviewer may switch from one pattern to the other several times depending on the subject matter.[2]

If you have done a good job in sequencing your questions, your interview will have unity; the seams do not show in a very good interview. Questions will flow smoothly from topic to topic. Ideally, you will find your next question in the answer to the previous question. One question flows into the next question because you use transitional words and phrases like you do in other forms of oral and written communication. When you change topics, you provide transition to bridge the gap. Or, you use mirror questions that have built-in transition.

2. Place difficult questions in the middle of the interview. If, from your analysis of the respondent, you judge that a

---

2. Cheryl Hamilton and Cordell Parker, *Communicating for Results,* 2nd ed. (Belmont, California: Wadsworth Publishing Company, 1987) 194–96.

questioning area may be sensitive, embarrassing, or threatening, probe this subject matter after establishing an atmosphere of trust and confidence with easier, safer, less offensive questions initially. If this delicate questioning does harm the rapport, you still have the opportunity later in the interview to rebuild the communication climate before wrapping up.

3. Ask short, simple questions. Avoid long, complicated questions that may be misunderstood. Avoid multiple-part queries, too. Both tax the respondent's memory and increase anxiety. An interview is not an inquisition or a grilling.

4. Choose your words carefully. Both parties must choose words carefully when framing and answering questions or when responding. An interviewer should be willing to explain and define if a question is unclear or too abstract. If the questioner is getting incorrect responses or the respondent has a quizzical expression, the interviewer should be quick to reframe the question to get a better response.

Another way to avoid these problems associated with perceptual and semantic noise is to avoid words that are emotionally loaded, words that are labels, stereotypes, or that have negative connotations. Words with emotional overtones make it more difficult for the other person to respond openly and honestly. A male interviewer who talks about the "girls in the typing pool" or indicates that the word processing staff consists mainly of married women who work for "pin money" is announcing to the interviewee that he has a sexist attitude about the value of working women. This message quite likely will inhibit the respondent from speaking frankly. The respondent fears antagonizing him with an alternate viewpoint.

5. Stay relevant and focused. Some interviewers lose sight of their purposes and go off into long speeches that waste time and destroy the forward momentum of the interview. Similarly, as an interviewee, keep responses short and to the point. Don't ramble off into unrelated areas. Help the interviewer maintain the focus and thrust of the information flow.

6. Take notes if the situation warrants it. Jot down questions you want to ask or points you want to make. Certainly, though, be judicious. Frantic, excessive note-taking may alarm and disorient the other person. Too much note-taking shifts attention away from the other person's verbal and non-verbal communication. Also, it interferes with listening, a process critical to good interviewing.

HOW CAN YOU BE MORE PERCEPTIVE IN INTERVIEWS?

Another skill good interviewers and interviewees have is perceptivity. In interviewing, perception means specifically *reading* the other party in the interview dyad and scanning the environment for clues that can improve the communication interaction.

Factors Affecting Interview Interaction

From personal experience, you know that communication is more difficult between strangers. Most people are conditioned to act in a restrained, guarded fashion when dealing with a person for the first time. It's especially true in an interview because the participants want to make a good impression and accomplish the interview purposes to their best personal advantage. So communication barriers must gradually be broken down for open, frank, and relaxed dyadic communication to take place.

We usually come to an interview with some perceptions of the other participants already formed in advance, and we change these perceptions as the interview goes along. From past informational interviews for newspaper stories, a business executive expects tough, probing questions from a certain reporter from a local paper. A supervisor is known for fair-mindedness, sensitivity, and a caring attitude in counseling interviews. On the other hand, another manager is tough and very direct in dealing with subordinates. A manufacturer's representative might be perceived as a smooth operator, one who drives a hard bargain in a sales interview. These people's interviews are influenced by their reputation.

We may be affected by the role relationship with the other interview participants. On the organization chart, are we superior, equal, or subordinate to the other party? Probably you perceive your boss as powerful (compared to you, anyway). Will your boss seize control of what you had planned to be a directive interview with you in charge? Will your boss misuse the power she has to frustrate you from achieving your interview purposes? Power inequities often complicate the interview process. Indeed, the style of interview, directive versus non-directive, may hinge on the power levels of the participants and how they use that power. Thus, interview interaction depends on how we perceive the other participants.

According to experts, three levels of interaction occur during interviews. The interaction level depends on the degree of self-disclosure, amount of personal risk, perceived meaning of the message, and the amount of important content exchanged:

Level 1 interactions deal with safe, nonthreatening areas of inquiry. Answers tend to be superficial, socially acceptable, comfortable, and ambiguous. Examples:

- Interviewer: How are you?
  Interviewee: Okay.
- Interviewer: How's the weather in Cleveland this winter?
  Interviewee: You know, cold and snowy.

Level 2 interactions deal with more intimate, controversial areas like behavior, thoughts, attitudes, beliefs, and feelings. Responses tend to be cautious, satisfying the interviewer but not revealing too much. For example:

- Interviewer: What do you think about the new health insurance plan?
- Interviewee: I'm pretty much satisfied. It paid for my entire appendectomy, but I got the run-around before all my emergency room bills were paid.

Level 3 interactions involve highly intimate and controversial areas. Often answers are very self-disclosing of feelings, beliefs, attitudes, and perceptions. Level 3 interactions are based on a high trust level, which often takes several interviews to develop. Example:

- Interviewer: Pat, output is 25 percent below last month. What's causing the production problems in your plant?
- Interviewee: I'm really demoralized about the staff cutbacks since the take-over. Who knows if my head's going to roll next? I've been nervous and edgy lately. Sometimes I drive my people too hard and fuss too much. Three weeks ago I got more bad news. One of my kids was arrested for drug possession and now the entire family is coping with that. It's been rough.

Compare these three interview interactions to doors. The door is ajar in Level 1, so general information passes through. The door is half open in Level 2, so more specific and revealing information comes through. In Level 3, the door is wide open; a high degree of self-disclosure occurs and very specific, revealing information passes through. Level 2 interactions are fairly common in interviews, especially when questions and responses are tactful and nonthreatening. Level 3 interactions are less common and require high levels of trust and motivation.[3]

Ways to Improve the Interview Climate

The following techniques will help you ease the other interview members into interaction Levels 2 and 3:

1. Keep other participants informed of your purposes and methods. Both interview parties need to know the interview's purposes and have clear expectations about what is to be accomplished. Not knowing the interview's purposes or operating at cross-purposes is frustrating, unproductive, and wasteful of time to interviewer and to interviewee. Be straightforward and honest. Avoid tricks, gimmicks, and lies.

2. Prepare well. As already mentioned, good preparation helps establish a positive communication climate. Your research helps you gain a clearer insight into the kind of person the interviewer or interviewee is. Thus, you and the other interview participants will interact more openly and effectively.

3. Build common frames of reference. Your preparation may have led you to a bit of information on which to launch the discussion, such as "I see you got your undergrad degree from CSU, too. Did you ever have Professor Browning for any of your social work courses?" If your preparation has not provided any leads, use a conversational wedge to break the ice without taking much risk. Asking questions such as "Gosh, it's a nice day, isn't it?" or "Have you watched any of the World Series games on TV?" may be trite, but they do get the conversation started. Then, you can listen for clues as to hobbies, sports interests, occupation, or family, for example, to build compatible lines of thinking and to open up the channels of communication.

4. Treat other interview participants as important individuals. Give them full attention and respect, even when their views are different from yours. More importantly, tackle the power differences that often exist between interview parties. Do not abuse

---

3. Charles J. Stewart and William B. Cash, Jr., *Interviewing Principles and Practices,* 3rd ed. (Dubuque, Iowa: Wm. C. Brown Company Publishers, 1982) 28–32.

the power that your position or circumstances may give you. Interviewer and interviewee should use their power and influence to accomplish mutual interview goals, not to sabotage them or to manipulate the other party. Power inequities can harm the interview interaction. Avoid such tactics as asking closed, leading, or loaded questions, misusing the funnel questioning pattern, or choosing home territory instead of neutral territory for the interview site. The interview may not move beyond Level 1 or even Level 2 interaction if you don't avoid these pitfalls.

5. Seem genuinely interested in the other party or the subject matter. Provide a self-introduction or information about your organization or task to create respondent interest. Develop a friendly relationship. If a warm rapport exists between the interviewer and the interviewee, both of you will be more motivated to participate in this purposeful, give and take conversation, work toward meeting interview's objectives, and go on to Level 2 or 3 interactions.

6. Motivate by rewarding. Evidence of potential personal benefit, money, copy of results, some kind of acknowledgment, note of appreciation, feeling of accomplishment, or pride in contribution may increase cooperation and commitment.

7. Be sensitive to nonverbal cues that convey (or betray) helpful information. This nonverbal language includes personal appearance (manner of dress and grooming), eye contact, mannerism (constantly changing seating position or fidgeting), blushing, handshake (cold, limp, sweaty or firm, confident, warm), frowning, smoking, or contradictory cues (saying "yes" hesitantly while shaking head "no"). Perceptive interviewers and interviewees *read* these factors and make adjustments in their questioning or responding pattern, word choice, and so on.

WHAT OTHER INTERVIEWING SKILLS ARE IMPORTANT?

A strong foundation for interviewing includes three other abilities—listening, paraphrasing, and responsiveness.

Listening

Listening is central to good interviewing. It can make or break an interview. Poor listening can be embarrassing. The interviewer might ask the same question over again, or the interviewee might respond to a question with incorrect or inappropriate information. An interviewer may be deciding on how to phrase the next question or wondering when a delicate subject should be raised, rather than focusing all attention on the other party's communication.

An active listener, on the other hand, is concentrating on the caliber of the interview interaction. You can apply this test to gauge your listening ability whether you are the interviewer or interviewee: If you are truly paying attention, you can repeat the content and intent of the message without much loss of accuracy or completeness.

Taking notes during an interview will improve your listening. Not only will you have some written reminder of the interview content for later reference, but writing forces you to pay more attention—to separate the important, relevant content from the rest and impose organization on the incoming information, if it needs such organization. Also, if you hear something that does not register completely, ask that the information be repeated or clarified. It may be the other party's fault because of poor enunciation or awkward phrasing but it could be the fault of your wandering, distracted mind.

You might want to review the section in Chapter 2 on listening. As you review, think about specific ways of putting the suggestions to work in the special context of interviewer or interviewee.

Paraphrasing

Interviewers and interviewees frequently use paraphrases. Paraphrasing restates communication content in your own words. It provides feedback to the other participant that you can use to judge the correctness of the information flow. If the paraphrase is inconsistent with what you meant to communicate, you can correct the misunderstanding. If you do not understand a question, ask for clarification ("I didn't quite follow what you meant by morale problems in my department") or paraphrase the question ("Are you asking if the training problems on the data processing equipment are connected to the problem of increased absenteeism since the new machines were installed?"). This follow-up ensures that you answer the correct question and indicates a reciprocal concern about fulfilling the interview's objectives.

Both content and intent can be paraphrased. When paraphrasing for content, you are restating the semantic meaning of the message. This is a content paraphrase: "You are saying, then, that the only way to improve morale in the engineering division is to replace its vice-president."

When you paraphrase for intent, you restate what you perceive the other person's feelings or motives to be. This, as you know from your own interpersonal relationships, is more difficult to do. Detecting underlying emotional intent demands greater perceptivity, an insight into the other person's frame of reference, and sharp listening. This is an intent paraphrase: "Do I understand correctly that you feel angry with Paul because he has gone over your head to the district manager two times?" If this is not a true reading of the other person's feelings, that misconception can be cleared up. Did you notice that this example is also a mirror question that invites further response?

Indicating Responsiveness

If one of the dyad shows detachment or boredom, the other party may sense it, back off, be less open, and become less committed to achieving the interview objectives. The interview interaction may fall off by a level or two as a result. Like paraphrasing, indicating responsiveness involves feedback. Both interview participants should show active and continuing interest in the interview's progress in two ways.

You can show your responsiveness verbally. Mirror questions perform this job in the questioning process. Also you can give some verbal cues that you are paying attention that will draw the other participant out. An interviewer might say, "Why?" "What do you mean?" "That's exciting, go on," "Uh huh," "I see," or "Really?" Your tone of voice will reinforce these cues. Sound sincerely interested, engrossed, and intrigued by the responses you are getting.

Other non-verbal cues can show your responsiveness. Maintain frequent and extended eye contact to indicate your interest level. Lively facial expressions are helpful as well. Eyes that are wide open and bright and a smile show pleasure and approval. A quizzical or surprised expression communicates misunderstanding or disbelief. A frown reveals disapproval. Body movements, like head nodding, signify agreement and coax the respondent.

HOW IS A GOOD INTERVIEW STRUCTURED?

As you have seen, interviewing is a complex combination of thinking and communication skills. You have also now realized that interviews follow a format and that some interview formats

FIGURE 6–1
Interview Structure

I. OPENING
    A. Establish good communication climate
        1. Introduction (if needed)
        2. Small talk
    B. Orient (as to purpose of interview, how data will be used, interview length, interview procedures, and so on)

II. BODY (use an interview guide if necessary)

III. CLOSING
    A. Summarize, indicate further action (as necessary)
    B. Express appreciation

are better than others. An interviewer can't just abruptly start asking questions and then shuffle the interviewee out the door when it's over.

The structure of an interview is shaped to some extent by its purpose and whether it is directive or non-directive. As with most complex communication tasks that business and professional people encounter, interviewing is more effective if a logical organization pattern is used. Rounding out this chapter is a look at the three-part format that most interviews use.

Let's examine this structure from the viewpoint of the interviewer responsible for controlling the interview. The interviewee's familiarity with this format is important, too. Knowing how an interview is likely to be structured helps him to relax during the interview and expedites the interview process. Of course, in a non-directive interview, both parties could jointly plan and execute the organizational pattern and the roles of interviewer and interviewee may switch back and forth. The three-part structure is summarized in Figure 6–1.

Opening

The first few minutes of an interview can be the most important and make the difference between a Level 1, 2, or 3 interview. A poor opener sometimes leads to no interview at all—the person may say no, walk away, or close the door. Spend time preparing an effective opener. Then take the time during the interview to encourage the open, caring, two-way communication flow both participants desire. Most interviews open with small talk to relax and orient both the interviewer and the interviewee. After this is done, the interview can proceed to the primary section—effective questioning.

Many people are intimidated by the prospect of a face-to-face encounter with a personnel recruiter, boss, counselor, or any business or professional person. They are apprehensive and perhaps unclear about what will happen. Therefore, aim to do two things in the interview opener to put the interviewee (and yourself) at ease and clarify your objectives.

First, build that important communication channel between yourself and the respondent that we mentioned earlier. In the first three or four minutes of an interview, each participant is trying to make a good impression on the other and to establish or to strengthen a conducive, interactive, open relationship.

Imagine you are conducting a counseling interview. Your goal is to resolve a conflict on a product development project between the engineering division representative and the sales division representative. Your chances are enhanced if all three of you first build a trusting, respectful, empathetic, relaxed rapport. Granted, this is often difficult to do, but failing to do so almost certainly dooms the interview.

How can you establish this positive communication climate? First, make the interview parties feel comfortable. Introduce yourself to the interviewees, if necessary. Shake hands and ask them to sit. Engage in a few minutes of sociable chit-chat. You can bring up an innocent subject on which you and respondents should be able to converse comfortably. It might be last night's ball game, a mutual friend, or the upcoming employee picnic. Don't overdo the first stage of the opening. Too much small talk wastes time, may raise the interviewees' suspicions, and can make you as the interviewer seem insincere.

Second, when both you and the interviewees feel more at ease, proceed to the orientation segment of the introduction. Make sure the respondent understands the interview's purpose and how it will be conducted. Never assume, even in an employment interview, that interviewees know the interview's purpose. In an informational interview, the interviewer should specify what information is needed or will be given. To encourage the respondent to answer questions frankly and specifically, tell how the information will be used. Assure the interviewee of the confidentiality of any sensitive data shared during the interview process, if that is the case. Finally, state how long the encounter will last, as a matter of common courtesy and to help both parties manage the time period.

Body

The longest part of the interview, the body, involves carrying out the pre-planned questioning strategy and perhaps recording information. This segment is the questioning/response/feedback part of the interview. Use the interview guide that you devised earlier to make sure that the interview's objectives are met. This outline or checklist will jog your memory about the sequence and content of questions. Ask your primary questions and follow up with secondary questions as conditions and time allow. During this part of the interview, budget your time to fulfil your purposes efficiently.

Close

If you have conducted all your business in one session, you are now ready to wrap up the interview. In some interviews, either the interviewer or the interviewee would be wise to summarize what was accomplished or to repeat the agreed upon resolution. The interviewer may also indicate any further action that is expected. If applicable, the interviewer tells the respondent what will happen next, like "This information will be presented to the Loan Review Committee on May 1. You will be notified by letter of their response to your loan application by May 15." Then each person should express appreciation for the other's time and cooperation.

An abrupt closing may undo the rapport established during the interview. If you are the interviewer, don't leave the interviewee with the impression that she has been used and discarded like an empty bottle. Future interviews will be strengthened by a good closing and marred by a poor one.

If the allotted time ran out for the interview, summarize progress so far and ask for additional time to complete the interview objectives. Don't sacrifice interview completeness or rush through your interview strategy just to finish on time. Check your calendars and set up another meeting to complete your purposes fully and unhurriedly.

SUMMING UP

As a business person or professional, you will be involved in many more interview situations than you might expect. Opportunities to use interviewing skills are frequent because an interview is really just a planned and purposeful conversation. Your purpose may be to get information, give information, persuade, or solve a problem.

In addition to personnel-management interviews that include employment, training, appraisal, and exit interviews, you are likely to conduct informational, persuasive, and counseling interviews many times in your career. You will use either the more common directive style in which the interviewer has almost complete responsibility for planning and conducting the interview or the nondirective style in which both participants jointly cooperate to plan and conduct the interview.

Successful interviews don't happen; they are well planned. Preparation involves determining the interview's purpose, analyzing the other participant, planning or anticipating the questioning plan, and making the interview arrangements.

As questioner, your most frequently used primary, or planned, questions, will be open questions that encourage longer, more expansive responses. You will use direct questions when you want specific, tightly-focused, time-efficient answers. You will also use mirror questions, which are restatement-probing queries. You will maintain flexibility to leave your primary questions temporarily to pursue secondary, or follow-up, questions.

Questions that should be used sparingly, if at all, are closed, loaded, and leading questions. Group questions together logically by topic and use either the funnel sequence—moving from general to specific questions—or the inverted funnel—progressing from specific to general questions—to build logical thinking and responding patterns.

Whether acting as questioner or respondent, experienced interview participants are perceptive. They read the other party in the interview dyad and scan the environment for clues to improve the interview's level of interaction. Level 1 interactions involve very safe, nonthreatening information; Level 2 interactions deal with more intimate thoughts and beliefs; and Level 3 interactions involve very personal, controversial content. To build the highest level of mutual trust and confidence, keep interview participants aware of interview goals, build common frames of reference, handle power differences, and be truly interested in the other party.

Also, interview participants should be active, focused listeners. They should paraphrase often for content and intent and indicate sincere interest in the interview encounter through verbal and nonverbal responses.

Most interviews have three parts. The opener establishes the desired relaxed, open communication climate and orients participants to the interview's purpose and methods. The body is the questioning/response/feedback portion of the interview where the interview's objective is fulfilled. The close reviews the findings or repeats the resolutions.

Application Exercises

1. Interview a business or professional person in your career area about interviewing. Find out:
   a. Amount of interviewing this person does (percentage of job time and communication time).
   b. Types of interviews conducted. (You might need to prompt your interviewee if he or she has an artificially narrow definition of interviewing.)
   c. Type of interview preparation engaged in.
   d. Person's interview style—directive, non-directive, or a combination.
   e. Techniques used to build good interview rapport.
   f. Advice on organizing various types of interviews (openings, questioning strategies, closings).
   g. Any tricks of the trade your expert will share with you (maybe on listening or paraphrasing).

   Present this information in an oral or written report as directed.

2. Watch a televised interview and evaluate the interview process. Audio- or video-tape it if possible so you can start and stop your playback for more detailed analysis and note-taking. You might evaluate an extended interview on a news program, a celebrity interview on a talk show, or an interview conducted by a professional like David Brinkley, Barbara Walters, or Ted Koppel. Evaluate concretely the interview's structure and interviewer and interviewee's skills in the areas of questioning, perceptivity, paraphrasing, listening, and responsiveness. Would you characterize the interviewer's style as directive, non-directive, or some combination? Describe instances of Level 1, 2, and 3 interaction.

3. Conduct 10-minute mock employment interviews. Audio- or videotape the interviews if practical. In pairs, role-play as interviewer and interviewee. To set the context, select a want ad for which you are reasonably qualified. Play back the tape and critique your skill as interviewer or interviewee. Evaluate interview structure, questioning/responding technique, perceptivity, listening, paraphrasing, and responsiveness. If you have time, repeat the process, playing the same role again or switching roles.

4. For one of the topics below, prepare examples of open, direct, leading, loaded, and closed questions. Assume you are conducting an information-getting interview.

a. current job
b. drug testing on the job or among athletes
c. nuclear energy
d. opinion of the president of the United States
e. tuition
f. sharing child-rearing responsibilities in two-income families
g. recreational interests

If circumstances allow, use your questions in interview role-plays. Analyze the effectiveness of different types of questions and the effect on the interview interaction.

5. Gather the data needed for an oral presentation by interviewing an expert on a topic related to your major or career interest. Apply the interview planning and conducting skills presented in this chapter. Here are some topic ideas and interviewee leads:
   a. corporate commitment to employee health fitness at a local business (interview a representative of a firm with an active and successful fitness program and in-house facilities)
   b. use of universal product code scanners at a nearby supermarket (interview supermarket manager)
   c. flexible work schedules at Metropolis Community Hospital (talk with director of nursing)
   d. inventory management at Gadzooks Industries (meet with vice-president of production)
   e. pros and cons of contingency fees in malpractice suits (interview lawyer with experience in this specialty)
6. Present a talk built on data collected in an interview with a business or professional person. Gather information about the history and operation of the organization in which the interviewee is a major part. The organization might be a large corporation, partnership, sole-owner business, hospital, community theater, or government agency such as your city's Department of Public Safety. To locate your interviewee, use your contacts—employers, parents, friends, and relatives. (For realistic interview interaction, do not interview friends and relatives.)

Tape the interview, if possible, and use audio excerpts in your presentation. Use presentations aids, too, if appropriate. (Get some samples of manufacturing materials or finished products. Take your camera and develop slides or photographs of interviewee, office and production facilities, products, and staff.)

In your interview, secure data on two dimensions of the organization: (1) its history—past, present, and future; and (2) all functional areas of operations—finance or funding, production, marketing, accounting, data processing, personnel, general management, economics, and so on. These sample questions will prime your planning process:

▶ When was the business (organization) founded? Under what circumstances?

- How much capital did you begin with?
- How do you obtain additional working capital?
- Is this your only location?
- How do you find employees?
- What are some of your operating problems (unions, government regulations, and so on)?
- What major changes in your products or services have occurred over the years?
- Are you planning to enlarge your operations or facilities in the next year or two?
- How do you advertise?

Some of this information is sensitive subject matter that your interviewee may be reluctant to discuss. If you work at planning and implementing your questioning strategy and building a high level of interview interaction, you might be surprised at the amount of cooperation and data you obtain for your presentation.

7. Evaluate the interview experience from Exercise Number 5 or 6 in a written report. Be truthful and frank in your assessment of your interview skills. The quality of your analysis and what you learned about the interviewing process are more important than whether the interview went well or not. Include the following in your analysis:
   a. Relevant background—who, when, where, and so on.
   b. Preparation for interview.
   c. Interview structure:
      (1) Nature of interview opening.
      (2) Content coverage and sequence.
      (3) Questioning strategy. For example: Was the interview directive, non-directive, or a combination? Did you and your subject ever switch interviewer/interviewee roles? Explain. What categories of questions did you use? Were secondary questions used? How? Did the questioning go smoothly and coherently?
      (4) Examples of question effectiveness and ineffectiveness. What factor(s) account for this?
      (5) Type of close.
   d. Judgment on levels of interview interaction reached. Was it predominantly Level 1, 2, or 3? Explain.
   e. Assessment of other interviewing skills—perceptivity, paraphrasing, listening, responsiveness.
   f. Unusual or interesting factors and illustration of their influence upon the interview.
   g. Overall evaluation of interview:
      (1) Personal perceptions and insights gained on interviewing.
      (2) Changes you would make if you were able to do the interview again.
8. Observe and evaluate a counseling interview. Secure permission to watch unobtrusively a counseling interview between an employee

and employer, instructor and student, marriage counselor and client, or psychologist and client, for instance. Discuss and critique the interviewer's:
   a. opening
   b. question and response pattern
   c. closing
   d. rapport with interviewee
   e. listening and paraphrasing skills
   f. nonverbal communication
9. Invite a salesperson to your home or office. Discuss and evaluate the same six points in Exercise 8 and share your reaction to the persuasive strategy used. If you are especially adventurous, you might experiment with some typical customer behaviors like nonresponsiveness, lack of decisiveness, or price resistance to determine the interviewer's response. Proceed carefully with this exercise or you may end up with a vacuum cleaner, encyclopedia, or new siding for your house!

Chapter 7

PLANNING SMALL GROUP COMMUNICATION

Do you like meetings? If you do, maybe you should be a CEO. John H. Bryan, Jr., chief executive officer of Sara Lee Corporation, logged 33½ hours of scheduled meetings in a typical 60-plus hour workweek. On Monday he scheduled his senior-managers' meeting as usual. In a small conference room near Bryan's office, this Monday's talk centered on weekly sales, product launches, and deals. At a board of directors' meeting later, he sought the okay to spend $600 million to add a new food company to Sara Lee. Late Monday, the acquisition team conferred with Bryan to plot strategy for the take-over. On Wednesday, he and senior vice-presidents had their quarterly meeting that he calls his "window on operations." Each manager takes his turn, and Bryan interrupts with questions. These were just the major meetings. Add plenty of impromptu meetings and business luncheons to get the full picture.[1]

You are not a high-powered top manager yet. Maybe your career path doesn't even include a lofty corporate position. But, if you are like most business and professional people, your schedule will contain its fair share of meetings. Meetings are unavoidable. But on the positive side, they are often the best way to carry out your job responsibilities.

Most of our emphasis so far has been on making a presentation to an audience in which the speaker controls the communication situation and interacts with the audience mainly through receiving feedback and answering their questions or on interviewing, one-on-one structured, goal-oriented conversation. In this chapter and the next, we move on to another important form of job communication—small group communication. Chapter 6 concentrates on the important role that small group communication plays in organizations and presents a systematic process for planning productive meetings and other forms of small group interaction. Specifically, we will:

- define small group communication,
- see how professionals and business people constructively use small group communication,
- expose disadvantages and misuses of small group communication,
- survey common types of small group interaction,
- explore the potential of a new alternative—teleconferencing,

---

1. "A Week in the Life of a CEO," *Business Week* Oct. 23, 1987: 46–49.

- examine a seven-step planning process for productive small group interaction,
- learn how to build an agenda.

SMALL GROUP COMMUNICATION DEFINED

Small group communication happens when several people engage in face-to-face interaction, working together toward a common goal. Ideally, "several people" means five to seven. Groups smaller than five often cannot develop an adequate information and talent pool to study an issue or make a decision. Groups bigger than seven do not allow maximum individual participation because members have to wait their turn to talk or respond. Or, individuals may hide, letting other people talk or volunteer. A small group is not an audience. Audiences are generally much larger groups with weaker goal orientation and group commitment.

In our definition face-to-face interaction means all group members are in the same space at the same time. Instant feedback and nonverbal communication are possible among group members. However, face-to-face interaction doesn't create a small group unless there is a common goal. Five people in a line to buy movie tickets discussing movie star gossip is not a group because the five people have no shared goal. If the theater sells out before their turn comes and they discuss other entertainment options for the evening, that's a small group since they now have a common goal.

People naturally seem to unite into small groups to work and play. To perform on-the-job tasks, business and professional people often prefer working in groups rather than individually. Perhaps you must make a decision. Instead of making the decision all by yourself, maybe with incomplete information or from your narrow personal perspective, you say, "Let's get the members of the department together for a staff meeting Thursday and discuss how to cut our budget ten percent." Such a group can examine the problem, input data from individual points of view, and, based on a large body of experience and information, work out a consensus decision.

Even if you make the final decision yourself, at least you have gotten involvement and feedback from your people. You know what your staff thinks and feels about this budget cut. You can factor this information into your own decision-making process. When you announce your decision, your staff members will be more likely to be receptive, understanding, and committed.

REASONS FOR WORKING IN SMALL GROUPS

Working together, whether it be a staff meeting, committee meeting, or workshop, can accomplish a variety of management and communication objectives. The following are valid reasons for small group interaction:

1. For discovering, analyzing, and solving a problem. Persons affected by a problem are brought together to share their experiences and give supporting or opposing information. From this data base, the leader and group participants can proceed through a systematic problem-solving process to arrive at conclusions and recommendations. Group interaction gives everyone who has a critical stake in the ultimate decision an opportunity to express a viewpoint. The resulting decision will probably reflect the wants and needs of the affected individuals better than if the decision were made solely by the boss.

2. To reconcile conflicting viewpoints. The meeting has replaced duels where two hundred years ago gentlemen of honor drew their pistols or swords to resolve differences. Fortunately, now most people with diverging points of view instead assemble for constructive discussion. Ideally, the contenders will work toward compromise or accommodation to relieve hostility and defuse a tense, unproductive work atmosphere. Group communication develops mutual understanding and creates empathy for other ways of looking at a problem. Give-and-take discussion brings misconceptions out into the open where they can be cleared up and where opposing views can be examined and perhaps reconciled.

3. To receive reports from individuals. Rather than merely distributing a written report, an executive may prefer to make an oral presentation to the intended readership. This small group presentation supplements the written report that everyone receives for further study or later reference. A speaker can relay information more emphatically, more convincingly, and in a more memorable fashion in a face-to-face setting. The speaker can use the force of her personality and enhance the message with nonverbal language. She may be able to use visual and other presentation aids more effectively than the purely graphic aids in a written report. The speaker can field questions and provide immediate responses.

Generally speaking, information that is presented in person seems to be more important or have greater impact on the listeners than written words in memorandums and reports. Bringing people together in a special meeting is a way to label the subject matter as more significant.

4. To obtain quick reactions. A small group leader can get reaction on the spot if the involved individuals are present to respond and give advice. In written communication, feedback is delayed because of the physical separation of the writer and the reader and perhaps by other distractions in the reader's environment. It may take hours or days to get back to the writer on the phone or in a memo. When the panic button is pushed and a decision must be made quickly, a common reaction is to call a meeting to get the participation of everyone involved with the least delay.

5. To train. Group sessions are used for orienting new staff members, to introduce a new procedure, or to present an idea or decision. This is more time-efficient than meeting with everyone one at a time.

6. To get around an administrative logjam. Say that a manager won't make a decision because it will be unpopular, it affects the manager personally or negatively, or it might create antagonism with co-workers. A way to bypass this reluctant decision-maker would be to set up a meeting to discuss the issue and act. In this way, the decision will be made by the group participants, not by one individual, who thus avoids having to absorb all the repercussions of an unpopular or difficult decision.

These six reasons show the considerable advantages of group communication in carrying out managerial responsibilities. So why does group interaction often have a negative connotation? Why are meetings something many business and professional people dread and avoid? The harried executive checks her appointment calendar and mutters, "That meeting of division heads is probably going to last the entire afternoon with precious few results to show for it. I'd be better off tending to business in my office." We'll look at how this dismal reputation developed in the next section.

Funky Winkerbean © 1988. Reprinted with special permission of NAS, Inc.

Meetings that are unplanned and ineffectively led are usually purposeless time-wasters.

THE OTHER SIDE OF SMALL GROUP COMMUNICATION

You have probably heard such disparaging remarks about meetings as these:

- "A committee is a gathering of the unfit appointed by the unwilling to do the unnecessary."
- "A conference is something at which, after all is said and done, more is said than is done."
- "A camel is a horse designed by a committee."

Despite such attitudes, executives are nonetheless spending 21 workweeks a year in meetings, according to a recent survey. Nearly a third of these meetings are considered a waste of time. This means the average executive, and probably the typical person in professional-level occupations, is spending almost 15 percent of his work time in unproductive small group communication! One respondent commented: "It's unfortunate, but calling a meeting has become a ritualized alternative to getting down to work."[2]

Somewhat tongue-in-cheek, an article from *The Wall Street Journal* suggests techniques that successful top managers use to cut meeting time while increasing meeting productivity.[3] For example, one executive conducts meetings in an office without chairs. He instituted this drastic practice when, in his words, "I realized that when people came into my office for a meeting, they would sit down with a cup of coffee, light up a cigarette, and get comfy.

---

2. "Survey: Meetings are Wasteful," *Management World,* Nov./Dec., 1986: 4.

3. Laurel Sorenson, "Time Wasted by Meetings Irks Business," *The Wall Street Journal,* Sept. 24, 1980: 23.

They had no reason to solve any problem quickly." When chairing a meeting, another executive keeps his wristwatch ready to time speakers and uses a buzzer to warn long-winded participants that they are monopolizing the group's time. Not surprisingly, he had to stop doing this because it was not a very popular or practical solution.

Other than this deservedly bad reputation and bad press, small group communication has other potentially serious problems that must be recognized and overcome.

Expense

One problem is expense. Meetings can get very costly, very quickly, considering the value received. When the personnel manager rounds up five subordinates for an hour-long staff meeting the first Tuesday of every month, the cost of their time may be surprising. For the sake of illustration, let's say their salaries average $25,000 annually. One hour of time for those six participants costs the company $144 in direct labor costs, as Figure 7–1 shows.

Consider the cost of a meeting with ten members, certainly not unusual, or a meeting that lasts for three or four hours, an all too-common occurrence. Worse, this is only half the dollar-and-cents picture. Indirect labor costs, such as payroll taxes, fringe benefits, general overhead, secretarial support for agenda preparation, distribution of the agenda, taking minutes, and each participant's preparation time, must all be added to the direct labor costs, as well as transportation time to and from the meeting.

FIGURE 7–1
Per Hour Direct Labor Cost of Group Interaction

Annual Salary	Number of Participants					
	8	7	6	5	4	3
$50,000	385	337	288	240	192	144
40,000	308	269	231	192	154	115
30,000	231	202	173	144	115	87
25,000	192	168	144	120	96	72
20,000	154	135	115	96	77	58

Source: Adapted from B. Y. Auger, *How to Run Better Business Meetings,* Minnesota Mining and Manufacturing Company, 1979: 19.

An easy-to-remember rule of thumb is that direct labor costs must be doubled to reflect the true meeting cost. So that monthly staff meeting is actually costing the business enterprise close to $300 per hour. Was $300 worth of value to the organization received from that staff meeting? Would the staff and company have been better off if no meeting had been held that month and each person had spent that hour on other job tasks?

In a well-run, necessary staff meeting, the answer, of course, would be "yes." Important information could be relayed and discussed, and departmental problems raised and perhaps settled. But such productivity is not a given and, unfortunately, may not be the norm.

Time Pressures

The next problem that commonly sabotages small group communication is time pressure. To expedite the flow of a meeting, group members often too willingly agree with each other just to speed up and shorten the meeting. They withhold important, relevant data so that they do not complicate the discussion anymore than it is already.

For example, Martha, attending the quarterly regional library directors' executive board meeting, looks at her watch and sighs. It's 3:45. This meeting has been going on for an hour and fifteen minutes. No end is in sight, and she has an appointment in her office at four. To shorten the meeting, she resorts to several potentially harmful tactics. She holds back her contributions. She stops commenting on her colleagues' facts and opinions. She casts her support to the bloc that will move the board to a decision and the meeting to an end. The meeting ends hastily at 4:05 with an unwise decision based on under-analyzed, incomplete data. Martha races to her four o'clock appointment.

Groupthink

Another factor can stifle discussion and hinder fully exploring the subject matter at hand. Groups bring pressure on individual members to conform with the expectations of the group because, by nature, groups want to agree. According to the "groupthink" theory, individual group members sometimes suspend careful, well-developed analysis in order to submit to the majority. The eight symptoms of groupthink are shown in Figure 7–2.

> **FIGURE 7–2**
>
> Groupthink Symptoms
>
> 1. *Invulnerability.* Members of the group share an mistaken sense of invulnerability. They feel their decisions cannot be wrong.
> 2. *Rationalization.* Victims of groupthink ignore warning signs. They collectively invent explanations to overlook negative feedback or justify their actions.
> 3. *Morality.* Group members believe unquestionably in the rightness of their decisions. They fail to consider any potential negative consequences.
> 4. *Stereotypes.* Group thinkers hold easily discounted views of people and situations. For example: "You know how our engineers are. They'd tinker with the design for years to get it perfected if we'd let them."
> 5. *Pressure.* Direct pressure is applied by the leader or group members to anyone who expresses doubts about the group's objectives. They make comments like "Let's not upset the apple cart," withdraw eye contact, move away from the problem person, or stop listening to encourage that person to re-establish harmony.
> 6. *Self-censorship.* To maintain harmony, groupthinkers conform and do not voice their misgivings and doubts.
> 7. *Unanimity.* Self-censorship leads to an illusion of unanimity when some members still have doubts.
> 8. *Mindguards.* Like bodyguards, members protect the leader and fellow members from adverse information that could cause the group to question its actions.
>
> *Source:* Adapted from Gene E. Burton, "The Group Process: Key to More Productive Management," *Management World,* May, 1981: 12–15.

For instance, some group members may not speak their minds for fear of disagreeing with a higher-status person. They may back off from group members who have more forceful, assertive personalities, even though the ideas these people are proposing are half-baked. Thus, for more timid individuals, avoiding conflict and promoting the appearance of agreement become more important than carefully considering the alternatives or achieving the correct solution.

Hidden Agendas

Finally, conflicting secondary goals may harm group interaction. Suppose the group's primary task is to find a solution to a given problem. As different solutions are suggested, judged, and criticized, some group members become more devoted to supporting a specific or favored position than achieving the best solution. A group member may have a hidden agenda, an ulterior motive or personal interest to which he or she is dedicated at the expense of full exploration of the issues. Often in response, the group resorts to bargaining, which produces a compromise solution that may be ineffective and have little real support from the members.

The benefits of small group communication are not guaranteed. Cost, time pressures, groupthink, and hidden agendas are problems that can compromise many of the advantages of group communication. When properly used, though, small group communication can be a powerful tool for building rapport and loyalty, solving problems, and making decisions.

TYPES OF SMALL GROUP INTERACTION

As a business person or professional, you will have many opportunities to capitalize on the advantages of small group communication in your day-to-day work. Here are the five major types of small group interactions you will encounter:

1. Staff meeting. The most common type of meeting, a staff meeting, brings together people who normally work together, a superior and subordinates usually. An office manager may conduct periodic staff meetings with the ten employees in the department. At a higher level, the president of a corporation may meet monthly with the firm's five senior vice-presidents. Staff meetings are used to present information that everyone in that organizational unit needs to know, to resolve problems affecting the unit as a whole, and to plan and coordinate individual tasks.

If the leader practices participative management techniques, the staff may make decisions through group consensus at these meetings. Or, he may seek input on critical matters that affect the organizational unit and later reach a decision on his own. This may be because the manager practices a more autocratic management style or because company regulations or other circumstances discourage delegating decision making to the group.

2. Committee. Also very frequently used, a committee is generally comprised of people brought together to carry out a special task. These individuals normally do not work closely together. They may be in different departments or locations or have job responsibilities that do not overlap. Each committee member has expert knowledge or a special point of view that is needed for accomplishing the committee's purpose, a purpose which cuts across the normal channels of management responsibility and communication. Some committees are permanent, standing committees charged to develop or carry out policy over a period of time. Other committees are temporary or ad hoc committees formed to resolve some particular issue and then disbanded.

An ad hoc committee might consist of six people, who function as a task force to study record storage and retrieval and recommend an up-to-date, cost-efficient records management system. To assure that all critical segments of the organization are included, the committee includes executives from each management area—one from research and development, engineering, production, sales and marketing, personnel, and general administration. Each committee member thus has a unique understanding of the filing demands of his or her specific staff. This increases the likelihood that each segment's special needs will be served by the records management system that is proposed by the committee.

3. Training or instructional conference. Obviously, this group's purpose is to inform or instruct through use of appropriate group strategies. Once the new records management system is installed, for instance, members of each organizational unit might participate in a training session conducted by the records manager on filing and accessing electronically stored records using desktop terminals and video displays.

4. Consultative conference. Here the group leader consults, counsels, or advises in a small group setting. Maybe a manager needs to make an important decision but wants to solicit data, viewpoints, and preferences from several persons. These people can be called together in a consultative conference to research the problem. With consideration of each member's input, the manager makes the decision.

5. Multiple-agenda meeting. These are larger, longer, generally more important conferences where participants are involved in numerous small and large group meetings with individual agendas and purposes. Multiple-agenda meetings in many ways are really a big meeting composed of many small meetings. Multiple-agenda meetings frequently consist of several large group general sessions that everyone attends. These sessions are characterized by more formal, large group interaction, such as lectures and panel discussions. Conference members also attend small group sessions aimed at participants with specialized interests or needs.

The annual state meeting of a professional press journalism association would fall into this category. So might a three-day conference for sales representatives held in Kansas City to introduce Neptune Enterprise's new line of electronic, "smart" telephones. A session with speakers from top management opens the sales conference. Most of the other meetings, however, are small group sessions designed to train the representatives in using and selling the new phones.

In all these group interactions, each participant is physically together in the same meeting space with the other participants. Teleconferencing is another form of small group communication that brings group members together using telecommunication equipment. Although meeting members are not in the same location, teleconferencing permits small group communication because instant feedback and perception of nonverbal communication are possible.

TELECONFERENCING

Since the Picturephone was introduced at the 1964 World's Fair by American Telephone and Telegraph, travel-weary business people and professionals have dreamed about the convenience of conducting business meetings over long distances on television screens. But high prices, fuzzy picture quality, and a hard-to-overcome resistance to any substitute for face-to-face meetings have delayed this dream from coming true. Now, with lower prices, improved video transmission equipment, and praises from early users, teleconferencing is coming into its own.

Teleconferencing uses telecommunication technology to bring participants together in an interactive group setting at a smaller cost in both time and money. Video, audio, and computer equipment is used to link meeting members through telephone lines and satellites in two or more locations.

Three main types of teleconferencing exist. In computer teleconferencing, the meeting is conducted from computer terminals that the meeting participants use to receive and transmit their print-based messages. Audio teleconferencing, which is the form of the common conference call, provides two-way audio connections with no picture transmission.

Video teleconferencing goes a step farther and completely fulfils the definition of small group communication. It provides two-way audio and video connections, so meeting members both hear and see one another. Conferees gather in specially equipped rooms outfitted with cameras, microphones, and monitors for full-motion picture and sound transmission (see Figure 7–3). Actually, you can do almost anything by video teleconferencing that you can do in a face-to-face meeting. Copyboard, transparency, slide, and document-facsimile transmission are possible with additional equipment.

Sears, Roebuck and Company installed a full-motion videoconferencing network in 1985 connecting 26 United States cities. Exxon, Xerox, IBM, J. C. Penney, and Boeing Company are other companies making the commitment to teleconferencing. Total costs per site average under $350,000 and prices are dropping quickly. Transportable room modules and desktop units will soon be available for $15,000 or so. Public teleconferencing—in which customers use teleconferencing facilities rented for a specific time period—is the answer for organizations that cannot justify the financial investment themselves. One major supplier is Hilton Hotels, which built a 35-site public network.[4]

The major advantage of teleconferencing is savings in travel costs and inconvenience. Aetna Life and Casualty Insurance Company estimated that 3,000 meetings took place in its teleconferencing facilities during its first year of operation, saving staff time worth approximately $327,000 that would have been spent in transportation to and from meeting sites. The four conference rooms cost $940,000 to outfit, but the system will pay for itself within three years.

An Aetna corporate communication manager said: "Before the system, when we had meetings [in Hartford, Chicago, or San Francisco], executives would fly out, meet over dinner, spend the night and return on the following day. That was two whole days lost, and now we only spend the actual time in the meeting." Even the ambience of a dinner meeting can be maintained by occasionally catering a meal in both conference rooms.[5]

Teleconferencing does have some drawbacks, even if the savings in travel outweigh equipment costs. Many people are camera-shy. They are intimidated by the television camera. They stiffen up and lose much of their communication effectiveness. Others just miss the travel and resist teleconferencing for that reason.

---

4. "Videoconferencing: No Longer Just a Sideshow," *Business Week,* Nov. 12, 1984: 116–120.

5. "Teleconferencing Reduces Cost at Aetna," *U. S. News and World Report,* March, 1984 (special section): S12–S14.

190 Chapter 7–Planning Small Group Communication

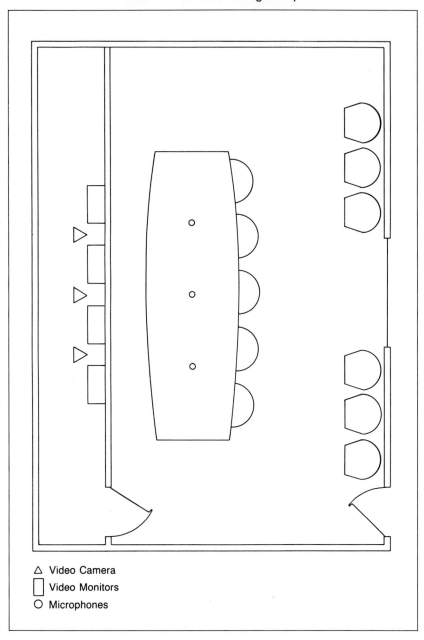

FIGURE 7–3

Video Teleconferencing Setup

△ Video Camera
☐ Video Monitors
○ Microphones

Also, some experts claim that teleconferencing increases the number of meetings and involves people who would not otherwise participate.

Although it is tough to put a dollar value on teleconferencing, users have discovered that video meetings can speed up the decision-making cycle. As fright, intimidation, and novelty disappear and are replaced by acceptance, familiarity and even dependence, perhaps teleconferencing will become comfortable enough to the meeting participants that they may forget they were brought together technologically. When that happens, video meetings might become just another option when planning a meeting.

PLANNING A MEETING

Meetings that accomplish their objectives are not lucky accidents; these group encounters are products of forethought and conscientious planning by group leaders and, to a lesser extent, by group participants. Like most human endeavors, a systematic approach simplifies the planning process of a meeting, saves time and effort in the long run, and puts in place all the required elements before the meeting starts.

"Should a meeting be called?" is the first big question that must be settled. Much of the negative reputation of meetings is due to their overuse. Therefore, a meeting planner must think carefully before calling a meeting. Maybe it's not warranted. Six valid reasons for small group interaction have already been cited; here are reasons *not* to call a meeting:

1. when a telephone, telegram, letter, or memo will produce the desired results,
2. when the leader and participants do not have enough time to prepare,
3. when key participants are not available,
4. when the meeting will likely be unsuccessful because of clashing personalities,
5. when the anticipated results do not justify the time and expense to hold the meeting.

Assuming that a meeting is necessary, what steps should be followed to set it up? Of course, the degree of complexity differs considerably for different kinds of group encounters, as does the

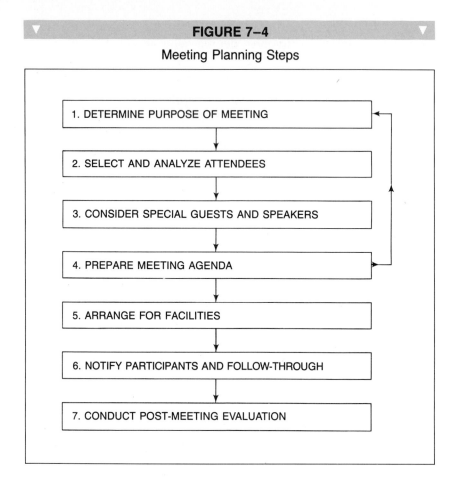

FIGURE 7-4

Meeting Planning Steps

amount of planning time. While the planning for the monthly staff meeting may be routine and delegated to an executive assistant, a three-day management retreat may require two months of planning and over one hundred hours of labor by several people.

Regardless, the same planning techniques are used. Model your meeting planning after the seven-part planning process that experienced meeting planners use (see Figure 7-4). Adapt it to fit the purpose, complexity, size, and length of your group encounter.

Step One: Determine the Meeting's Purpose

The meeting planner's first job is to state a purpose in specific, action-oriented terms that will unify the group members into a work team and focus them on a group goal. Remember, working toward common goals is an identifying characteristic of small group communication. A management retreat's goal could develop this way: "Re-examine the Consumer Appliance Division's five-year long-range product design strategy, revise it for three new product roll-outs, and build the management team's commitment to achieving the new strategy."

The rest of the planning consists of getting the time, people, and facilities required to carry out meeting objectives. The final evaluation of the meeting involves deciding how well these objectives were achieved.

Step Two: Select and Analyze the Participants

The meeting's purpose, of course, is accomplished through the dynamic interaction of the right participants. First, invite only those people whose presence is required to carry out your group objective(s). Running a meeting and meeting its goals is more efficient if the group is smaller. It is also less expensive. Recall how quickly true meeting costs mount up when the expense of each participant's time is considered. Limit the number of attendees, but make sure to invite all key people:

1. who have important information to contribute,
2. whose approval may be needed at the meeting,
3. who will carry out the decisions that are reached.

Second, study the roster of people you have invited. Ask yourself questions like these about the attendees: What is an individual's relationship to the subject matter of the meeting? What is his or her knowledge and interest level? As a group, are the members receptive or hostile, informed or uninformed, motivated or apathetic? Have the attendees worked together before? What are their work relationships? Is there a common goal or interest that can be appealed to in order to forge a sense of group loyalty and motivation?

Step Three: Determine What Additional Resources Are Required

Next, the meeting planner looks beyond the group's purposes and its members to determine what special expertise, presentation aids, and equipment will be needed to carry out the group's objectives. You might have to invite guests and speakers who have in-depth knowledge and practical experience on the subject matter. Enlarging the group's membership and bringing in outsiders with fresh perspectives are tactics that combat groupthink. Special guests and speakers, especially those coming from out of town, may entail additional complications, such as advance travel arrangements, lodging, cost reimbursement, and professional fees.

In planning the training session on using the new electronic records management system, the records manager will need to make arrangements for a vendor representative to be there. Also she decides to invite her counterpart from another firm in the area to give suggestions to the trainees based on his experience in smoothly and quickly adjusting to the new system. The record manager decides that a set of visual aids should be designed and produced to acquaint system users with the capabilities of the new records management system, examples of storing and retrieving data in the data banks, access passwords, special keyboard codes, and so on. She will work with the company's graphics department to produce these transparencies that she will use in her part of the training session.

Step Four: Prepare a Meeting Agenda

The agenda is the plan for the group's interaction and a timetable for all activities. A good agenda gives a meeting a logical, well-unified structure. Topics, speakers, and group interaction techniques are arranged in the best sequence to give the meeting forward movement. The conference leader uses the agenda to keep on track and to manage time to complete intended goals efficiently.

Conference participants use the agenda to plan and prepare, too. It is usually sent to the meeting participants in advance so they can clear their calendars for the meeting and, if necessary, make travel and other arrangements. For either background or for presentation, the participants may need to gather data from files, review and organize it, develop speaking notes and presentation aids, and so forth.

In Figure 7–4, you noticed a loop from step four back to step one. This point in the process of planning a meeting is a good time to evaluate, assess, and analyze before going any farther. Have you planned the right activities to accomplish your objectives? Do all the meeting activities directly and defensibly contribute to accomplishing the meeting's goals? Anything that does not clearly move toward the meeting's goals is a time-waster and a distraction. Drop such activities from the meeting's agenda. Your analysis may indicate that agenda items may have to be added, another group approach substituted, or another expert guest invited.

Agenda planning is challenging. You are dealing with human beings engaged in a complex, ever-changing, and dynamic communication process. A background of experience certainly helps when designing an agenda for a meeting, especially an important one. We'll look more at agenda construction at the end of this chapter. For the meantime, let's assume your planning is going along well enough for you to move to the next step.

Step Five: Arrange for Meeting Facilities

As far as the meeting environment goes, skilled meeting managers plan in advance down to the last detail, leaving nothing to chance. Productive meetings are held in attractive, conducive, well-equipped surroundings. Everything is pre-planned and on hand before the group assembles.

If the roster is very small, the meeting can be held in a group member's office, or a company conference room can be reserved. More important, more formal, or larger meetings may even be housed in special, off-site meeting facilities. This means checking potential meeting sites, negotiating with hotel/restaurant personnel, and overseeing the preparation of the meeting site. Specifically, the following meeting environment details must be resolved:

▶ **Meeting room(s)** Consider these factors: The facilities should be the appropriate size. You don't want members of a small meeting feeling lost and detached in a cavernous, arena-sized space, nor do you want members of a larger meeting feeling like they are squeezed into a stuffy little box. Comfortable seating should be available that can be arranged depending on the type of group interaction desired. If needed, tables should be provided.

Planning for the physical comfort of the conferees dictates investigating ventilation, heating, air conditioning, lighting, restroom facilities, and provisions for handling the needs of handicapped attendees. Also, check to see if the space is appropriate for using any intended presentation aids—light control, screens, and electrical outlets, for example.

▶ **Equipment** If audio-visual equipment will be used, plan accordingly. Equipment may be provided by the speaker, your organization, or rented from the conference facility. Make sure that the equipment will be available when needed, that it has been set up, and that it has been tested. Thought should be given to little things, like writing pads, pencils, and ashtrays. Speaking of ashtrays, will smoking be permitted? If so, how will it be controlled to avoid irritating non-smokers?

▶ **Banquet and lodging facilities** If the meeting lasts more than a half day, meals become a planning consideration. Are people on their own for dining or do you want to serve meals? If meals are part of the planned activities, menu planning, food preparation, and serving must be arranged. For an even longer meeting with out-of-town participants, sleeping accommodations are necessary. Arrangements with hotels or motels must be made, either by the meeting planner for the entire group or by each participant for his or her individual needs.

Step Six: Notify and Follow-Through with Participants

In a short, routine meeting situation, this step consists of simply sending a brief memo containing the agenda and meeting details. Give ample lead time so that each attendee has a chance to prepare. On the other hand, if a meeting requires out-of-town travel or will extend for several days, this step becomes more complicated. A letter or memo including invitation and details along with enclosures, like agenda and travel arrangement details, should be sent weeks in advance.

Step Seven: Conduct Post-Meeting Analysis

Although this step is done after the meeting is over, post-meeting analysis is nevertheless an important planning step, mainly to improve similar meetings in the future. Even the best planned, best conducted meeting will have shortcomings, flaws that can be eliminated next time around. Look back at step one objectives and judge how well they were fulfilled. With perfect 20/20 hindsight, you will see improvements or changes that will make future meetings even more productive.

For example, you think, "Next time we will have mid-morning and mid-afternoon coffee breaks so the attendees can move about and relax more. Two tough, long work sessions in a row was too much." Or, "I didn't exercise adequate control over the agenda, and we ran 15 minutes over time. I must manage time better at the next meeting."

Your impressions, though, can be biased and incomplete. For especially important meetings, you might want to get reaction to the group encounter from the participants through a brief questionnaire. Request their evaluation of the meeting's objectives, speakers, group techniques, meeting facilities, and so on. Another way to solicit feedback is to ask several participants in person or over the phone for their candid reactions. With this learning-from-experience orientation, a meeting manager can learn from past mistakes and, quite likely, avoid them the next time.

MORE ON AGENDA PLANNING

Good agenda planning results in time saved, not time wasted, and goes a long way to overcoming the major problems with too many meetings—lack of commitment, little focus, and few results. These three tips will guide you in designing a first-rate agenda:

1. Break down the total block of time into smaller blocks of time, each with specific subgoals leading to a major goal. In this way, you develop the parts in relationship to the whole. It is less frightening to plan an eight-hour workshop when you think of it as having four separate parts with subgoals. Furthermore, it makes time management easier. You give speakers and topics specific time limits. Thus, you can keep time allocation and subject matter emphasis where it ought to be.

2. Build variety into your meeting plans. The longer the program, the more important this suggestion becomes. To prevent an endurance marathon, punctuate a longer meeting with coffee breaks or break-out sessions. Allow participants to stretch their legs, get refreshments, and talk informally. It's basic human nature: People have short attention spans. They become restless after sitting too long or being engaged in one activity too long. Attendees appreciate a snack or want to visit the restroom. These change-of-pace activities do not waste meeting time. They heighten the general interest and energy level of the men and women involved in the group interaction. They enhance the likelihood of a successful meeting.

Another thing you can do is choose a good mix of group interaction techniques. Chapter 8 presents your small group interaction options. In a longer or more stressful meeting, variety in the way group members accomplish their objectives and communicate with each other will recharge participant involvement and interest.

3. Deliberately build some leeway into the time schedule. If the meeting begins to run behind, whether due to circumstances within or beyond your control, there will be some room for flexibility. One purpose of coffee breaks, in addition to their obvious primary benefit, is that they can be shortened or lengthened when necessary. Shortening a 30-minute break to 15 minutes will probably not have a big effect on the participants, but it will allow the meeting leader to make up some lost time. If you load up every minute of the meeting, flexibility is sharply reduced. Having painted yourself into a corner like this, it may take a major reshuffling of your plans to salvage the meeting's effectiveness.

For many kinds of small group communication, especially staff, committee, and consultative meetings, the agenda format guide shown in Figure 7–5 will help strengthen your meeting planning and give you a good guide to follow during the meeting. It shows

FIGURE 7–5
Meeting Agenda Format

Date: _____
Time: _____
Location: _____
Roster: Responsible for items:
1. _____   _____
2. _____   _____
3. _____   _____
4. _____   _____

Approx. Time		Item	Decision	Person Respons.	Deadline
_____	1.	_____	_____	_____	_____
		Points to consider:			
		a. _____			
		b. _____			
		c. _____			
_____	2.	_____	_____	_____	_____
		Points to consider:			
		a. _____			
		b. _____			
		c. _____			
_____	3.	_____	_____	_____	_____
		Points to consider:			
		a. _____			
		b. _____			
		c. _____			

Source: Adapted from R. Alex MacKenzie and Billie Sorensen, "It's About Time . . . ," *The Secretary*, Nov. 1979: 12.

when and where the meeting is, who should attend, and what the major items of business are. Spaces for recording decisions, responsibility assignments, and deadlines are built right into the form. These spaces will be filled in as the meeting progresses. Record-keeping like this increases the likelihood that action will be taken, responsibility for follow-through will be assigned to a specific accountable person, and that a date for action will be agreed on. The finished form may also serve as a guide when preparing minutes of a meeting.

SUMMING UP

Small group communication occurs when several people, usually five to seven, engage in working toward a common goal using face-to-face interaction. Small group communication is used to discover, analyze, or solve on-the-job problems; reconcile divergent points of view; receive reports from individuals; obtain immediate feedback and quick reactions; instruct or orient; and circumvent a reluctant decision-maker.

Considering all the potential value of small group communication, meetings have developed a rather questionable reputation. Several problem areas must be dealt with successfully for small group communication to achieve its promise. Meetings are expensive when direct and indirect labor costs of all participants are calculated. Often the value of small group communication does not justify the costs. Time pressures may cause group members to agree readily with the majority or to withhold important information to expedite a meeting. Group members are susceptible to the "groupthink" phenomenon in which they suspend careful, thoughtful analysis to avoid conflict, instead promoting an illusion of agreement. Some participants may have hidden agendas to which they are personally committed at the expense of group objectives.

The most common and routine of the five major types of small group interaction is the staff meeting, which brings together members of an organizational or work unit to present information, coordinate individual responsibilities, and resolve mutual problems. Committees bring together persons who usually do not work together to undertake a special task, either of a permanent or temporary nature. Training and consultative conferences are two more types. Multiple-agenda meetings are larger, longer conferences in which the participants engage in a series of small and large group meetings with individual agendas and purposes.

No longer do business and professional people have to travel to one conference room to engage in these group encounters. Teleconferencing, especially videoconferencing, uses telecommunication hardware to bring participants together at less cost and with little sacrifice of the interactive group atmosphere.

Productive, efficient small group interaction requires careful planning. Use a seven-part planning process adapted to the purpose, length, complexity, and size of the group encounter. 1) Determine the meeting's purpose specifically. 2) Select and analyze the attendees. 3) Determine what additional resources, such as special guests, presentation aids, and equipment, are needed. 4) Prepare the meeting agenda to give the group encounter a logical structure and timetable. Well-run meetings are broken down into manageable, smaller time blocks providing a mix of small group techniques to maintain participant interest and freshness. 5) Select meeting facilities. Arrange for an appropriately sized and outfitted conference room. Longer meetings may require meal planning, banquet facilities, and sleeping accommodations for attendees. 6) Announce meeting to participants and send them the agenda. 7) After the group encounter, conduct a post-meeting analysis to ensure even more successful small group communication at future similar meetings.

Chapter 8

USING SMALL GROUP COMMUNICATION

A successful meeting requires the two *Rs*—*rapport* and *results*. A friendly, interactive meeting without results wastes each participant's time. Long-lasting, worthwhile outcomes seldom result from meetings without an established rapport. Chapter 7 presented half of the building blocks for harmonious, productive meetings: an understanding of small group dynamics, systematic meeting planning, and agenda building. This chapter presents the other half: the knowledge and skills that meeting planners need in order to become meeting implementers. In this chapter, you will learn how to:

- select and use the appropriate kind of small group interaction to build rapport and accomplish meeting goals,
- put a problem-solving process to work in meetings to achieve desired results in the least time,
- apply effective leadership skills,
- contribute positively as a member of a small group.

GROUP PROCESS TECHNIQUES

Business people and professionals have plenty of opportunities to use group process techniques, methods of interacting and communicating in small groups. Unfortunately, it is easy to resort to worn-out and limited techniques. Lecturing is often wrongly used with small groups. The lecture—the platform speaking situation in which one speaker presents information on a subject to listeners—is a large group technique that *can* be ideal for giving information to people efficiently. The problem with lecturing is the one-speaker-to-audience orientation. A small group is not an audience. An effective small group leader aims to maximize member communication, involvement, and commitment as the group strives to complete its task. However, the prospects for such interaction are limited using the lecture format. A lecturer is set off from the audience, which is made up of primarily listeners, not contributors or doers.

Fortunately, when you are in charge of on-the-job small group situations, you have many group process techniques from which to choose. And, when you are a group member, you make the leader's job easier and the group more productive if you are familiar with the group process being used. As a leader, you will probably choose the small group technique. You decide based on time/space factors and the group's purpose, size, and composition.

With what techniques of group interaction should you be comfortable (or at least acquainted)? Although not an exhaustive list, this section examines group process techniques for gathering and analyzing data, solving problems, making decisions, informing, instructing, and persuading.

Group Discussion

The most often used and probably most familiar small group process is group discussion. Commonly used in staff and committee meetings, the leader, probably the manager of the work team or the chairperson, defines the subject or problem which is the group's focus. Group members then participate in a discussion to exchange information, criticize and evaluate, or thrash out a problem, often using a formalized problem-solving procedure. (More on managing group discussion and using problem-solving techniques follows.)

The group leader may read the consensus of the group (judge what the majority believes), the determination of which becomes the basis for making policy. She may even ask for a formal vote. Another option is polling members one at a time, asking them for their final reactions. Both approaches risk reducing group unity. Participants may break into two camps—for and against. In cases where decision making cannot be delegated to the group, the group leader will make the final decision after considering the group's input.

Nominal Grouping Technique

Even with a skilled and perceptive leader, the group discussion approach can stifle creative and innovative thinking in ways we examined in Chapter 7. Group members defer to others with greater status or more forceful personalities. Group members sometimes feel pressure to fit the mold. By conforming to the group consensus, some members stop participating in the discussion and evaluation process.

A self-evaluating process begins; participants judge their own contributions based on an internal perception of their own competency, not based on the value of the idea. When this happens, minority viewpoints that can be especially insightful, unique, or creative are lost. Participants limit their participation according to their perception of their status in the group. It is a rare subordinate who would feel confident to enter into a free-wheeling group discussion on an equal level with the boss.

Nominal grouping technique (NGT) combats many of these harmful tendencies of group interaction by deliberately reducing the group members' physical interaction. NGT is a highly structured method of group interaction. A low-profile leader guides the group participants through the five NGT steps:

1. Idea listing. After the leader has carefully outlined the problem at hand, everyone, working independently, prepares a list of ideas in response to the problem. By beginning with an individual writing process, each person is unaffected by other group members and has time to think ideas through logically.

2. Recording. Each group member offers ideas in turn to the group leader, who records all ideas on a master list on a chalkboard or other visual aid.

3. Preliminary voting. All members vote on their preferences as to the best ideas on the master list, with respect to their priority, cost-effectiveness, or some other criterion. For example, participants may be asked to list their preferences in order of practicality for five proposed solutions. They vote on a 5, 4, 3, 2, 1 basis (assigning five points for the most practical idea, four points for the next most practical idea, and so on). The results are tallied, and the scores posted on the master list. Notice that during the first three steps, no verbal interaction has taken place, except to explain or clarify.

4. Discussion. The group leader moderates a focused discussion of the items on the master list. As in any other group discussion, members explain, develop, clarify, and advocate their viewpoints. On the master list, ideas are revised, combined, deleted, or added. The leader tries for equal participation from everyone.

5. Final voting. Group members vote a second time, again ranking ideas on some criterion of acceptability using the 5, 4, 3, 2, 1 format. Revealing the final results, the group leader can adopt the winning proposal. Or, having secured group ideas and preferences, the group leader can make the final decision in consideration of the group's input.

If the group is large, let's say 20 or more, the leader usually divides the entire group into subgroups of 5 to 7 for Steps 1, 2, and 3. The entire group is convened for Steps 4 and 5.

Because Step 1 permits time to think ideas through and Step 3 gives a first impression about the whole group's reception to their ideas, participants have more confidence in the more valid ideas and feel more secure in defending them. For instance, an idea Sarah volunteered hesitantly in Step 1 no longer seems so outlandish because it ranked high in Step 3s preliminary voting. Sarah speaks up confidently, knowing the idea received a strong initial group reaction.

Brain-storming

Unlike NGT, brain-storming is a very unstructured, free-wheeling way to encourage fresh thinking. Think of brain-storming as *directed daydreaming.* In brain-storming sessions everyone thinks out loud. Participants throw out off-the-top-of-the-head ideas as quickly as possible.

Someone writes the ideas on a chalkboard, transparency, or flip chart. Keeping ideas on view encourages contribution. Seeing the idea in black and white makes the contributor feel good, too. Yet at the same time, when placed on public display, the idea becomes the group's property. No judging or criticism of ideas is permitted yet. At this point, premature criticism would have an inhibiting effect on participants. Evaluating too soon censors expression of novel ideas or problem-solving approaches.

Brain-storming sessions are characterized by loose, informal leadership. Leadership may change several times during the session. If the atmosphere is free and uninhibited, a spontaneous stream of ideas flows. One person's ideas spark another's thinking—participants leap-frog on other group members' ideas.

Time is usually limited. Subtle pressure seems to spur creativity. The goal is to produce ideas in quantity, and quantity breeds quality. From the long list of ideas, the brain-stormers will be able to cull several original, imaginative, innovative, and workable approaches. The hits will be pursued further during a separate analysis and evaluation stage.

For example, a marketing manager might use a brain-storming session to determine ways to increase the sales volume of the company's line of frozen dinners. Some of these ideas might emerge from a brain-storming session with the marketing staff and other company representatives: Cut prices 10 percent. Advertise dinners as light cuisine because many consumers are weight- and nutrition-conscious. Cut prices 20 percent. Consumers of frozen entrees often dine alone, so include a page of light reading in the box to amuse the diner. Keep the same print and media ads but increase the advertising budget 25 percent to hit more prospective buyers. Cut prices 30 percent. Package assorted dinners in six-packs at a 10 percent lower price. Enclose 50 cents discount coupons with each dinner usable on a repeat purchase. Cut prices 40 percent. The brain-stormers joke and laugh a lot. That's a good sign. Productive brain-storming sessions have a relaxed, humorous, free-wheeling atmosphere.

Close your eyes and daydream about this problem. What other unique, creative approaches can you think of? Some of the suggestions may be far-fetched, impractical, even facetious. Some ideas, though, may bubble to the surface that would not have been thought of otherwise. These ideas can be plugged into the evaluation step of a problem-solving procedure for further scrutiny.

Question-and-Answer Session

In a question-and-answer session, there is no formal presentation other than a short introduction or briefing. The bulk of the meeting consists of group members asking questions and one or more experts responding to them. Through this focused questioning/answering process, information can be exchanged and clarified.

The caliber of communication in this group process, of course, depends on the quality of the questions and responses. To successfully take part in a Q & A session, you might want to review the suggestions for handling questions and formulating responses in Chapter 4.

Round-Table Discussion

Interacting in a large group is cumbersome and sometimes ineffective. Since only one person can speak or participate at a time, the potential for interaction is limited. To bring some of the advantages of small group communication into a large group situation, use round-table discussion, sometimes called buzz groups. To multiply the opportunities for involvement, divide a large group into smaller groups of five to ten people that then meet simultaneously in a large room or separate rooms. Each small group's goals might be discussion, brain-storming, or problem-solving. The entire large group reconvenes, and a spokesperson from each buzz group shares the results of their small group interaction.

Role Playing

Role playing is a group process that is especially useful in personnel training and development for learning how to use more effective forms of behaving or interacting in job situations. Role playing creates simulations of face-to-face encounters in which the participants put themselves into make-believe situations. Members of a role play are usually given written role descriptions and a brief outline of the setting to study in advance. They then role play the fictitious situation through to resolution using the new form of behavior they are learning.

The role players often perform before the rest of the group. The spectators then critique behavior and offer suggestions for improved interaction. Frequently, the role plays are videotaped for evaluation by the participants themselves. The role play might be repeated so that the participants can improve the way they interact using this feedback. The participants may change roles. This way, they gain a better understanding of the other person's perspective.

Role playing is a valuable technique for experimenting with new patterns of behavior. Participants can practice them in a non-threatening, relatively risk-free environment. When comfortable, they can begin using their improved behavior patterns on the job. Role plays might reenact interactions between supervisor and employee, interviewer and interviewee, or salesperson and customer. Role playing can be used to develop leadership abilities, communication skills, decision-making abilities, planning skills, and how to give or receive criticism.

Case Study

The case study method is very common in higher education and is used in on-the-job training. Members of the case study group analyze written descriptions of realistic problem situations, often based on actual events. Using a problem-solving approach, they act as a management or consulting team. The group identifies and studies the problem illustrated in the case, evaluates options, and makes decisions. Finally, they formulate plans to implement and evaluate the recommended solution.

Knowing something from reading or from a lecture is not the same thing as *doing* something with it. Group members use case analysis to bridge the gap from merely understanding abstract theoretical knowledge to applying it in realistic job situations. Feeling more comfortable and capable about putting their knowledge to work, case study group members are more likely to transfer their knowledge to on-the-job situations.

Games and Simulations

Games and simulations can be used to accomplish training objectives. Participants (players) simulate a real-life situation in a competitive atmosphere. Like case studies, games and simulations develop problem-solving and decision-making skills, but the environment is more realistic and interactive. They teach the participants how to devise practical applications based on textbook knowledge.

More and more, games and simulations involve computers. Players input data on decisions using a terminal or personal computer. The computer manipulates variables in a computer program model that mimics as much as possible the real-world situation. The results of the game players' decisions are then printed out or displayed, and the next round of decision-making or problem-solving begins. Economic decision-making or designing and carrying out a marketing plan could be practiced this way.

Summarizing Group Process Techniques

After looking at eight group process techniques, aren't there many more ways of working with small groups of colleagues, employees, customers, clients, and so on than you thought at first? Some techniques are more time-consuming and unfamiliar than others. When using less familiar group processes, like nominal grouping technique or role playing, you may need to train your group first. The results, however, are worth it if freer, more equal group interaction produces better results.

When using group process techniques as a small group leader, remember these suggestions. 1) Become more flexible in your approach to small group communication—be more adventuresome and experiment. 2) Develop skill in using as many as possible. Then you will be able to choose the single technique or combination of techniques to build group commitment and fulfil group objectives most successfully. 3) Use techniques with well-chosen, well-produced, and well-used presentation aids for maximum returns.

PROBLEM-SOLVING PROCESS

Meetings and group process techniques play an important part in identifying and solving on-the-job problems, as you have already seen. Through your own experience and observation, you have discovered that there's more than one way to solve a problem. Indeed, management experts have developed a number of problem-solving techniques. Each is invariably better than an unfocused, hit-or-miss approach. Managers and other professionals usually take a solid problem-solving formula and, through experience and use, hone it to a high level of usefulness for their particular needs.

Six Steps in Good Problem Solving

Because problem solving is a fundamental purpose of small group activity, let's examine one problem-solving procedure (diagrammed in Figure 8-1) that is logical, structured, yet adaptable, and then see how it would be used in an on-the-job situation. The group leader usually guides the problem-solving team through these steps:

1. Identify problem. Many times no one clearly understands the problem. Some group members may have a fuzzy grasp of the problem. Other members may define the problem differently or have an opposite view of its severity. Some members of the group may not even perceive the situation as a problem. The first step in the problem-solving process, therefore, is to define the problem.

FIGURE 8-1

Problem-Solving Process

1. Identify problem 2. Analyze problem 3. List possible solutions 4. Determine selection criteria	Investigation and Inquiry Stage
5. Analyze proposed solutions critically	Discussion and Debate Stage
6. Reach decision and implement	Decision-Making and Implementation Stage

The problem may be interwoven with related problems. Or, the problem situation may be so complex that it must be split into subproblems for easier manipulation. Problem-solvers face another task—separating the problem from causes and symptoms. A problem is a condition that is different from what someone thinks it *ought* to be. Problems exist in people's heads; one person's problem is another person's opportunity. Causes are contributing factors to the problem. Symptoms are signs or results of problems. Rather than treat the symptoms, like a doctor, aim to treat the underlying disease or problem.

The following example illustrates problem/cause/symptom connections: Suppose your organization is suffering 50 percent employee turnover yearly in the shipping department. The shipping department supervisor believes this is a problem because, in his opinion, the turnover rate should be less than 20 percent annually. Assuming he can convince other people to define the employee turnover situation as a problem, causes might be poor employee hiring practices, poor communication between supervisors and department members, or less-than-competitive wages. Symptoms might be low morale on the shipping dock, poor productivity, higher incidence of damaged goods, and higher level of employee injuries.

Notice a tree-like relationship among the problem, symptoms, and causes. Symptoms correspond to leaves, which lead to causes—that is, the branches—which in turn lead to the actual problem, the trunk or root. Low morale among shipping department employees is symptomatic of poor communication within the department, which may be one of the causes of the excessive turnover rate.

2. Analyze problem. The second step is the fact-finding stage. Having defined the problem, group members analyze as much relevant information as possible regarding the problem, its contributing causes, its symptoms, and its relationship to other problems. They determine the why, what, where, when, who, and how. People are interviewed or surveyed. Correspondence, reports, and meeting minutes are examined. External sources of data, like books, periodicals, and newspapers, are researched. Causes, effects, and interrelationships are outlined clearly and specifically.

3. List all possible solutions. Using the brain-storming technique in a very free, permissive, and uncritical atmosphere, the work group lists possible solutions to the problem. By not evaluating, criticizing, or passing judgment at this stage, everyone stays out of their traditional, boxed-in thinking patterns and proposes solutions to the problem situation from new perspectives. If this step is done well, the group has compiled a thorough list of possible solutions. The list contains some bizarre, impractical ideas; some solutions that promise little success or that have already been tried unsuccessfully; and some original, untried, but promising approaches.

4. Decide on selection criteria. The next step is to decide on criteria for judging the items on the solutions list. These selection criteria become the basis for judging each of the solutions generated in Step 3. What set of goals should the ideal solution possess? Possible criteria include the following: Benefits must outweigh the costs. The solution can be implemented within a reasonable time. The approach must be new and untried. Key personnel or departments must agree to support the solution. The solution must be compatible with long-term goals. The solution must substantially attack the basic problem, not just treat the symptoms. Once group members have reached agreement on selection criteria, they can move to the next problem-solving step.

5. Evaluate solutions critically. Steps 1 through 4 fall into the investigation and inquiry stage; Step 5 involves discussion and debate. The team weighs the pros and cons of each Step 3 solution in terms of Step 4 criteria. The group leader conducts a reasoned examination of each solution and its potential effects. The list is gradually narrowed down. Several solutions are obviously unworkable and quickly scratched. Other solutions are eliminated after more discussion. Two or three options survive this shakedown process.

6. Reach defensible decision and implement it. In the final step, the group leader sums up the arguments for and against each of the remaining solutions. The group leader may informally read the group's consensus, such as, "After hearing your debate on solutions 2 and 4, I believe the group has decided solution 4 is the best way to go." Or, the group leader may poll each person for his or her opinion. The majority decides which solution to implement. If the problem-solving group was mainly consultative, the group leader considers the group's discussion and suggested recommendation and then independently makes the final decision. All that remains, then, is deciding how to implement the solution and assigning responsibilities.

This six-step problem-solving process does not always move forward in a straight line. Back-tracking is common. Running into a barrier along the way, the problem-solving team might go back to re-analyze the problem, seeking more data, for example. Ready to move forward again, they go on to re-examine selection criteria and solutions.

The Process in Action

An example shows this problem-solving procedure in operation. Barbara Wong is administrative manager of the Proto Corporation. She is responsible for a staff of 100 office and clerical employees in five departments: mail handling, records management, word processing, copying, and general office services. Each of these departments is managed by a supervisor who reports to her. During part of three staff or special meetings, she and her supervisors grapple with reducing absenteeism.

Barbara's first step is to delineate the problem clearly. At the January meeting, she tells her five supervisors that the absenteeism rate has reached epidemic proportions. On a typical workday, 15 percent of the staff calls in sick.

Barbara spends fifteen minutes acquainting each supervisor with the problem situation. The records management supervisor was not even conscious of a problem because absenteeism in her section is the lowest, hovering around five percent. High absenteeism is seriously affecting the entire office's productivity. Absenteeism in the mail room has been running 25 percent, most frequently on Mondays, Fridays, and days before and after holidays. In word processing and the mail room, temporary office agency help has been used to fill in. This practice increases labor costs 50 percent. Vacations have been postponed or cancelled to keep up with the workload. Overtime costs are $4000 over budget.

When all five staff members' questions have been answered and each fully understands the problem and its effects, Barbara proceeds to the problem-analysis step. She asks each staff member to gather data for the February staff meeting. Each supervisor will analyze absenteeism problems in his or her department by examining payroll and personnel records. Who is absent? How often? On what days? Does there seem to be any pattern connected to missed workdays? And so forth. Each supervisor is requested to interview three of his or her employees to get employee viewpoints on missed work, its causes, and possible solutions. Barbara also distributes copies of a report that the accounting and data processing departments prepared when they had similar absenteeism problems six months ago. Finally, she gives her people a copy of a *Management World* article on white-collar absenteeism. It will give them ideas on what other companies have done.

At the February staff meeting, Barbara and her colleagues devote 30 minutes to sharing and discussing the results of each person's fact-finding. The group now enters the solution-listing stage. Everyone brain-storms and Barbara records fifteen ideas on the chalkboard. Among the staff's ideas: Firing any employee with more than two absences a month; raising all salaries 20 percent to increase job loyalty; giving employees more flexibility in setting up their individual work schedules; sponsoring a company day-care center so employees would not be at the mercy of unreliable baby-sitters.

Next, Barbara moves the group into the judgment-criteria stage. Fifteen minutes is spent establishing these criteria with which the ultimate solution must agree:

1. The solution is acceptable to the majority of the six group members. Barbara practices participative management and believes in this case she can delegate the decision-making responsibility to the group. In case of a tie, she will cast the deciding vote.

2. The solution will not create problems greater than the problem it is supposed to solve. For example, requiring excessive record-keeping to document absences in order to establish just cause for firing an employee.

3. The solution is practical to execute. It can be implemented within 30 days.

4. The solution is cost-effective. The predicted dollar savings must exceed the cost of implementing the solution.

5. The solution is acceptable to top management. It must be approved by the vice-president of human resources.

6. The solution must cut the absenteeism rate to 5 percent within three months.

Because time is running short in this meeting, Barbara tells her supervisors to evaluate critically each of the brain-stormed solutions on the basis of these six criteria and meet again in one week to propose an acceptable solution.

One week later, the staff reconvenes to discuss and debate the possible solutions. Ten solutions are discarded immediately because they are illegal, impractical, too expensive, or too burdensome to administer. After 30 minutes of further give-and-take discussion on the five remaining absenteeism-reduction approaches, two solutions remain that best meet the criteria.

Moving to the decision and implementation stage, Barbara asks for a show of hands. Proposal 12—establish a flex-time work schedule—wins 5 votes to 1. Barbara assumes responsibility for developing the new schedule and clearing it with the vice-president. The flex-time schedule will begin in three weeks on March 5 for a three-month trial period, during which time she will monitor absenteeism, payroll costs, and productivity figures.

At the June staff meeting, Barbara and her five supervisors will re-evaluate the flex-time solution. After three months, how much has the absenteeism rate been cut? How close to the five percent goal is it? Based on the data from the flex-time trial, they will decide whether to continue flex-time scheduling unchanged, alter it to increase its performance, or investigate another absenteeism reduction plan to replace it.

To get the most out of small group communication, business and professional people need to know more than just how to plan meetings and use small group processes and problem-solving techniques. Plans and agendas don't make or break meetings, people do. Successful, productive meetings demand a leader and group members who know their roles and carry them out competently.

LEADER'S ROLE IN MEETINGS

Leading a group boils down to doing three things well:

▶ A leader *guides* the participants. This job includes developing the agenda, selecting and using the most appropriate group processes, and proceeding smoothly from one item or activity to the next on the agenda.

▶ A leader *stimulates*. She creates an atmosphere of involvement and rapport. By using such tools as questioning technique and presentation aids, the leader maintains lively interest in the meeting's subject matter and commitment to the meeting's goals.

▶ A leader *controls*. A meeting is not a gab fest. The leader exercises control, probably the most important leadership responsibility, to insure that the meeting's purpose is accomplished effectively and efficiently. He interprets group consensus, if required. Through organizational and communication channels, the leader follows through at the direction or the advice of group members.

A person's leadership style depends on many factors, including the leader's personality, management beliefs, and use of power, plus time pressures and group characteristics. Leadership styles range from the permissive, hands-off, power-delegating style to the democratic, participative, power-sharing style to the autocratic, power-retaining style. Each is appropriate in the right circumstances. Regardless of the label attached to a person's leadership style, a good leader must control. Exercising control does not necessarily make one less democratic or more autocratic.

Forging a collection of people with different goals, personalities, and backgrounds into a cohesive, motivated, results-oriented group will be a challenging task when you are leading a group. Notice how the guiding, stimulating, and controlling responsibilities are woven into the following eight recommendations for skillful group leadership.

1. Begin with a Statement of Objectives

As in any communication endeavor, it is risky to assume that group members, merely by virtue of their attendance, are aware of the why and how of the meeting. First off, orient and motivate the group participants. If you cannot clearly and concisely describe the meeting's purpose and its value, that may be a very good sign you have not prepared well or have called an unnecessary meeting.

Offering the tentative agenda to the group for approval or modification may be enough in some meeting situations. At other times, something more is needed. Motivate by explaining how the group as a whole and each conferee individually will benefit if group interaction is successful. For instance: "Each of you has felt the effects of recent data processing foul-ups—errors, delays, and so on. Some of our biggest clients have complained. Our job today is to begin investigating whether a centralized data processing department might improve how we deliver DP services. If we're successful in making the right changes, you'll be able to give your clients the kind of efficient, accurate accounting services that they demand from our firm and you know they deserve."

2. Manage Time Rigorously throughout the Meeting

Because time pressures can be destructive to group interaction, use every minute of meeting time to advantage. Start on time. Late starts almost guarantee the meeting will run overtime or the planned business will not be covered. Waiting for latecomers wastes the time of those attendees who are ready and present on time and paradoxically rewards those who are late. (Of course, there are exceptions to this rule: Waiting a few minutes for the boss or a special guest is usually wise.)

Your agenda specifies time limits for speakers. As meeting leader, stick to the agenda to keep time allocation and subject matter emphasis where it ought to be. If a speaker is going on too long or getting off the subject, you should courteously prompt the speaker to get back on the topic or abbreviate the rest of the presentation.

If you believe that the second topic on the agenda deserves ten minutes, keep to your plans unless, as the meeting evolves, some reallocation of time is justified. When the program falls behind the agenda, it has a cumulative effect. Later speakers and activities on the agenda may get short shrift or be omitted entirely. Such things possibly compromise achieving group objectives and reduce the entire meeting's value.

Finally, end on time. Attendees have almost certainly planned to do other things after the scheduled adjournment time. They expect and appreciate being able to follow their day's schedule, whether it be catching a plane or getting to a luncheon appointment on time.

3. Keep the Discussion Moving toward Goals

One way to keep the discussion focused is to restate your purpose if participants are diverging from the agenda's intended subject matter. By resetting the limits of the work session, you clarify what's in and what's out of bounds, like this: "Today's job is solve Problem X, not Problem Y. We'll tackle Problem Y at another meeting."

You will also need to suggest useful information, present evidence, ask questions, and actively solicit opinions from all involved. Encourage silent members to express their viewpoints. For example, "Aaron, you work in accounting. How would the accounting department be affected by centralizing data processing operations?"

Of course, you may face the opposite problem—coping with the long-winded or wandering group member. Gently, but clearly, discourage these people from making speeches or injecting irrelevant information. Maybe like this: "Mary, selection of accounting software will be a problem whether data processing services are centralized or decentralized. The group wants to focus directly on the centralization issue right now. Software selection questions can be resolved later."

4. Maintain Good Rapport Among Group Members

As leader, monitor the interaction process for signs of deteriorating rapport. Group members will react to poor meeting design, hostile and attacking group interaction, lack of progress, and lack of control with stress responses. Participant behavior, such as the following, are often stress symptoms:

- emotional attacks,
- ego battles,
- negativism, refusing to cooperate
- competition,
- dictating,
- straying from the subject,
- joking and kidding,
- reading, daydreaming,
- empty agreement (saying "Yeah, sure, no problem" to avoid attention or shorten the meeting).

When you notice these signs, take corrective action before mounting stress levels destroy rapport. Maybe you must minimize interpersonal rivalries, conflicts, and tensions. Trying to keep the atmosphere friendly, permissive, and informal is important because rapport is a precondition for achieving results. However, building and keeping a positive communication climate is not always easy, even for the most experienced and able group leader.

Encourage participants to address contributions to everyone, especially their contributions of a negative or controversial nature, not to specific individuals or departments. Group members consider their ideas as personal property. Attacking an idea is like attacking the individual personally. Hostile exchanges separate group members into opposing factions. The sought-after goal of group cohesiveness is destroyed. Tempers flare, and honest differences grow into personal animosity and stubbornness. When speakers word sensitive contributions carefully and give them a more general focus, attention remains on the issues, not on personalities.

If matters have already gotten out of hand and the free investigation of the subject at hand is jeopardized, you must exercise your control function and steer the group's interaction back into more fruitful channels. How? Try to summarize or paraphrase contributions to soften them or redirect criticism. For example, you may recast the direct criticism, "Epstein knows perfectly well bringing in another DP consultant won't work. It just takes the pressure to make a decision off him for a few months." to "Almost every corporate unit has hired consultants in the past with limited results. We need to make a decision now, promptly, using our own considerable pool of expertise." This takes the heat off of Epstein, softens and broadens the criticism, and redirects the discussion toward meeting objectives.

Other strategies often work if group interaction is charged with tension or worn down by fatigue. Try injecting some humor into the situation. Permit group members to back-track into more agreeable territory. If the attendees are fatigued or bored, you might switch to another group technique to accomplish the same goal or call a ten-minute recess so everyone can walk around some and get coffee. Maybe your restless group is telling you the meeting is over, and you should continue the group's business at a follow-up meeting. If the conference room is becoming hot and smokey, open the door or turn up the air conditioning.

5. Coordinate Group Thinking

Group members will be making contributions from their unique perspectives. As group leader, help unite separate ideas into a pattern so a clear train of thought is apparent to everybody. To make the emerging pattern or direction even more graphic, use a chalkboard or overhead projector to outline, diagram, or list ideas as they are presented and reacted to.

Another way to coordinate group thinking is by making frequent summaries during meetings. Summaries during a meeting emphasize that subgoals are being accomplished and they reinforce the group's feeling of forward momentum. Internal summaries also paraphrase content or intent. This kind of review brings misunderstanding into the open. And, summaries serve as transitions to the next stage of the meeting.

A summary at the meeting's conclusion is wise, too. Here, you can recap the major results of the group's deliberation, indicate any points of disagreement that still need resolution, restate any decisions arrived at, and remind conferees about their individual assignments and deadlines. One caution: summaries can become repetitive, time wasting, and insulting to the group's intelligence if they are too detailed or too frequent. Use them sparingly and for effect.

6. Use Questions as a Potent Tool

Statements push people, questions lead people. Questions ask people to think and stretch their imaginations. Skilled group leaders ask questions often to draw out conferees and explore important concerns. Especially where your objective is persuasion or problem solving, as much as possible, substitute questioning for lecturing. You accomplish the same purposes but with a stronger team orientation and more feedback. Even in an information-giving meeting, questions help determine the attendees' level of understanding, clear up misconceptions, review, and link abstract points to on-the-job action.

For these reasons, talented meeting leaders rely on questions. Most of the one-on-one questioning strategies you recall from Chapter 6 on interviewing can be adapted for small group communication. Here are several more questioning strategies that you can apply in small group settings:

Overhead questions. Questions directed to the entire group are called overhead questions. They are effective in generating ideas and getting discussion going. Example: "What are your ideas on reducing the six-week backlog in the print shop?" After asking the question, there will be a pause, sometimes a long one, while conferees ponder their responses. Don't panic and quickly throw out another question. Doing so only confuses the audience as they stop working on the first question and begin thinking about the second. Instead, give the group enough time to think and then share their responses.

Directed questions. Ask directed questions of specific people to obtain further information, to probe, or to involve shy or inattentive people. Direct questions also help to start discussion if overhead questions don't. Always put the individual's name before the question. If the respondent is deep in thought (or has lapsed into reverie), hearing his or her name generally breaks the trance, gives the person a chance to get set mentally for the question, and avoids a potentially embarrassing incident. Be stingy in using directed questions. When overused, they create a schoolroom or interrogation-type atmosphere.

Relay questions. Directing the same question to a second, third, fourth person to broaden the discussion or to gauge the level of commitment is done in a relay question. Example: "Mrs. Brown, do you have anything to add to Peter's answer?" "Margaret, how do you feel about Peter's idea?"

Reverse questions. This technique is used by the respondent to throw the ball back into the questioner's court. When asked a question, like "Paul, do you think enough press operators would agree to work Sunday even for double-time?" Paul might reverse the question and ask, "Since you're a former supervisor in that department, what do you think?" Reverse questions probe the thinking of the person who raised the question. They also allow a person to remain non-committal.

Hypothetical questions. These questions work well to extend thinking on an item under discussion. The questioner creates an imaginary scenario and asks the group what they would do. A hypothetical question may appear more concrete and effective than repeating a question that did not get much of a response. Example: "What if the print shop supervisor were to hire ten additional part-time employees during November? Would that cut the backlog down to manageable proportions?"

Personal experience questions. A good way to get a discussion started is to ask someone to describe an actual personal experience that relates to the discussion. Example: "Bob, you used to work in the print shop at Zenith Corporation. Didn't they hire temps for the rush season? How did that work out?"

Some question types don't work any better in small group settings than they did in interviewing—for example, closed questions that can be answered "yes" or "no." They often kill discussion, as do leading questions that can bias a response. Better than "Do you agree with me?" is asking "You're directly by affected the slowdown, Sara. What do you think about it?"

7. Obtain Honest and Valid Conclusions

Honest and valid conclusions are often hard to achieve because of the common weaknesses of small group communication—groupthink, clock-watching, growing fatigue as the meeting drags on, and so forth. A good group leader is alert for symptoms of these negative forces and attempts to reduce or resist these pressures.

You can minimize time pressures and fatigue by exercising control over agenda construction and by sticking to the agenda order and its time frame. If time is running out and the meeting's objectives cannot be completed properly, your group may be better off scheduling another meeting than making an expeditious, but improperly thought-out, decision.

To avoid groupthink, put these suggestions to work:

▶ First, deliberately bring in outsiders whose opinions differ from those of the group members. This action forces group members to explore a broader base of data and viewpoints.

▶ Second, encourage group participants to be critical evaluators, people who look at all sides of a problem regardless of personal opinion or personal advantage. Stimulate critical thinking by asking good questions. Request proof for doubtful statements.

▶ Third, consciously solicit alternative viewpoints. Draw out quiet or submissive members. Ask people with opposing viewpoints to defend and develop their positions. Keep personal opinions to yourself until others have aired their viewpoints. Since most people don't like to disagree with the boss, group leaders, especially when meeting with subordinates, must be careful in expressing personal opinions. Avoid advocating a position. This usually telegraphs to the conferees that the decision has already been made in your mind. Why, they may wonder, should they risk voicing alternative viewpoints when it will have no positive effect? Although you should remain as impartial as possible, of course inject valid input into the discussion where needed.

▶ Fourth, give members a second chance to re-evaluate their first decision and dispute it before committing to the final decision.

8. Follow-through with Results.

Meetings are a waste of time if people talk and talk and talk—but nothing comes of all the talking. As a competent group leader, you don't let this happen. Make sure members leave the meeting knowing that they have done something—solved a problem, shared knowledge, acquired new skills—and that their valuable time has been profitably invested in completing worthwhile organizational, group, and personal objectives.

As the person in charge, one of your final tasks is to see that any group decision is communicated to the right persons and departments. Conferees need to know what will happen next. Assign specific follow-up responsibilities. Maintain accountability. People assigned tasks should give progress reports at pre-determined intervals so the meeting leader and other members can monitor progress. Prepare minutes of meetings and distribute them within 48 hours to all participants, absentees, and non-group members who need the information.

MEMBER'S ROLE IN MEETINGS

Strong, capable group leadership is critical to productive group interaction, but good group *membership* is just as important. Not surprisingly, companies spend millions of dollars yearly on leadership training. However, with a bulge of baby-boom managers in their 30s and 40s who are coping with being stuck on career plateaus, companies like American Telephone and Telegraph and Mellon Bank Corporation are now teaching employees how to be better followers. One proponent of "followship" training says "people actually play both roles and need both skills, but the quest for being a good leader can be hampered by not being a good follower."[1] Effective followers are team players who profit in the long run by putting organizational and work group objectives above their own career objectives. In this way, followers build the skills and reputation needed for the day when they are rewarded with leadership positions.

Not only do good followers eventually become leaders themselves, but in the meantime they make their leaders' jobs immeasurably easier. Leading a group is less difficult if group members are cooperative, understanding, and sympathetic.

You will probably be a participant in many more meetings than you will chair, especially as you launch your professional or business career. To be a better group participant, demonstrate the following behavior:

---

1. Timothy D. Schellhardt, "Companies Try to Teach Art of Following," *The Wall Street Journal,* April 6, 1988, p. 21.

1. Be prompt and regular in attendance. Come prepared and on time to make your best contribution. Lateness indicates lack of courtesy and, as we've seen before, may waste time.

2. Participate fully in group discussions and other activities. Everyone who is invited to a meeting is there for a reason. You have a contribution to make to the group's interaction and ultimately help accomplish the group's objectives. Why make the person in charge pry information out of you? Enter into discussions enthusiastically, freely sharing your special perspective, knowledge, and experience with colleagues. Maintain an attitude of inquiry and empathy.

3. Stay relevant. Remember that the group leader is trying to maintain a developing train of thought. Don't interrupt this train. Elaborate on other's contributions, support or refute them with evidence. If your mind is especially fresh or fertile, maybe an avalanche of ideas, some pertinent and some not so pertinent, will suddenly occur to you. Jot down the irrelevant ideas for the meantime and use them later when they fit in. Share the relevant ideas at the appropriate time with the group.

Help the leader to stay on the agenda and on schedule. We all know of participants in meetings or students in classes who talk constantly to attract attention to themselves. What they say does not move the discussion forward. They merely waste time and obscure the evolving thought pattern. Other people we know say little, but when they do speak, their words are important. Their contributions are carefully reasoned, concise, and persuasive. The discussion is moved along toward its goals. Take a lesson: don't make speeches or monopolize discussion opportunities. Aim to make your contributions short, clear, and one point at a time.

4. Keep remarks impersonal and free from prejudice. If you have an opposing viewpoint, disagree tactfully. Don't carp or whine. Conferees owe one another courtesy and respect. Address sensitive remarks to the group as a whole, not to particular group members or departments who may take personal offense. In this way, the leader will not have to repeatedly try to defuse potentially explosive conflicts between you and dissenters.

5. Assist in reaching conclusions. Good conferees are constructive, actively involved, and committed to group goals. They put group and organizational benefits before personal, selfish gain. They help the leader avoid groupthink.

Offering input into analysis and decision making doesn't mean being a "yes-person," someone who always agrees with the boss

FIGURE 8–2

Getting More from Meetings

1. **Consider alternatives to meetings.** First of all, does the situation really require group interaction? Might it be better just to make the decision yourself and announce it in a memo to avoid calling everyone together. Perhaps a conference call could substitute for a face-to-face meeting. These techniques reduce the number of meetings business people and professionals must clear time for on their busy calendars.

2. **If possible, attend fewer meetings.** Send a representative. This saves your time but gives a subordinate experience, more responsibility, and enhanced visibility. Or, attend part of the meeting (with the leader's consent). In either case, you will have minutes or your subordinate's report to fill you in on what you missed. Meetings often can be consolidated. Perhaps every-other month staff meetings will be just as effective as monthly meetings. Stagger attendance at meetings. Go to, say, every other policy review committee meeting. Or send a written report of your contribution for presentation at the meeting.

3. **Seat participants strategically**—shy members next to outgoing members, newcomers between more experienced members, and so on.

4. **Make sure everyone is acquainted.** If necessary, introduce guests or newcomers, or begin with introductions. Provide name tags.

5. **Explain functions**—what will the leader's role be and what will be the attendees' roles? If the agenda is complicated or an unfamiliar group process is used, this will orient group members.

6. **Establish the correct emotional climate.** The leader's behavior generally has more effect on the group climate than any other member's. The leader's demeanor determines whether the climate will be formal or informal, cold or warm, rejecting or accepting. Dispense with stuffy formalities in small, informal meetings, such as raising hands for permission to speak or elaborate parliamentary procedures. When possible start on a upbeat note. Begin the session with some good news so people are glad they showed up.

7. **When talking before even a small group, whether impromptu or extemporaneously, use all the principles of good organization and delivery:** Present your ideas logically and persuasively, show enthusiasm, be conversational, aim for vocal color, and use natural body language.

8. **For important meetings, contact selected attendees before the meeting.** This practice permits you to build preparedness and interest. You can read group sentiment, too, in order to anticipate clashes, avoid hopeless battles, or devise a new plan of attack.

FIGURE 8-2 (continued)
Getting More from Meetings

9. **Use presentation aids for maximum affect.** They arouse and maintain interest, call attention to specific ideas, and save time. Their use also forces you to do your homework more thoroughly.
10. **Work for consensus, not total agreement.** A consensus means that most people agree on the action to be taken or the decision to be made. Unanimous support for important or complex issues is rare. Meetings usually require give-and-take, and consensus can still provide workable solutions.

no matter what. Don't be a manipulator either, one who is constantly studying the political rewards and consequences of an action and working to mold group action for personal favor. Don't be a saboteur with a hidden agenda that you hope to fulfil, even if you don't harm the group's best interests. And, lastly, don't be a "stand-patter," a person who doggedly resists new ideas and frustrates any efforts to change.

6. Listen actively, paraphrase often, and ask questions. Such behavior reduces misunderstanding, error, and unnecessary back-tracking to clear up a point. Questioning is just as useful for meeting participants as for meeting leaders. Use the same good questioning techniques to draw out colleagues or to encourage more critical thinking.

7. Be a good sport, even if the group consensus goes against you. No one convinces everyone of the worthiness of his or her ideas 100 percent of the time. Graceful losers gain the respect of their colleagues by accepting negative decisions with dignity and by supporting the will of the majority.

See Figure 8-2 for many more ideas, tips, and suggestions that group leaders and participants alike can put into practice for more productive, relaxed, and efficient small group communication.

SUMMING UP

Rapport and good results are the goals of successful meetings. When working in small group situations, business people and professionals use the group process technique that creates the communication climate and the results they want.

The most common small group format is group discussion, a focused, goal-oriented exchange of information and evaluation. NGT uses a tightly structured, five-step process (idea listing, recording, preliminary voting, discussion, and final voting). Since only in the discussion stage can group members explain their positions and seek support, NGT minimizes the effects of harmful group pressures. For generating ideas and solutions, brain-storming is ideal. In an unstructured, highly interactive, non-critical atmosphere, group members suggest ideas that are recorded for later analysis. Question-and-answer sessions can be used for information exchanges in small groups. Round-table discussions are a way to make small group communication practical within a large group. Role-playing, case study, games, and simulations are especially useful group techniques where training or application of textbook knowledge to on-the-job behavior is the objective.

These group process techniques are often employed in various combinations when the work team's goal is problem solving. Approaching problem solving systematically sharply increases the possibility of identifying the best solution efficiently and with less frustration. First, identify the problem, sorting it out from its causes and symptoms. Break the problem into subproblems for easier study. Second, analyze the problem. Scrutinize the problem from all angles in this fact-finding stage. Third, list all possible solutions using the brain-storming technique. Fourth, decide on selection criteria on which to, fifth, evaluate the solutions list. Sixth, make and carry out the decision.

Using group formats and problem-solving formulas well calls for group leaders and participants who competently perform their roles. To be a capable group leader you must guide, stimulate, and control. You will 1) begin meetings with a statement of purpose to provide orientation and incentive; 2) manage time carefully during the meeting; 3) keep group discussion moving toward goals; 4) maintain good rapport among group members; 5) coordinate group thinking; 6) use questioning to probe topics and involve participants; 7) seek honest and valid results; and 8) see that decisions are implemented, communicated, and monitored.

From the perspective of an effective group member, you must cooperate with the team leader by: 1) being prompt and regular in attendance; 2) fully engaging in group interaction; 3) sticking to the subject matter; 4) keeping remarks impersonal and unprejudiced; 5) assisting in reaching group conclusions; 6) using good listening, paraphrasing, and questioning skills; and 7) accepting negative decisions and supporting the will of the majority.

Application Exercises

1. Divide the class into groups of five to seven people. Select a topic related to group interests and experience. Conduct a 20-minute group discussion before other class members using effective group leadership and participant techniques. One person, appointed by the instructor or chosen by the group, will act as leader to introduce group members, present the discussion topic, guide the discussion, and summarize the discussion. If possible, videotape group interaction.

    Group members and/or class members then evaluate the discussion. Criticize the leader and each group member on his/her group interaction using the suggestions on effective leader/participant behavior presented in this chapter. Give specific instances of effective and ineffective behavior. Offer suggestions for improvement where possible.

2. Experiment with nominal grouping technique. In work groups of five to seven, work through the NGT process. For your problem select a current-events issue from the local newspaper that requires resolution. A reporter from each group should report to the other groups on the following:
    a. A summary of the problem and group's suggested solution.
    b. Reactions to the nominal group technique. Were there problems implementing any of the NGT steps? What strengths and weaknesses did your team discover about NGT? How practical and valuable would you predict NGT to be on the job?

3. Use the brain-storming technique to generate a thorough list of approaches to a school or work problem. Examples: ways to lower school tuition, how to increase school spirit and attendance at campus sporting and social events, how to eliminate the parking space shortage, or possible improvements to include in the next update of "X" brand word processor you all use. Brain-storm for ten minutes. One group member will record the idea flow. Afterwards, evaluate the brain-storming process. Did your group display all the characteristics of effective brain-storming? How could the group's idea generation be improved?

4. Conduct a town meeting to examine and resolve a problem your city or town faces (reducing local taxes, attracting new industry, improving municipal services, for instance). Each person should research the problem before the meeting. Appoint a mayor to lead the town meeting through the six-step problem-solving procedure recommended in this chapter. After your town meeting, conduct a debriefing session to evaluate your group's performance. If you can videotape your meeting, playbacks will help your analysis. How well did each step go? Note any special successes or problems related to group leadership or participation, also.

5. Critique a meeting. Options: Attend a business meeting where you

are employed. Go to a meeting of a school, social, service, or church group to which you belong. Or, attend a meeting of an organization to which you don't belong, such as a business, professional, or civic group (get permission first). Observe and evaluate the meeting. If you can, interview the meeting leader and several meeting members for additional insights. Report on the following in written or oral format as directed:

    a. Meeting agenda. If possible, obtain a copy of the agenda before the meeting. Compare the agenda to the actual order of the meeting's business. Was the agenda followed closely? What deviations from the planned schedule occurred? Were they justified?

    b. Time management. Did the meeting begin and end on time? Did the leader and participants exercise effective time management techniques?

    c. Meeting purpose. Define the meeting's purpose(s). How well were they accomplished? What were the meeting's outcomes? What follow-up and implementation plans were made?

    d. Negative aspects of small group communication. Did the value received by each participant justify his or her time away from regular job tasks? Were time pressures exerting any harmful effects on the group's interaction and decision making? Did you observe any symptoms of groupthink? Did you sense any participants had hidden agendas?

    e. Group process techniques. What group interaction and problem-solving techniques were used? Were they appropriate and successful?

    f. Leadership. Evaluate how well the leader carried out his or her role. Would you describe the leader's style as permissive, participative, or autocratic? What behaviors were successful? Unsuccessful? In what ways did the leader use questions effectively or ineffectively?

    g. Participant involvement. Describe attendees' behavior and interaction. Describe and evaluate specific instances of effective and ineffective participant behavior.

6. Interview a person who runs and participates in meetings and conferences frequently. Record this person's judgments on:

    a. Frequency and value of meetings. How many meetings does he or she attend weekly on the average? How many are productive, valid uses of work time? Does your expert use any methods for decreasing the number of meetings attended? What are these methods?

    b. Meeting purposes. In this person's organization, for what purposes are meetings held?

    c. Meeting disadvantages. Probe for your expert's experiences and opinions on negatives aspects of small group communication, like unjustifiable costs, time pressures, groupthink, and hidden agen-

das. What advice can he or she offer on coping with these potentially destructive problems?
- d. Meeting planning and agenda construction. Does this person have any tricks of the trade?
- e. Characteristics of an effective meeting leader.
- f. Characteristics of an effective meeting participant.
- g. Techniques for coping with difficult attendee personalities, such as a shy, introverted, noninteracting person; talkative member who makes speeches or frequent irrelevant remarks; hostile, dominating person; submissive, yielding individual; "yes-person"; manipulator; saboteur; or "stand-patter."
- h. Meeting follow-up. What recommendations does your expert have for following-up on meeting decisions. How does he or she monitor carrying out of group decisions and directives?
- i. Meeting evaluation. Does your expert engage in post-meeting analysis. How?
7. Meeting Planning Case—an individual project

Imagine the organization you work for is presenting a staff development workshop. You are assigned to plan and run it.

Your boss gives you this general format to follow:

▶ Plan a four-hour program to take place approximately two months from now.

▶ Invite 12 of your organization's professional staff. Three staff education seminars are held yearly, and one third of the 36-member staff attends each one.

▶ Select a topic on which your seminar participants need further training. For example: Using an unfamiliar software package; strengthening interviewing skills; using better employee evaluation methods; reducing stress in the workplace; providing an update on a new product, manufacturing method, or technology.

▶ Use your organization's conference and audio-visual facilities.

▶ Engage two speakers for your workshop. You might hire consultants, professors from local colleges and universities, or business and professional people in the area who are experts on your workshop's subject matter.

▶ Use group process techniques and presentation aids innovatively and creatively in a workshop atmosphere. You may need to break your 12 participants into smaller groups at times to use small group process techniques more successfully. Your boss wants the staff attending the meeting to do more than listen. Have them see, do, become involved. Motivate workshop attendees to put what they learn into practice their next day on the job.

Prepare a report (oral or written as instructed) detailing:
   a. Specific purposes of the meeting.
   b. Date and time.
   c. Facility arrangements including room layout and presentation aid requirements.
   d. Agenda, including group activities and media usage.
   e. Follow-up evaluation procedure you will use to capture information on workshop's acceptance and usefulness.
   f. Memo to attendees announcing meeting and agenda.
8. Meeting Planning Case—a small group project

I. OBJECTIVES

You are an assistant to Deborah Denton, regional vice-president of marketing, and have been assigned to plan the regional sales meeting held yearly at your company's headquarters. The meeting's primary purposes will be to:
   a. Reveal the three-year corporate strategy to improve market position and profitability.
   b. Introduce the new 2001.1 model, a technologically superior product to those already marketed by your company and its competitors.
   c. Unveil the marketing program to push the 2001.1 very strongly in your regional sales territory. Your company will have a six-month lead on its competitors in the introduction of this next-generation product.

You and the other members of the five- to seven-member planning committee are responsible for a meeting three months from now for the 20 sales representatives in your region. This gives you a good lead time to plan all aspects of the sales meeting and to report back to Deborah and other members of upper management with your detailed plans.

II. BACKGROUND AND ASSUMPTIONS

Your company serves a national market, divided into 15 regional sales territories, each composed of 3 or 4 states, each with a local sales office. Each region holds a sales meeting yearly.

Assume your sales region covers three states. Your home state is one state in the territory. The regional and state office are located in a city of your choice in your home state. Eight sales representatives work out of this office. Select two adjoining states to complete your sales region. Choose a city in each state as the location of that state's sales office. One state office has seven reps and the other, five reps. For example, if you live in Ohio, you could choose Cleveland as your regional and state office, Indiana as the second state in the sales territory with the state office in Fort Wayne, and Pennsylvania as the third state with the state office in Pittsburgh.

After fifty years of operation, your company is well respected in the industry and has established a reputation for high-quality products, competitive prices, and reliable service. However, it has never been an industry leader as far as product development and sales aggressiveness are concerned.

Your company's market share has been stable for five years and it has been moderately profitable. The field is dominated by four other major companies that service 90 percent of the market (the remaining 10 percent is divided among three small newcomers serving only small markets at present). Industry position and market percentages are: Competitor A, 35 percent; Competitor B, 25 percent; your company, 20 percent; and Competitor C, 10 percent.

David Bishop, your company's president, has set a company goal to move into second place within three years and first place within six years. This goal will be accomplished by a large capital investment in new manufacturing facilities, the introduction of improved models, and more aggressive and effective marketing.

III. PLANNING RESPONSIBILITIES

Here is a partial, certainly not exhaustive, list of committee responsibilities:

- ▶ Select dates and develop agenda to fulfil meeting objectives.
- ▶ Arrange for suitable meeting and lodging facilities.
- ▶ Invite sales representatives, speakers, and other participants, and arrange for their transportation to and from their home cities and to the meeting site.
- ▶ Arrange for food, refreshments, and entertainment.
- ▶ Develop a defensible budget.

IV. GUIDELINES

Deborah, in consultation with David, has given the planning committee these guidelines:
1. The meeting will be two days long, not including travel time of attendees.
2. The 20-person regional sales force will attend at company expense.
3. Deborah will open the meeting with a welcome and overview of the purposes and agenda of the meeting.
4. Immediately after this opening presentation, David will present the company's three-year plan.

5. Work sessions on the following subjects should be organized and scheduled:
   a. Training in operation of 2001.1. Each rep should have two hours hands-on experience so he/she can demonstrate it confidently to prospects. Make all equipment and trainer arrangements.
   b. Discussion of marketing plans for the 2001.1 by corporate headquarter's Marketing Division staff. Also, Robert Reese of Reese, Barnes, Reese, and Phillips, your company's new advertising agency, will be scheduled to acquaint reps with the extensive national advertising program planned to launch the 2001.1.
   c. Successful sales techniques for 2001.1. Use suitable group process techniques for effective training.
   d. Assessment of probable competitor reactions and development of counter-strategies.

   Speakers, trainers, and session leaders may be company staff and/or outside consultants. Your committee may need to break the 20 participants into smaller groups at times to use small group process techniques more successfully.
6. Hotel/motel that is selected should meet needs of participants relative to transportation, lodging, meeting space, audio-visual equipment, food, free-time entertainment, and so on. A suite (living room-meeting-room-bedroom combination) should be reserved for one member of your planning team who will serve as the meeting coordinator.
7. Food and beverages should be arranged as appropriate. Some meals may be left to the discretion of the attendees. Morning and afternoon coffee breaks should be scheduled. One hospitality or cocktail hour should be planned.
8. Entertainment and leisure-time activities should be available for participants during the free time in the evenings and for change of pace, especially during afternoon sessions. (Spouses will not accompany sales reps.) Light, motivational, relevant after-dinner speakers should be scheduled for some functions. Be sure to schedule 30 minutes at one meal function for presentation of sales awards by Keith Rossino, national sales director, to recognize the best sales reps in your sales region. Hire a photographer to take pictures of the awards ceremony for the company newsletter.
9. Regarding costs, the planning committee will be assigned a budget level to work within: **generous** budget (company projects a successful, prosperous corporate image without being extravagant, wasteful, or tasteless), **moderate** budget (a middle position), or an **inexpensive** budget (the company projects a spartan image; it is very cost conscious; meeting should be conducted at minimum expense without appearing cheap).

   All expenditures must be justifiable in terms of completing meeting objectives and maintaining the desired corporate image in the industry and among employees.

Use community resources to develop realistic and accurate plans. For example, correct cost data for travel, hotel facilities, and meals; realistic honorariums for speakers; actual entertainment options in your city during the time of the meeting. (Caution: Do not misrepresent yourself and your objectives when seeking data from your sources.)

V. GROUP PRESENTATION SPECIFICATIONS

The planning committee will report back to upper management (other class members) with a comprehensive, detailed, well-organized, and professional oral presentation.

Implement these guidelines in your group presentation:

- Each group will have _____ minutes to present all its plans and the rationale for those plans. This formal presentation will be followed by a _____-minute question-and-answer session led by the meeting coordinator.
- Each group member must make an approximately equal oral contribution to the presentation in terms of time and content.
- One member will make an opening orienting statement announcing the company's name, its product, and any special assumptions the group made. (Feel free to fill in the details not provided in this case or make additional assumptions, but do not ignore or contradict the facts and specifications presented.)

Here's some helpful advice: Develop clear and explicit objectives and make sure meeting plans accomplish these objectives efficiently. Make the meeting interesting as well as informative and productive. Use group processes and presentation aids innovatively. Figure that if your committee does not plan it, it will not get done. **Provide rationale for all your planning and budget decisions so that your listeners not only know what you plan to do, but why.**

APPENDIX

Student evaluators and the instructor may use the following evaluation form for evaluating presentations and providing feedback. The ten-item form can be used as provided; or it may be adapted.

To make evaluating easier, more precise, and more objective, please refer to the assessment scale that follows. This scale has two benefits: One, it helps you as evaluator select the rating on the five-point scale that best describes the speaker's performance on that item. Choose the rating that best sums up the speaker's strengths and weaknesses. Use the comments column of the evaluation form to provide additional helpful, specific, and supportive advice.

Two, the assessment scale helps you as presenter to prepare well for talk opportunities. Select a realistic goal for each item. Aim for that goal as you prepare for, practice, and deliver your presentation. For more advice on realistic goal-setting, refer to Chapter 4, "Putting It All Together."

EVALUATION FORM

Time _____ Presentation by _____

ITEM EVALUATED (see assessment scale)	EXC.	GOOD	SAT.	FAIR	POOR	COMMENTS
1. Content/ Time Management						
Organization						
2. Opener						
3. Body						
4. Close						
Delivery						
5. Reference to Outline/ Eye Contact						
6. Poise						
7. Voice/ Language Use						
8. Body Language						
9. Communication Climate						
10. Presentation Aids						

ASSESSMENT SCALE

Item	Excellent	Good
1. Content Time management	Related to audience perspective and use (plus next two columns) Efficient time management (within 15 seconds of time limit)	Provided concrete material—facts, figures, examples (plus next column)
2. Opener	Especially unique or creative; audience and self involved in opener (plus next two columns)	Attention getting (plus next column)
3. Body	Especially well-chosen organizational pattern; smooth transition from point to point	Well organized; transition provided; logical flow of points
4. Close	Unique or creative close; tied to opener	Effective close; makes talk seem complete but lacks creativity
5. Reference to Talk Outline Eye Contact	Virtually no reference to outline; talk went smoothly with no gaps; strong talked quality (conversational, spontaneous) Eye contact to all sections of audience; real contact for almost the entire time	Some reference to outline, but very smoothly done; few pauses Eye contact to all parts of audience more than half the time

	Satisfactory	Fair	Poor
	Data and interpretation correct. Relevant topics included. Acceptable time management (within 30 seconds of time limit)	Weak support of material; little listener orientation	No attempt to relate content to audience; vague; lack of development Inefficient time management (more than 60 seconds over or under time limit)
	Statement of purpose; nothing extraordinary	Omitted statement of purpose; does not lead smoothly into body of talk	Missing or had nothing to do with topic of talk
	Logical flow of points; lacks enough transition	Loosely organized; no transition provided	Unorganized; rambling and incoherent; illogical flow of points
	Standard closing; lacks uniqueness or originality	Abrupt closing; loose ends hanging; uninteresting	No close provided; close has nothing to do with topic; contains new factual material
	Frequent reference to outline; a few hesitations; read or recited quality at times Eye contact about half the time	Frequent reference to outline; halting or hesitant delivery (seeming unfamiliarlty with outline) Infrequent contact (less than half the time; looking away from audience or at outline frequently); eye contact to limited section of audience	Read outline or manuscript to audience Little eye contact; eye contact to only part of audience

ASSESSMENT SCALE (continued)

Item	Excellent	Good
6. Poise	Speaker completely at ease; relaxed; no signs of nervousness; seems in total control	Speaker seems at ease; few signs of nervousness
7. Voice	Pleasant speaking voice; appropriate volume and rate; uses vocal expressiveness to show interest and enthusiasm throughout talk	Pleasant voice; appropriate volume and rate; uses some vocal expressiveness
Language Use	Words chosen well for audience; no errors in grammar; no pause words; no jargon or slang; no errors in pronunciation	Words chosen well for audience; few pause words used; few errors in grammar or pronunciation
8. Body Language	Speaker uses body as communication tool; effective and natural use of gestures and facial expressions; no distracting mannerisms	Speaker uses some gestures and/or facial expressions; no distracting mannerisms
9. Communication Climate	Exceptionally warm, enthusiastic, dynamic speaker-listener rapport (plus next two columns)	Receptive to questions; detailed responses (plus next column)

Satisfactory	Fair	Poor
Speaker seems a little ill at ease; some signs of nervousness	Speaker seems nervous; several signs of nervousness	Speaker seems very nervous; anxiety keeps speaker from delivering a coherent talk
Pleasant voice; appropriate volume and rate; lacks enough vocal expressiveness	Voice too soft or loud; monotone (no vocal expressiveness); rate too fast or too slow; some slurred words and phrases	Voice is inaudible or irritating; no vocal expressiveness; rate too fast or too slow; frequent slurred words and phrases
Words chosen appropriate for audience; some pause words used; some grammatical and/or pronunciation errors	Inappropriate word choice for audience; frequent use of pause words; several grammatical and/or pronunciation errors	Inappropriate word choice for audience; frequent use of pause words; frequent grammatical and/or pronunciation errors
Neutral body language—speaker uses no gestures or facial expressions; has no distracting mannerisms	Speaker had one or more distracting mannerisms	Negative body language—speaker has several distracting mannerisms
Professional appearance and manner	Vague or unresponsive to listener questions	Seemed cold: mechanical in audience interaction; unresponsive

ASSESSMENT SCALE (continued)

Item	Excellent	Good
10. Presentation Aids: Appearance	Easy to read or see; very effective use of color and graphic design; unique or creative design	Well designed; easy to read or see; some creativity in design
Use	Speaker very familiar with aids; aids add much to audience understanding; speaker smoothly introduces and uses aids; no problems using aid	Speaker familiar with aids; used in talk with minor problems

Satisfactory	Fair	Poor
Easy to read and see; simple, straightforward design; little creativity in design	Difficult to read or see; carelessly designed and constructed; lack of imagination	Impossible to read or see; little attention to design and construction; lack of imagination
Speaker fairly familiar with aids; not smoothly used in talk (some problems using aids or equipment)	Speaker unfamiliar with aids or equipment; aids add little value to presentation	Speaker unfamiliar with aids; aids add no value to presentation or distract from presentation

INDEX

Agenda, 215–216
  preparation of, 194–195, 197–199
Appeals, in persuasive presentations, 29–31, 61–63
Appraisal interview, 149
Attention-getter, 54–55
Attitudes, in audience analysis, 30–31
Audience
  analysis of, 25–33, 70–71
  differentiated from small group, 179
  heterogeneous, 26–27
  homogeneous, 26
  involvement in opener, 54–55
  kinds of, 31–33
  question-and-answer sessions with. *See* Question-and-answer sessions

Body
  of interview, 170
  of presentation, 57–58
Body language, 88–93
  facial expressions, 91
  gestures, 91–93
  personal appearance, 89
  posture, 90
  speaking position, 89–90
Brainstorming, 205–206, 210
Briefings, 7
Business speaking, 6–8

Carnegie, Dale, 52
Categorical organizational pattern, 50
Cause and effect organizational pattern, 50
Charts, 125–26, 137
Chronological organizational pattern, 48–49
Closed questions, 158
Closings
  of interviews, 170
  of meetings, 221–222
  of presentations, 58–60
Color, using in presentation aids, 119–120

Committees, 186–187. *See also* Small group communication
Communication, 20, 21–25
  barriers during interviewing, 162
  complexity of, 20
  process of, 20–25
Conferences, 7. *See also* Small group communication
Conflict resolution
  in interviews, 150
  in small group communicaton, 180
Consultative conference, 187
Conventions, 7. *See also* Small group communication
Counseling interview, 150

Delivery, 80–93
  body language, 88–93
  eye contact, 86–88
  goal-setting for, 100–102
  with presentation aids, 114–115, 136–141
  voice, 81–86
Demographic factors, in audience analysis, 27–28
Direct presentation aids, 125–127, 132–133
Directed questions, 219–220
Directive interviews, 151

Emotional appeals, in persuasive presentations, 62–63
Employment interview, 149
Enunciation, 85–86
ESCAP-E planning formula, 43–48, 70–71
Exit interview, 149
Extemporaneous presentations, 11–13, 64–67
Eye contact, 16, 86–88, 126, 139

Facial expressions, 91
Facilities for meetings, 195–196
Feedback, 23–24, 87
Film projectors, 129–130, 138
Filmstrip projectors, 129–130

Flip charts, 127, 137, 141
Format guide
 for agendas, 198–199
 for extemporaneous presentations, 66–67
Forum, 7
Funnel sequence, in interview questioning, 160

Games, 208
Gestures, 91–93
Goal-setting, for delivery techniques, 100–101
Graphs, 125–126, 137
Group discussion, 203
Group leader, 202–203
Group process techniques, 197, 202–208
Groupthink, 184–185

Handouts, 126
Heterogeneous audience, 26–27
Hidden agendas, 185–186
Homogeneous audience, 26
Humor, 93–95
 in meetings, 218
 in question-and-answer sessions, 99–100
 spontaneous, 168
Hypothetical questions, 220

Idea development, in planning extemporaneous presentations, 45–48
Impromptu presentations, 10–11, 12–13
 opener for, 54
 preparing for, 11, 42, 48
Informational interview, 149–150
Interaction in interviews, 162–164, 168
Interviewing, 6, 146–172
 climate, ways to improve, 164–165
 example of preparation for, 155–156
 indicating responsiveness during, 167
 listening, 165–166
 paraphrasing, 166–167
 perceptivity, 162–165
 preparation, 153–156
 purposes, 147–148
 questioning skills, 156–161
 responding skills, 159–161
 structure, 167–170
 styles, 151–153

Inverted funnel sequence, in interview questioning, 160

Knowledge-to-date factor, in audience analysis, 31

Leader behavior, in small group communication, 202–203, 214–222, 224–225
Leading questions, 158–159
Lectern, use of, 89–90
Lectures, 7, 202
Listening, 33–37
 as group member, 225
 barriers to, 35–36
 communication process, role in, 33–35
 in interviews, 165–166
 techniques of, 36–37
Loaded questions, 158

Markerboards, 126–127, 137, 141
Maslow, Abraham, H., 29–30
Mass communication, 7–8
Meetings. *See* Small group communication
Meeting members, 193
 behavior, analysis of, 222–225
Memorized presentations, 8–9
Mental filters, 22
Mental processing, 21–22
Message, 23
Mirror questions, 158
Miscommunication, 23
Models, as presentation aids, 125, 137
Multiple-agenda meetings, 187–188
Murphy, Thomas A., 14

Needs, in audience analysis, 29–30
Noise, in communication process, 24–25
Nominal grouping technique, 203–205
Non-directive interviews, 151–153
Nonverbal language, in interviews, 165, 167
Notes for presentations, 64–67, 72–73
 format of, 66–67

Opaque projectors, 129
Open questions, 156–157
Openers, 53–57
 of direct presentations, 53–57

of impromptu presentations, 54, 56
of interviews, 168–169
of persuasive presentations, 61
Oral communication, 3–6
Order of importance organizational pattern, 51
Organization, of interviews, 167–170
Organization, of presentations, 46–47, 48–52, 74–76
  body, 57–58
  close, 58–60
  opener, 53–57
Organizational patterns, 48–52
  categorical, 50
  cause and effect, 50
  chronological, 48–49
  combination approach, 52
  direct, 60
  indirect, 60–64
  order of importance, 51
  persuasive, 60–64
  problem-solution, 50–51
  spatial, 51–52
  topical, 51
Overhead projectors, 128–129, 135, 140–141
Overhead questions, 219

Paraphrasing
  as group member, 225
  feedback, form of, 23
  in interviews, 166–167
Perception
  in communication process, 21–22
  in interviewing, 162–165
Perceptual noise, 24
Personal appearance, 89
Personal computers, 132–135
Personal experience questions, 220
Persuasion, needs analysis for, 29–31
Persuasive interview, 150
Persuasive presentations, 60–64
Physical noise, 24
Physiological noise, 24
Pictures, as presentation aids, 125–126, 137
Planning procedure for presentations. See ESCAP-E planning formula
Platform speaking, 7
Posture, 90
Practicing, 67–70, 71–74
  speaking anxiety, 15
  suggestions for, 67–70
Preparation
  for interviewing, 153–156
  for meetings, 191–197
  for presentations. See ESCAP-E planning formula
  for question-and-answer sessions, 96–97
Presentation aids, 110–142
  computer-generated presentation graphics, 132–135
  design of, 118–124
  practicing with, 70
  selection of, 115–116, 136, 137–138
  types of, 125–135, 137–138
  use in presentations, 136–141
  use in small group comunication, 195, 225
Presentation graphics, 132–135
Presentation options, 8–13
Presentation structure. See Organization
Primary questions, 157
Problem-solution organizational pattern, 50–51
Problem-solving process, 209–214
  in small groups, 180
  steps in, 209–212
Professional speaking, 6–8
Projected presentation aids, 127–132, 134–135, 140–141
Pronunciation, 69
Proodian, Ralph, 81–82
Props, 125, 137
Psychographic data, in audience analysis, 29–31, 62
Psychological noise, 24
Purpose statement
  in interviews, 153, 168–169
  in presentations, 44–45, 56
  in small group communication, 192–193, 215

Question-and-answer sessions, 7, 95–100, 200
  preparing for, 96–97
  techniques for, 97–100
Questioning, 156–161, 219–220, 225

Rapport. See also Perception
  in interviewing, 153–154, 164–165,

Rapport (cont.)
   167, 168–169, 170
   in small group communication, 202, 217–218, 223, 224
Rate of speaking, 83–84
Rational appeals, in persuasive presentations, 62
Read presentations, 9–10
Receiver, 23
Recording during interviews, 161, 166
Rehearsing. See Practicing
Relaxation techniques, 16, 101–102
Relay questions, 220
Responding skills, 159–161
Reverse questions, 220
Rockefeller, David, 3–4
Role-playing, 207
Round-table discussions, 206

Secondary questions, 157
Self-involvement, in opener, 55–56
Semantic noise, 25
Sender, 22
Simulations, 208
Slide projectors, 129–130
Slides, 129–130, 134, 138
Small group communication, 6–7, 178–226
   expense of, 183–184
   group process techniques, 202–208
   groupthink, effect of, 184–185
   hidden agendas, effects of, 185–186
   leader behavior, 214–222
   member behavior, 222–225
   planning for, 191–199
   problem-solving process for, 209–214
   reasons for using, 180–181
   teleconferencing, 188–191
   time pressures, effects of, 184
   types of, 186–188
Spatial organizational patern, 51–52
Speaking anxiety, 13–17, 87, 100–102

Speaking opportunities, 6–8
Speaking position, 89–90
Staff meetings, 186
Structure. See Organization; Organizational patterns.
Summaries
   in interviewing, 158, 170
   during meetings, 218–219
   as presentation close, 59

Tables, as presentation aids, 125–126
Talk structure. See Organizaton, of presentations; Organizational patterns.
Teleconferencing, 188–191
Time management
   during interviews, 170
   of meetings, 215–216, 221, 223
   during presentations, 44–45, 69–70
Topical organizational pattern, 51
Training conferences, 187
Training interviews, 149
Transition
   in interviews, 160
   in presentations, 57–58, 76
Transparencies, 133–134, 137. See also Overhead projectors

Values, in audience analysis, 30–31
Verbal filler, 84
Verbal support of ideas, 47, 64
Video, 130–131, 133–135, 138
Visual aids. See Presentation aids.
Visual support of ideas, 47. See also Presentation aids.
Voice, 81–86
   enunciation, 85–86
   pitch, 82–83
   rate, 83–84
   volume, 84–85

Word charts, 125–126, 133
Word choice, 25, 161